*Praise for faithfully feminist*

"What a brave and powerful exa[m]ment; of living within boundari[e]reveal. The importance of apprec[...]beauty of living inside of a system of observance cannot be overemphasized. This compilation does all of that and more."

–Mayim Bialik, Emmy-nominated actor, "The Big Bang Theory"

"One after another these Faithful Feminists from Abrahamic traditions tell of their journey through bias and discrimination to clarity and peace. The struggle can come within religious traditions or in secular settings, but all lead to a fuller understanding of fidelity in a complex world. In their telling many of their stories mirror and nourish my own. I am grateful for their bold willingness to share their insights and stimulate my reflection giving rise to the certainty that we are all sisters in this quest. Thank you!

–Sr. Simone Campbell, executive director of
NETWORK and founder of Nuns on the Bus

"*Faithfully Feminist* is a must read for anyone eager to tear down biases and stereotypes surrounding the loaded concepts of both religion and feminism. This beautifully written anthology finally provides a loud and clear voice for women who are proud to call themselves feminists and believers, and serves as a wakeup call to those that believe feminism is incompatible with religion. An inspiring book!"

–Shaheen Pasha, Assistant Professor of international
Journalism at University of Massachusetts-Amherst and
former reporter for Dow Jones, CNN and Thomson Reuters

"The stories shared in *Faithfully Feminist* paint for us the varied and textured reality of women's feminist expressions of faith in all their complexity. They defy any claim to simple, dualistic perspectives of how feminists should relate to patriarchal religious traditions. Life cannot be so reduced. These women's stories are a testimony to the vastness of human strength and creativity and the transformation that is possible at the intersection of feminisms and religions. These women speak for themselves and we are the better if we received their gift and listen to their voices."

–Xochitl Alvizo, co-Founder of FeminismandReligion.com

"What brings one to faith and keeps one 'faithful,' especially in religious communities that remain densely patriarchal? As the narratives in this anthology attest, these are such ineffably personal questions that no woman can answer them for another. Perhaps that is just as well since it allows us to learn from each other's struggles how to be present to the divine in our own distinctive ways."

–Dr. Asma Barlas, Professor of Politics at Ithaca College
and author of *"Believing Women" in Islam: Unreading
Patriarchal Interpretations of the Qur'an*

"*Faithfully Feminist* is a creative collage of witty, tantalizing, courageous, honest, and provocative faith stories. The writers share from the sacred places in the heart and urge us to answer the question, 'why do we stay?' Their diverse stories affirm that feminism is necessary to the faith and practice of us all for we are all God's people. These heartwarming stories challenge the boundaries that patriarchal religions place on women and celebrates the significance of listening and attending to women's faith voices."

–Grace Ji-Sun Kim, author of *The Grace of Sophia:
A Korean North American Women's Christology*

"This is a richly textured, intellectually and ethically challenging book—especially for readers like me. As a religious traditionalist, I need to hear these voices. I may not always want to hear them, but I need to hear them. Their honesty, depth, commitment, and energy are compelling. This book attests to the vitality of our several traditions and to the moral integrity of the thinkers who work to stay within them."

–Alan Mittleman, Professor of Jewish Philosophy,
The Jewish Theological Seminary and author of
*A Short History of Jewish Ethics*

"In today's world, expressing faith is often as contentious as claiming feminism. *Faithfully Feminist* brings the two together like cinders in a fire longing for oxygen. Sparks fly as Muslim, Jewish, and Christian women invite us into their stories of standing up for their equality and full humanity while deepen their faith. The diversities and continuities of their experiences of the divine and commitment to their communities ignite and illuminate faith and feminism in ways that enrich each tradition. Stunningly eloquent, powerfully honest, a must read!"

–Kate Ott, author of *Sex + Faith*

"Read this book—to plunge immediately into the world of why women bother sticking with the worlds' sexist religious traditions—because they want to transform them! In the words of the savvy editors of *Faithfully Feminist*, 'to live a feminist and religious life is an art . . . it requires being graceful and bold, cunning and creative.' This is precisely what this strong collection of writing is all about."

–Laura Levitt, Professor of Religion, Jewish
Studies and Gender, Temple University

# faithfully
# feminist

## A Note about the *I Speak for Myself* series:

I Speak for Myself ® is an inclusive platform through which people can make themselves heard and where everyone's voice has a place. ISFM®'s mission focuses on delivering one core product, a "narrative collection," that is mindset-altering, inspiring, relatable, and teachable. We aim to deliver interfaith, intercultural titles that are narrow in scope but rich in diversity.

Please be sure to check out our website, www.ISpeakforMyself.com, to learn more about the series, join the conversation, and even create an I Speak for Myself ® book of your own!

Sincerely,

Zahra T. Suratwala and Maria M. Ebrahimji

Co-Founders, I Speak for Myself ®

### Books in the Series

**Volume 1**: *I Speak for Myself: American Women on Being Muslim*

**Volume 2**: *American Men on Being Muslim: 45 American Men on Being Muslim*

**Volume 3**: *Demanding Dignity: Young Voices from the Front Lines of the Arab Revolutions*

**Volume 4**: *Talking Taboo: American Christian Women Get Frank About Faith*

**Volume 5**: *Father Factor: American Christian Men on Fatherhood and Faith*

# faithfully feminist

## Jewish, Christian, & Muslim Feminists on Why We Stay

*edited by*

Gina Messina-Dysert, Jennifer Zobair, & Amy Levin

*Foreword* by Judith Plaskow, Rosemary Radford Ruether, & Amina Wadud

White Cloud Press
Ashland, Oregon

*The views and opinions expressed by each contributing writer in this book are theirs alone and do not necessarily represent those of the series' editors or I Speak for Myself, Inc.*

White Cloud Press books may be purchased for educational, business, or sales promotional use. For information, please write:

Special Market Department
White Cloud Press
PO Box 3400
Ashland, OR 97520
Website: www.whitecloudpress.com

Cover and Interior Design by C Book Services

Printed in the United States of America
First edition: 2015
15  16  17  18  19      10 9 8 7 6 5 4 3 2 1

Library of Congress Cataloging-in-Publication Data
Faithfully feminist : Jewish, Christian, and Muslim feminists on why we stay / edited by Gina Messina-Dysert, Jennifer Zobair, and Amy  Levin. -- First edition.
    pages cm. -- (I speak for myself series ; 6)
  ISBN 978-1-935952-48-0 (paperback)
1. Women and religion. 2. Feminism--Religious aspects. I. Messina-Dysert, Gina. II. Zobair, Jennifer. III. Levin, Amy, 1986-
  BL458.F36 2015
  200.82--dc23
                        2015012985

# Dedication

For the future generation; that they embrace a feminist ethic and recognize that while change may not happen all at once, it is possible with ongoing commitment.

Especially for Sarah Messina-Dysert, Tariq Zobair, Hannah Zobair, Zach Zobair, Noah Freud, Sivan Freud, and Elie Allal.

# Acknowledgements

We would like to express our sincere thanks to Zahra Suratwala and Maria Ebrahimji for recognizing the value in this project and providing support and encouragement from conception to birth.

We also deeply acknowledge our unending gratitude to our foresisters who have paved the way and made it possible to empower voice among all persons committed to feminist praxis. We would like to especially thank Judith Plaskow, Rosemary Radford Ruether, and Amina Wadud for their graciousness and willingness to support this project.

Finally, we would like to thank our loved ones for offering a community to exist where we can continue to explore feminist ideas and theological practice as active agents. A special thank you to Ann and Richard Levin, Joel Mittleman, Christopher Messina-Dysert, Talha Zobair, Xochitl Alvizo, Kristan Smith-Park, and Asma Barlas.

# Contents

# Foreword

## by Judith Plaskow, Rosemary Radford Ruether, and Amina Wadud

"Feminism saved my faith" is the concluding phrase of one of the writers in *Faithfully Feminist*, and though not everyone would say it that way, most of these women have found feminism and faith vibrantly interrelated. The contributors to this anthology articulate a range of reasons that feminists might choose to remain within a patriarchal religious tradition. They also remind us that women reconcile their faith and feminist identities in diverse ways. This volume testifies to the dynamism within the religious communities of Judaism, Christianity, and Islam in the United States, and to their internal diversity. This diversity allows for the contributors to engage in a process of their own development as feminists of faith that interacts with similar processes of development going on in their religious communities.

The overriding common bond for these women of faith is the shared conviction that the conflict between religion and feminism is real—even when it is generated by other people's expectations that those two identities are separate and irreconcilable. Once each woman arrived at a place where she no longer felt an imperative to abide by an either/or dichotomy, she was able to define the terms of her religion and feminism for herself and to own both identities as significant.

Multiply the individual accounts in this volume by tens of thousands, and the effect of these women's decisions and the concerted actions for change that have flowed from them has been enormous. For example, feminism has profoundly altered American Judaism in the last forty-plus years. Women are ordained in all branches of liberal Judaism and, in all but name, in modern Orthodoxy. New denominational prayer books written in English use inclusive language and incorporate writings by women. Feminists have written Torah commentaries, designed rituals for important turning points in women's lives, and created new scholarship on women that contributes to a fuller history of the Jewish people.

Likewise, Christianity has been significantly impacted by the work of feminist theology. While some branches continue to refuse leadership roles to women, many others have acknowledged that every person embodies the spirit of Christ and have embraced the ordination of women. In 2006 the Episcopalian Church ordained its first woman bishop, the highest office in the church. Inclusive language has found its way into the prayers and rituals of many churches and feminist commentaries have shifted thinking on scriptural interpretations. Dialogue within and across branches of Christianity are expanding borders, and movements like Woman Church and online feminist spaces have created opportunities for women to claim agency and participate in roles that have been traditionally withheld.

In the long road to Islamic feminism, women have sometimes lacked agency to define either Islam or feminism. Traditional definitions of these words which operate as a constraint on work within Islam towards justice, equality and dignity; feminism was connected to Western imperialism and invasion into Muslim-majority nation states, and centuries of patriarchal control and interpretation stifled women's efforts to claim Islam for themselves. This is changing, aided by campaigns such as the 2009 launching of the Musawah movement for equality and justice in Muslim family law. A new freedom is emerging that allows Muslim women the dignity and honor of defining Islam and feminism for themselves—no matter how little they might know of global discourses and historical traditions. All that was necessary was to, identify as a believer and expect a life of justice within that belief. Islam has also witnessed women-led prayers and a move toward inclusive prayer spaces.

The profound changes feminists have inspired and worked for do not mean that all problems have been solved and that women's subordination is a thing of the past; there is plenty of work for a new generation. The difficulties with overcoming the glass ceiling and balancing work and life that women within the larger society face also bedevil women in all three religious communities. Panels, boards, and publications often exclude women's voices completely or have only token female participation. Ordained women in Judaism are paid less than their male counterparts and rarely become senior rabbis in large or prestigious congregations. If women "choose" to serve smaller synagogues —the explanation often tendered to explain these gaps—that is partly because the expectations surrounding the rabbinate have not kept pace with its changing demographic, and women who want to combine rabbinic work with raising a family face considerable obstacles. Christian ordained women face similar obstacles within the priesthood and continue to be denied leadership roles in some branches, including Catholicism and Mormonism. Similarly, Muslim women are often excluded from panels at religious conferences and are underrepresented on the boards of religious institutions. The idea of women leading Muslim prayers remains controversial. And too often, discussions about women's role in Islam still revolve around the issue of hijab, or covering.

The challenge for feminists today is passing on feminist insights and gains to the next generation. Is women's history being incorporated into elementary and high school texts, or are students being taught the same parade of male names and faces? More particularly for Jews, Christians, and Muslims, when a girl or woman wants to mark some nontraditional ritual occasion, is it clear where to turn for resources? Do most Jews, Christians, and Muslims even know that it is possible to create new rituals that feel deeply meaningful and religiously authentic?

Finally, when teachers—and parents—talk about God, how is God imagined? Are children still growing up thinking about God as a distant male figure, or are they offered a range of images, and emboldened to create their own? Are children being encouraged to talk about and challenge passages in and interpretations of the Torah, Bible, and Qur'an that are misogynist or otherwise unethical? Are they developing critical tools that will allow them to engage with and transform difficult parts of tradition?

The next generation of feminists should consider a move beyond rhetoric and terminology towards substance and personal affirmation. Identifying as feminists of faith helps forge global alliances towards meaningful dialogue across difference—even the differences within. It is only when these deeper levels of change are addressed that the question, "Why stay?" will cease to be relevant.

# Introduction
## by Jennifer Zobair, Amy Levin, and Gina Messina-Dysert

Faith and feminism….an oxymoron?

Too often, claiming to be a feminist and a person of faith is met with skepticism and negation. Many feminists wonder how we can remain in patriarchal religious traditions. Strictly traditional Jews, Christians, and Muslims accuse us of renouncing our "God-given" gender roles and succumbing to secular ideals.

At the same time that feminism has become more complex, with its many waves crashing at all times, religion has become an ocean of complexity that is often misunderstood. Religion is criticized in the progressive, secular sphere as violence inducing, irrational, and anti-feminist. Where does this leave religious women who identify as feminists? Simply put, we are doubly "othered." In a time where women of faith are often viewed as submissive, naive, and self-defeating, it is necessary to acknowledge the feminist side of faith.

That is why we need space to speak frankly, honestly, and personally about what it means to live everyday as a practicing religious feminist—to debunk the stereotypes and binaries, but more importantly, to raise consciousness once again. Now that our feminist foremothers like Judith Plaskow, Amina Wadud, and Rosemary Radford Reuther have cracked the stained glass ceiling, there are a myriad of new feminist rituals, traditions, and movements within Judaism, Islam, and Christianity. Whether or not we choose to don our *hijabs* (headscarves), *tallitot* (prayer shawls), or crosses is a multifaceted choice based not on the simple question, "is this feminist" but on a hybrid of influences and ideas as sacred as religion, as poignant as feminism, as personal as family, and as mundane as fashion.

To live a feminist and religious life is an art in itself; it requires being graceful and bold, cunning and creative. These words describe the women in this anthology. They are Jewish, Christian, and Muslim women who come from the same prophetic tradition, hold feminist values, and are relentlessly asked why they stay. The Abrahamic traditions are also patriarchal ones, and the perception seems to be that it is a feminist act only to *leave* such a religion.

We contend that it is also a feminist act to *stay*.

The time for an anthology like this has never been more urgent. Feminists struggle to find footing within their faiths. Just within the last year, several Jewish women who were part of the Women of the Wall (WOW) movement were assaulted and arrested for asserting their rights to pray collectively at the Western Wall, the holiest site for Jews. Within Christianity, a faithful woman is equated with Candace Cameron, former child star of "Full House" and *New York Times* best-selling author who claims to be biblically submissive to her husband. And to be a perfect woman is impossible, since no woman can be like Mary the mother of Jesus, both a virgin and a mother. Muslim women are often told by traditional clerics to appreciate their equal but separate status and to find comfort in their gender-specific roles. FEMEN[1] assumes Muslim women cannot speak for themselves and bare their collective breasts to save Muslim women, thereby "speaking" for them. It is no wonder that empowered women struggle to remain in their faith traditions.

We've been asked what this project symbolizes to us. In response, we've tried to express what it means to provide a platform for empowered women of faith to speak. Once, one of us said simply, "Understanding. Hope. Love." We get emotional when we think of the women who are routinely told they have to choose, that they cannot be both a person of (an Abrahamic) faith and a feminist, but who persevere in both faith and feminism anyway. But this anthology is more than just feminists of a particular religion making their case through their honest and brave stories of strength and struggle. This collection includes women from different faiths—faiths which often appear to be in conflict—standing shoulder to shoulder to reclaim

---

1. FEMEN is an international women's movement of topless female activists painted with slogans and crowned with flowers. They regularly protest events, especially those that are connected to patriarchal religion.

sacred space, illustrate our commonalities, and show that we are more alike than we are different. These narratives also respect and highlight the differences, ambiguities, and multiplicities between and within our own traditions. While there is no monolithic response to the tension between feminism and religion, our experiences weave together overlapping themes among our different religions, denominations, ages, ethnicities, sexualities, and professions. We believe this book represents the strongest statement of sisterhood: We respect and support each other, honor our differences, and join together with affection and solidarity to speak our truth.

Recently there has been some scholarship criticizing the telling of personal narratives by women of faith, especially by Muslim women. The critics argue that such narratives only take place in the context of "proof"—that the writers are trying to prove that they are as "normal" as everyone else, and that therefore these stories are not authentic or empowering. We reject these claims. We believe that dispelling stereotypes—which can impact lives in real and devastating ways—is an acceptable context in which to speak. In fact, we believe that any context in which a woman feels misunderstood, or maligned, or where she simply wishes to tell her story, is an acceptable context in which to speak.

The practice of women telling their personal stories isn't new. Ever since feminist pioneer Kathie Sarachild coined the term "consciousness-raising" in the late 1960s, feminist groups and collectives have been using the power of personal narrative to better understand women's oppression and make the "personal" become "political." In a culture where technology and media both connect and isolate us, it is more important than ever to create new platforms to bring women together to discuss and analyze their personal lives.

This book is such a platform. We are speaking both to those who would deny our full participation in faith or feminism and to fellow women of faith who struggle. Ultimately, through storytelling and sharing we come to know ourselves—our fears, our compromises, our refusals to compromise, and our paths to self-actualization. We've been doubly "othered" and yet, slowly we're reclaiming and redefining this otherness. In some communities we are now the majority, and ideologies of sexism and female exclusion are the new "other." The journey is not over, but we've come a long way. We are living realities.

That's why we have weaved together the testimony of these forty-five women. We believe that hearing such stories is lifesaving. We've felt isolated and alienated, we've found new communities, and we've found God as a woman and in unlikely places. We've blended tradition with innovation. We've made feminism just as sacred as our religious traditions. Even in the moments when we compromise or bend, we never fully compromise our feminism nor our faith. That is the spirit of this project—sharing our stories, being empowered through voice, and acknowledging that being feminist doesn't mean giving up on your faith.

# Speaking Forward
## by Deonna Kelli Sayed

DEONNA KELLI SAYED is a writer, cultural commentator, and digital story-teller. She is the author of *Paranormal Obsession: America's Fascination with Ghosts & Hauntings, Spooks & Spirit,* a cultural studies discussion regarding the paranormal in post-9/11 American society. Her work has appeared in the *New York Times* featured anthology, *Love, Inshallah: The Secret Love Lives of American Muslim Women,* and she is one editor of the accompanying website, loveinshallah.com. Deonna has contributed to storyandchai.com, altmuslimah.com, and Muslim Media Watch. She is currently working on a memoir partially supported by a 2013 North Carolina United Arts Council Regional Artist Grant. Follow Deonna's musings on Twitter @deonnakelli.

1.  My husband held me in bed on one lazy Sunday morning. I rested gently tucked in his arms as our sleepy conversation turned to various theological matters. For some reason, the concept of sin came up. "Men are responsible in heaven for the wife's sins, even more so than they are for their children's sins," he postulated as he kissed my forehead. I curdled. My heart quaked all the way to the bone marrow.

"I don't believe this," I replied. "It doesn't make theological sense." I was accustomed to strange pronouncements from some Muslims regarding the nature of female souls, but these normally did not come from my husband. As an Afghan, he followed the Hanafi[1] school of thought and held conservative views on many issues, but he also

---

1. Hanafi "school" is one of the four Sunni schools of Islamic jurisprudence regarding social and personal matters.

actively supported women's voting and educational rights in the Muslim world.

One particular hadith informed the belief he expressed that morning. Yet, I surmised, it was one that contradicted Qur'anic injunctions of individual sovereignty when it came to matters of personal thoughts and actions. I know that my husband had shared this hadith with me in affection, but the paternalistic assumption on that drowsy morning made me ache.

I experienced what scholar Abou El Fadl calls a "conscientious pause," which, in my understanding, is when one encounters a faith assumption that doesn't feel right in the heart. One has a spiritual obligation to confront these ruptures. Nothing that I knew about Islam affirmed that women were so incompetent that we couldn't represent ourselves in front of Allah. It was at that moment, in the arms of a marriage already floundering, and at the cusp of a spiritual state where I longed to redefine my experience with Islam, that I heard a quiet murmuring: *If you ever want to rediscover your faith and claim it as your own, then you have to leave this space.* It was then that I understood that honoring what you intuitively feel to be Divine, even if it disrupts those who control the story, is empowerment. Part of my decision to leave my marriage arrived over that hadith. It brought the journey full circle: I had decided to love a man in the name of Islam; and, later, I decided to leave in order to own my Islamic identity. I initially thought fleeing an unhappy marriage to a decent man was a typical white girl thing to do. Later, I realized that ownership of my faith was a powerful Muslim woman thing to do.

◆◆◆

The root word of Islam means both peace and surrender. These concepts are easy to understand at one level: when one surrenders to Allah, one will find peace. Yet, many Muslims have a hard time defining the boundaries of surrender. Some fall to rigid clarifications of what is halal (permitted) and haram (forbidden) at the expense of inner spiritual development. Others give up their sense of individual agency because they feel too timid to critically engage the faith by questioning aspects of interpretation. In Western feminism, concepts like agency and empowerment are canonized. The idea of surrender (the term submission is also used) is almost an offensive, naughty word. I struggled with this dichotomy when I left my twelve-year marriage. I wanted to find personal authenticity with my identity as a writer and as a Muslim woman. The "authentic self" is an idea arguably very privileged and American. My realities that day I lay in my husband's arms were those of an educated, middle-class, white, American woman who knew my marriage was failing. I could not see any surrender to the realities of my marriage, which tasted brittle and dry at that point. My urge was to get up and go, and good riddance. During a few conversations with my ex-husband (and especially during every episode of Zakir Naik on Salaam TV), I'd feel words choke in my throat that would eventually end up diverted in the synapsis between my mind and my heart.

There are parts of the Qur'an interpreted in ways that alienate me as a woman and as a member of humanity, and I'd stifle a scream when I heard men (and women) bow to these interpretations. I thought, *This doesn't intuitively feel right. I don't like it.* Yet, I did not know how to argue these assumptions. Using the same rhetoric (the Qur'an, the hadith) as counter points merely affirmed that the capital-T "Truth" stayed lodged in place. Someone always knew a saying from Mohammad that I did not, or produced a *tafsir* (interpretation) as counterpoint. The dialogues seemed consistently trapped in a closed circle, and could ultimately be declared *bida* (forbidden innovation) if one dared to jump beyond the lines. I became fatigued of talking back to something for which I could not locate an efficient language. I wanted to enunciate new possibilities, but I came up dry every time. What bothered me about the assumptions some Muslims made about women in Islam were not only structural issues like access to educational and economic resources, but also certain interpretations that denied women ownership of our faith experience. Author Bushra Rehman summed it up nicely when she said to me that many Muslim women feel that other people have more ownership than we do over our personal stories of faith and identity. But there is fear in claiming the story because many Muslim women are told that we don't have the right to even ask for it. There is a deep faith-based feminist action in ownership that belongs to all women (and men, to be fair): personal authenticity is a spiritual journey and a component of living belief. If I cannot be my authentic self in front of Allah, then how can I be authentic in other relationships in my life, particularly with my spouse?

In the months after I left my marriage, I remembered a conversation I once had with Sheikh Tala Al-Alawani, the founder of the Fiqh Council of North America. We were sitting in an Afghan restaurant in Georgetown when he suggested that everyone needed to "read the Qur'an at least once like Prophet Muhammad was merely a postal worker who delivered the book just for you. Tear it apart. Question Allah over verses that do not feel right." Almost fifteen years later, I struggled with how to define Islam as a divorced, forty-year-old white Muslim woman. Sheikh Taha gave me permission to tell Allah how I felt. And on the day that my ex-husband offered his hadith, I realized that I would never be able to own my story if I was not allowed, at bare minimum, to own my sins.

2. I am an academic feminist in the sense that part of my college studies included feminist and social theory. It never occurred to me that I might also be a "faith-based feminist" in my daily life. The first type of feminist—the one able to namedrop scholars and use exclusive lingo—seems like a cool version of feminism. To be a faith-based feminist conjures less erudite images. Yet, when I reflect upon my journey, I realize that most major decisions in my adult life have revolved around my Islamic identity. Let me tell you two short stories about ownership and love: I asked my husband to marry me. It happened one day while riding down Sixteenth Street in Washington, DC. I found myself at a stage in my life where I wanted a partner, a good Muslim man, and I had found one. There is an Islamic precedent to a woman securing a man in marriage: Khadija, Prophet Muhammad's first wife and the one he was monogamously married to the longest, asked *him* to marry *her*. So I took this legacy as my own.

This is the second story: Khadija was also the first person to acknowledge the significance of the first Islamic revelation. She lovingly assured Prophet Muhammad his sanity was intact after he received this revelation; an event he initially found frightening and assumed to be some sort of hallucination. She recognized the importance of the message before he did, and she called on a Christian relative to confirm the event as spiritually significant. Imagine what might have happened to Islam if Prophet Muhammad had walked into his home on that day and Khadija had responded, "Boy, you are crazy!" Her feminist agency as a supportive, intellectually and spiritually engaged wife secured the future of a global faith community. She owned the moment, and she encouraged Prophet Muhammad to do so, as well. Ownership matters, and it even comes with an Islamic precedent.

3. Religion has always existed as a female centered experience for me, even prior to my Islamization. I grew up in the rural American South and attended a Southern Baptist church. In my world, men did not attend church or deal with spiritual matters. The women-folk took me to God. I stumbled into Islam during college through Palestinian activism and association with Islamic scholars and intellectuals. Muslim women guided me as friends, mentors, and religious instructors. They discussed the things that really mattered: the negotiation of love, female oriented understandings of the Divine, and women's empowerment. Many were daughters and granddaughters of Arab activists. One friend recalled her grandmother leading a women's meeting on each full moon so women could travel through their village at night in brightness and safety; her aunt was also one of the first women in her country to wear the *jilbab* (a non-black, modest "robe") as a spiritual and political statement to counteract secular, Arab nationalism.

Other women were descendants of the Muslim Brotherhood of the '60s and '70s, back when the movement honored intellectual pursuits and pulsed with inclusive excitement on college campuses across the United States. Women played vibrant roles as the institutional shape of the American Muslim community took root. African-American Muslim women exhibited vivacious personalities as community activists and pioneers of American Muslim identity. For me, Islam emerged as a female-filtered experience. Men were Islam's showpieces. Women were the stealthy gears that got stuff done.

I spent my marriage adhering to my ex-husband's interpretation of Islam—a kind version, but one that did not fit well with my spiritual contours. I struggled with how to redefine my faith post-divorce. Just like in the beginning of my journey, Muslim women once again guided me towards a new orientation in Islam, and it had everything to do with owning my story. After I had an essay featured in a book, *Love, Inshallah: The Secret Love Lives of American Muslim Women,* the book editors asked me to join the editorial board of the book's accompanying website. A global community of Muslim women took me into their fold and accepted my journey as completely legitimate. I was writing and editing material for a small but growing world audience that understood the power of narratives. Storytelling became one way to honor new realities facing Muslim women (and men) at the global scale. A small yet growing segment of Muslims started deconstructing the faith through prose and fiction in compelling, transformative ways. We weren't merely speaking back; we were now speaking forward.

Where does feminism come into this? I surrendered to the journey of finally owning my identity as a Muslim woman, and this surrender became empowerment. Surrender arrives in the struggle of personal authenticity in front of Allah. Surrender arrives in the moment of accepting imperfections and acknowledging that there isn't one story of Islam. We don't have to accept the interpretations that make us feel small; we can surrender to our intuition and our questions. There are other stories, other wonders in the text, other ways to know Allah and our faith.

To surrender can be profoundly feminist. I know a brilliant young Muslim poet, Key Ballah, who summed this up well for me. "Islam isn't an easy thing to fit whole inside of your mouth," she shared. "Sometimes it needs to be broken apart so you can swallow it bit by bit." Ballah continued, "I have fallen in and out of love with Islam in the same way I've fallen in and out of love with myself. My honesty is the only thing that has saved me from drowning in the patriarchal, overreaching interpretations of my religion. My ability to speak about the way that these interpretations push me out and ostracize me and make me feel uncomfortable in my own skin has been what has saved me."

To surrender is acknowledgment that personal authenticity is a disjointed, ongoing endeavor. Yet, one cannot worship their God without embarking on that journey. Feminism can be the political struggle against structural and patriarchal oppression, but it can also be the quiet personal choice to honor your faith—indeed, to fight for your place in it—and to carve out spaces for others to do so, as well. I still struggle with surrender and agency in my life, as I am in constant fear of personal and spiritual inertia. Yet, I understand that the journey towards ownership is not one act but a collection of surrenders over a lifetime. The Muslim declaration of faith suggests this is part of the journey; there may sometimes be distance in the "there is no God" moments, but they end with the return "but Allah." Sometimes, you faithfully give yourself over to the process of being occasionally lost, but eventually found again. The most profound moments of personal clarity are often waiting on the other side.

# Leading from Here
## by Dasi Fruchter

DASI FRUCHTER holds an MPA from the New York University (NYU) Wagner School of Public Service and is a third-year student at Yeshivat Maharat, the first institution to ordain Orthodox women as clergy. While she works towards her ordination and an M.A. in Jewish Studies at NYU, she is hosting festive Shabbat meals, teaching Torah, and working within the Jewish community and across faiths towards a better world.

My decision to enroll in Yeshivat Maharat, the first institution to ordain female clergy in the Jewish Orthodox movement, had its first stirrings while I was sitting on a balcony.

Over time, I've learned that I am an expert on "singing from here." From where? From the balcony, or from the other side of the *mechitza* (a partition separating men and women in Orthodox Jewish prayer spaces). Over the last ten years, dozens of women have come up to me after prayer services, their faces either bashful or smiling, thanking me for choosing to sing loudly from "here," telling me that I've enhanced their prayer experience or given them permission to be audible. But many years before they thanked me, they thanked my mother for singing beautifully and confidently, even though it was my father whose job it was to sing. He's the cantor, and his voice was supposed to reach the heavens, loaded with the desires and prayers of the whole congregation.

I always describe my father's *chazzanus* (cantorial style) as unique and sweet. He leaves the flowery trills and extended vibrato of a classical cantorial style behind, but he is still able to unearth a deep sense of tradition. Year after year, on the eve of Rosh Hashanah, the Jewish New Year, my sisters and I accompanied my mother as we walked up the creaky wooden stairs of the synagogue to the balcony. The sanctuary smelled like a full library and aging wood, and a reverent hush filled the corners of the room. We did our best to get center seats since they looked directly upon my father's head. We were birds, sitting up there with the other women in their colorful hats, observing the beauty and choreography of the High Holiday experience from above. I almost wonder what it would be like to watch myself, year after year, listening to his haunting prayers up in the balcony. I was sometimes playing with a toy, eating a bag of snacks, sucking on a honey stick, reading a book, or wearing my first splash of perfume as a young adult—and always awakened and startled to alertness by the gravity of the environment, the smells and sounds.

During the services, we were physically quite far from my father. But my mother set a beautiful example of singing from the balcony. Her beautiful voice, bursting loud and without shame, entreated us to join along with her. As we grew older, we sang with harmony, likely louder than what was socially acceptable, but the way our harmonies blended with my father's was pleasing to the women around us. Most of all, it was our moment as the women in the family to unite and draw close to God with our voices. These are treasured memories that I file away and bring forward when I need strength.

When he was old enough, my brother was allowed to join my father on the *bimah* and sing harmony with him. Meanwhile, my sisters and my mother continued being experts at singing from "here." I wanted so badly to join my brother and father, "there." I remember feeling anger and frustration, year after year, because I wanted to reach the whole congregation. I knew I could bring a sense of holiness to the room with my voice.

Those moments on the balcony, when I knew I couldn't stand there with my brother and father, were when I began asking questions. From the balcony, I saw the same holy scene, year after year. There was something beautiful about that, but I also wondered if a woman would ever be visible as a part of the service, even if she wasn't leading the prayers. I knew that by denying the space of a woman's voice, we were losing out on a sense of the sacred in the room.

The reason we sang from the balcony, as I understood it, was the way we understood halakhah (Jewish law). I honestly struggle with the framework of halakhah, but as a person who tightly grasps this spiritual and ethical framework, I often find myself bringing Godliness into my life through existing and fixed structures. The life of an observant Jew, regardless of gender, is governed completely by time. With the rising of the sun in the morning comes a dozen ways I am meant to interact with community, the Creator, and myself. By the time the sun sets, I would ideally be bursting with the satisfaction of at least a hundred blessings, three *ashreis* (a prayerful recitation of Psalm 145), and other rituals along the way. Every day is an intricate weave, with the holy punctuating the mundane like an earth tone stitch braided with a gleaming thread of gold. When I try to describe this framework that holds me in all of its Godliness, I sometimes talk about a moving flow of molasses: sweet, sticky, and slow. Much like molasses, Orthodox Judaism can be deeply sweet but is also sticky and moves at a snail-like pace.

That slowness is evident in ancient rabbinic texts—which can take easily dozens of pages to discuss a single blessing said over a certain type of food. My teachers taught that important decisions about Jewish law and spirituality should and would take time. There was a sense of holiness about being held by time. The best example of this is Shabbat, the seventh day, the day of rest. Since Shabbat's time-holiness meant that there were many things we could not do on Friday night and Saturday itself, Friday afternoon would culminate in a frenetic rush of chicken roasting, putting up the hot water pot, and taping lights in the bathroom so we wouldn't accidentally turn them off and have to brush our teeth in the dark. From the time the sun dipped on Friday to the emergence of three stars on Saturday night, we were held by a sense of law that both prohibited and allowed. We were forced to be extremely intentional with every moment. "We don't kill time," my mother says, "time is holy." Similarly, tradition is holy. We respect the time it takes to make a decision, to change something. We sit in the stickiness until we're sure, even when it seems like our skin is beginning to prune. So my mother and my sisters and I stayed in that balcony, and continued to sing from "here."

Within halakhah, in addition to personal and communal ritual, is an obligation to those who are broken and downtrodden in the world. I often find myself struggling alongside people whose work is centered around the pursuit of treatment or rights that affirm a God-given human dignity. So I've stood on metaphoric balconies as well, asking larger questions about poverty, hunger, or privilege. I was asking the questions from a distance, but I had to ask them from somewhere. Asking them from "here" was a great start.

Whether in the realm of feminism or other fields of searching for human dignity, my life has been dotted by these balcony moments where a respect for time and tradition in Orthodoxy comes into conflict with movement towards justice. I realized that the activist world sometimes moves too quickly for the slow pace of Orthodox Judaism. The issue comes when a respect for tradition and time bumps up against a real need, a disadvantaged voice, or an injustice. While some do struggle with the issue of a partition separating men and women, on my personal Orthodox path, it does not feel like an injustice to me to sit on the other side of the mechitza. Choosing to separate by gender in prayer spaces is a legitimate and powerful choice that I make, guided by halakhah. However, denying women a voice in all areas of public synagogue life is an injustice and most importantly, a disservice.

I could have gone three ways in these seemingly contradicting moments. I could have chosen a different way to engage with my Judaism that wasn't as challenging. I could have swallowed my desire to give voice to myself and to other women. But I chose a third path. For me, those moments on the balcony told me that there is a communal need for women to hear and to be heard. I needed to step down from the balcony somehow, in a way that respected time and tradition. This path helps me to uncover where progress is necessary and possible within the framework of the tradition, even as it pushes its boundaries.

One of the moments in the bible that resonates most with me is when Jacob stays up all night struggling with what we understand may have been an angel. After the struggle, Jacob is renamed "Israel"—the one who struggles with God. I am grateful that the concept of struggle is given honor by being part of the name of our people, since struggle is an integral part of what it means for me to be an observant Jew.

Choosing this direction—and its attendant struggles—led me to a name change of my own. More specifically, it has led me to a place where I wear the identity of "Orthodox Feminist" on my forehead. In my community and to many others, this means that I am not a devout and quiet scholar. Instead, I am a change-maker, a struggler and sometimes a downright rabble-rouser. The choice not to pursue my spiritual leadership in a way that is palatable to more of my peers, and could be more easily affirmed and supported by more of the Orthodox community at large, is a difficult one sometimes. This choice, however, is the fullest and most robust understanding that I have of the Torah, for "its ways are ways of pleasantness, and all its paths are peace."

I've chosen to make my Jewish life look a little different by devoting my life to female spiritual leadership in the Orthodox world, and allowing for a deep, communal, spiritual struggle. Sometimes, I'll sing from "here," with my mother and sisters like I always have, and sometimes I'll be "there," somewhere new, giving a sermon or facilitating spiritual space, but still grasping Jewish law tightly. The fusion of action and tradition, movement and rootedness, can be found all over my life today. It happens when I create intentional prayer spaces with male colleagues. And it happens in the work my peers and I do to revive the practice of the monthly ritual immersion after a woman's menstrual cycle; we strive to address the issues of women's health, sexuality, and body positivity in the ritual.

There is fear and discomfort, and yet I wake up every morning to witness increasingly more women who want to be heard from the balcony or in the main sanctuary, *within* their tradition. I think a great deal about the questions that come from living a Torah lifestyle that have implications for the health of our communities. Who is organizing around institutional power for women in the Jewish community? Are we taking rituals crafted by men and making them uniquely our own? Can we struggle as our genuine selves while still being true to Jewish law? And are we doing it from above? From within? From here, or from there?

In the Yeshivat Maharat program, my days are spent with my head buried in ancient rabbinic texts, exploring and wrestling with the complex nuances of Jewish law. The more I can understand the laws and study them, the deeper I'm engaged in the tradition. I fall in love more every day with how the framework grasps me lightly, holds my community, and envelops the world. I'm not going anywhere. Halakhah is home. I will continue to cling to the Tree of Life while singing loudly from the balcony. But sometimes, I'll walk down those stairs and work with others to make room for a strong, participatory, and spiritually robust community.

Please God, give me the ability to respect the beauty and the sanctity of time in this process. Please God, give me the strength necessary to step down from the balcony when necessary and also the humility and wisdom to stay and sing from "here." I can't profess to know what's right, but I am making a commitment to listen to the voices of those women who sing around me.

# My Mother's Bat Mitzvah
## by Miriam Peskowitz

MIRIAM PESKOWITZ is the New York Times bestselling author of *The Daring Book for Girls* and the *Double Daring Book for Girls*. She is also the author of *The Truth Behind the Mommy Wars*, *Spinning Fantasies: Gender, Rabbis and History*, and, with Laura Levitt, *Judaism Since Gender*. She has taught at the University of Florida, Emory University, Temple University and the Reconstructionist Rabbinical College.

**Friday Night Service at Community Reform Temple. Westbury, New York. Sometime in the mid-1970s.**

The congregation is singing the *Avot* (patriarchs) prayer. Ann Middleman sits in the brown, velvety pew in front of us. We've just mentioned the forefathers Abraham, Isaac, and Jacob; Ann, who has a clarion strong singing voice, inserts the foremothers Sarah, Rebecca, Rachel, and Leah. Ann is my mom's friend. It's a moment of confusion. Some in the congregation keep going. Some wait for her to finish her brief, female-focused, four-beat cadenza. Eventually everyone finds the new rhythm and the prayer continues.

This may be one of my earliest memories of synagogue Judaism. I am ten or eleven or twelve. I find it thrilling.

Ann does this at every service I can remember. She makes the whole congregation slow down and include the matriarchs even if some people might laugh. Even if some might cock their heads, and think she is brash or weird or out of place. Even if, perhaps, it causes some to try to understand the world that is changing all around them.

Years later, the Reform movement issues a new edition of their prayerbook, *Gates of Prayer*. The liturgy has changed, thanks to women and men around the country who, like Ann, added the foremothers on their own. The prayer is given a new name, the *Avot V'Imahot* (patriarchs and matriarchs). The kids now don't even realize that within our lifetimes, this prayer was an argument, an option, a question. Now it's just the way things are, and possibly, have always been.

### Simchat Torah Morning Service at Temple Adas Israel. Sag Harbor, New York. October 2012.

My job this morning is to pick up my grandmother. Roz is ninety-five. She lives at the San Simeon by the Sound nursing home. We're running late. When I reach her room, Roz hasn't finished dressing. The nurse hasn't yet poured her medicines. And just because she's ninety-five doesn't mean she wants to skip putting her lipstick on right.

Why am I in a rush to get her moving? Today is a big deal. It's the bat mitzvah of her oldest daughter—my mom, Myra, seventy-three—and the service starts in a half-hour. I pack my grandma into the front seat, stash her wheelchair in the hatch, and we're off.

My mother made sure I had a bat mitzvah. It was the '70s—still the semi-early days for girls' bat mitzvahs, but totally the norm for Reform Jews. Her friend Sonya had been put in charge of finding my *kippah* (skullcap) and tallit (prayer shawl). This is common now. Four clicks on Etsy.com gets any prayer shawl you like delivered to your front door, but it wasn't that way then. Sonya had visited Jerusalem that winter, and she'd gone tallit shopping for me. In store after store, they'd show her the usual garb. She'd say, "But where are the nice colors for girls?" There would be a tumult. "Girls?! Tallitot?!" It was shopping as feminist activism. Sonya returned to New York with a turquoise, white, and gold tallit. We agreed that indeed, she had done a great job. These were lovely colors for girls.

Sonya and my mom tell this story for decades.

Three and a half decades later, it's my mom's turn.

I wheel my grandmother into her place in the first row. The small congregation, worried by our lateness, breathes a collective sigh of relief. My mom is already on the *bimah*. Several women had been in her Hebrew class, which turned into the bat mitzvah class. At first, my mom continued out of loyalty to her friends. One by one they dropped out, but she continued. For herself. After so many years of being a synagogue volunteer, she wanted to feel like a leader. For her, this meant knowing Hebrew, knowing the liturgy, being able to lead the service without faking it. Today, my mom is radiant. Her long silver hair is tucked into a chiffon. Her flowing silver-gray dress looks like it was designed for the head teacher of the angels. She leads prayers. She chants from Torah. She gives her own *d'var Torah* (interpretation of a part of the Torah). Her friends beam up at her. In fact, everyone in the pews beam up at her. Her gentle rabbi is so proud. She has made herself into the Jewish leader she dreamt of being.

Because it is also Simchat Torah, when she's done, we promenade with the Torah. Imagine this: My grandmother in her wheelchair carrying a Torah in her arms for the first time ever; women her age missed nearly all the religious change of the last century. Pushing her is my newly bat-mitzvahed mother, followed by me and my youngest daughter, age seven. Four generations of women, at the ritual center, in a synagogue founded by watch factory workers in an historic whaling town.

I came of age while feminists were still singing from the margins of an unwritten text. My introduction to Judaism came through passionate, committed feminist interventions, like Ann's; women who used their voices and bodies to carve out more space for them to be Jews. It was weaned on long conversations with Sonya and my mom. These women were my Torah, my Jewish learning.

What Jewish feminists have accomplished in the last forty years, in liberal Jewish communities, is extraordinary. Historically speaking, never have so many Jewish women been as empowered in their traditions. Yes, there's always more to fix. There are people who don't get it. There are holdout communities where Jewish men grab tightly onto their leadership and every possible power over women. Still, in all of

Jewish history, Jewish women have never been so included, educated, or collectively liturgically and religiously creative as now. This present moment is worth appreciating. Enormous amounts of feminist religious change have occurred.

Consider this question, then: What does it mean for those of us who grew up, and learned Jewishness, within traditions of feminist critique, now that so much has been achieved in our progressive Jewish communities? Coming of age this way, the fight, the challenge, the creative newness of change was a spark through which religious life was experienced. One gets used to this, to ritual as activism, activism as ritual. When there's no longer as much to argue about, ritual and learning and all the rest feel different; nice, but perhaps a little flat.

**Kaddish. Florida. January 2014.**

A year after my mom's bat mitzvah, my grandmother dies. My mom is saying Kaddish. She and my dad go to Florida for three months in the winter, and she wants to continue her practice. Is there a congregation in West Palm Beach that is traditional enough to gather a daily minyan, and egalitarian enough to include her? Two seconds on Google finds an egalitarian conservative minyan ten minutes from her apartment that meets six days a week at 8 a.m.

My mom tells me her news. I think of Esther Broner's book, *On Mornings and Mourning: A Kaddish Journal*. Published in 1994, Broner wrote about her experience of the eleven-month mourning period after her father died. She went to an Orthodox synagogue where she sat in the segregated women's section, wasn't counted in the minyan, and in general, had to fight to matter.

I think for a moment about sending my mom the book. Then I realize how anachronistic that would be. Kaddish isn't a fight for my mom. It's just Kaddish, and very meaningful as such. The new minyan welcomes her with open arms. She counts. She matters. The Adon Olam prayer ends and she is offered everything from a chocolate-covered Entenmann's donut to a splash of whiskey in her coffee, and if that isn't inclusion, I don't know what is. She falls in love with her new minyan-mates, and they with her.

One day I attend with her. We meet one of the minyan women in the parking lot. She hands my mom a bag filled with pretty hair clips. "I found these while cleaning out," she says, very kindly. "I thought they might look nice in your hair." My mom thanks her, and they walk inside. Both women put on a kippah. A man hands me one, too. My mother wraps herself in her tallit. I hadn't seen her bring it in. Turns out she stows her tallit bag on a shelf in the minyan room, because, you know, she's become a regular. The two women don't wrap tefillin: the black boxes with leather straps, with the biblical commandment inside, placed on one's forehead and on one's arm, and used at week-day morning prayer. Many of the men do; tefillin has always been a commandment directed at men, and from which women have been restricted. Some women who aren't there that day do pray with tefillin, my mom tells me. This has inspired my mother. She decides to ask her home rabbi to teach her how it's done, but that's another story.

My mom's Kaddish experience has come a long way from what Esther Broner describes in *Mornings and Mourning*. There's no friction. There's no feminist angst or intervention. My mom gets to perform rituals that at many points in her life would have seemed impossible or would have been highly contested.

Honestly, what a joy. This is the new religion of the mothers. Things have changed. This is why I stay.

There's another reason, too.

### Rosh Hashanah. Philadelphia, Pennsylvania. Fall 2013.

If feminism and conflict were part of what made Judaism meaningful, how do we enjoy the new traditions? Is it boring now that there are fewer angels to wrestle? When we've mixed and matched the Passover Haggadah so much, for example, that we expect to find the orange on the seder plate, and see Miriam's cup on the table? We'd be terribly disappointed if the twenty-year-olds *didn't* bring in the special Haggadah supplement that explains the terrible mass incarceration of black and brown men and the new Jim Crow. Explaining these things is now on par with explaining the horseradish and the *matzah* (unleavened bread).

Enjoyable, yes. But not boring. Because there will always be those delightful twenty-somethings who bring in the Incarceration Four Questions, or whatever the next oppression that we must respond to. For them, these ritual interventions still feel risky, still create a religious buzz. And every time, it challenges me. And that ubiquitous orange on the seder plate? Some aging Jewish feminist has to remind everyone that it wasn't always an orange, and it wasn't always about Jewish women, and tell the story of how the orange started out as a truly radical crust of bread that Oberlin College students placed on the seder plate in the mid-1980s, and then wrote about it: as a charge to remind us of issues facing lesbians and gays.

In 2013, I pop into Rosh Hashana services in the lower room of the Mennonite Church, which a new congregation has rented out for the day. Rabbi Linda Holtzman is leading services. The room is filled with LGBT kids, I'm assuming from West Philly. I can barely tell who is which gender, and isn't that the point? Some people have brought their aging parents in wheelchairs, which makes it a gloriously loving, multicultural room. Could I even have imagined this when I was a college Jewish feminist whose friends were putting bread crusts on the seder plate? Perhaps that's the point in this transgender revolution that began well after I came of age, and which I am still trying to understand in all of its complexity. My older daughter babysits for a trans male rabbinic student, who gave birth to his own (adorable) baby. I could feel like an earlier, older generation of Jewish feminist, exempt from understanding the next generation, allowed to pretend the world isn't changing around me. Except that Linda Holtzman's on the bimah, and Rebecca Alpert's in the room. Both are first-generation feminist and lesbian rabbis. Both are my spiritual elders.

Look what Jewish feminism opened up: communities and inclusions that I've had to blink a few times to understand, communities that bust open new barriers, as once I was part of an earlier wave of busting and opening.

The buzz of change is my Jewish tradition, and it never ends. Overt religious change has become a new spirituality.

# The Faith of My Mothers and Sisters
## by Elise M. Edwards

ELISE M. EDWARDS, PH.D., is visiting professor of Christian Ethics at Baylor University. Her interdisciplinary work examines issues of civic engagement and how beliefs and commitments are expressed publicly. As a black feminist, she primarily focuses on cultural expressions by, for, and about women and marginalized communities. Elise regularly blogs at FeminismandReligion.com and can be followed on Twitter @EliseME.

"I don't know where I'd be without Jesus."

This is a statement I heard over and over during the weekend my family laid my Aunt Ruby to rest. There were two memorial services—one at the church my aunt attended in suburban Maryland, and another at a chapel in rural Virginia close to where she was born and buried. It seemed particularly appropriate for a woman who was praised for her godly life, who died on Easter Sunday, and who loved church to have two Christian services to mourn and remember her. My cousins, parents, and the extended community of friends and family assembled at these services repeatedly confessed to each other, "I don't know how I could make it through this without faith" and "I don't know where I'd be without Jesus."

The faith that has sustained my family through difficult times is centered on Jesus. Because I was raised with their faith, Jesus has long been the center of my spiritual life. Well before I knew that women could not be ordained in some Christian traditions, or that many Christians use the Bible to keep women silent and submissive, I knew that Jesus loved me and that I loved him. While Jesus is the central figure in my faith, love is its defining principle. John 3:16 was the first Bible verse I memorized. (This is fairly typical for children who attend Sunday School in their early years.) It is a verse that speaks of God's love for the world, and Jesus' presence in the world as a sign of that love. As a young person, I felt special believing that the God who created the whole world loves me and that the son of God loves me, too. I simply cannot imagine what my life would be like without that love and without the Christian teachings and traditions so inextricably woven into the tapestry of my family's life.

There have been times that I thought of leaving a particular church (and I have), but I have never wanted to leave the Church, which is the universal body of believers of Jesus. I am a Christian because Christianity is the faith tradition that has sustained the women in my family for generations and continues to sustain me through its doctrines and practices. I know that Christian theology is centered on a male Savior (Jesus) and a God too-often imagined as male (the Father). I know that some Christians teach that women should be submissive to men, that women are inherently more sinful than men, and that women's leadership in the church should be restricted. But I first learned the Christian faith from women. It was mostly women who nurtured my faith, and they found within Christianity a hope and a purpose and a calling that surpasses any patriarchal agenda.

I have not had the same crisis of faith that many feminists have had—to feel that I have to choose feminism over Christianity. As an undergraduate student, I became quite aware of the ways in which Christianity has been and continues to be misogynistic; there are texts that denigrate womanhood and practices that keep females silent and submissive. While I understand criticisms about Christianity's irredeemably patriarchal character, the arguments have never been convincing enough to outweigh my experiential knowledge. My walk with Jesus, the spiritual lives of women who inspire me, and my understanding of the gospel convince me of the realities and possibilities for Christianity to support the fight for gender equality and justice.

I want Jesus to walk with me,
I want Jesus to walk with me.
All along my pilgrim journey,
I want Jesus to walk with me.

TRADITIONAL NEGRO SPIRITUAL

The faith of my matriarchs is rooted in the black Baptist church, and although I have tended to worship in more internationally-based or predominantly white Baptist churches, it has been the faith that the women of my family modeled that I practice. My mother, my maternal grandmother, and my sister helped me experience the joy and connection with the divine that comes from singing in the church choir and belting out gospel tunes or spirituals when I am alone.

My mother taught me how to pray. The first bedtime prayer she taught my sister and me showed me how to entrust my soul to the Lord as I sleep. However morbid it may sound, the phrase, "If I should die before I wake, I pray the Lord my soul to take" gave me some comfort despite my childhood fears of tornadoes, robbers, and other dangers hiding in the deep of night. The beginning of the prayer, "Now I lay me down to sleep, I pray the Lord my soul to keep" still soothes when anxiety, loneliness, fear, or unexplained insomnia prevent me from falling asleep. It calms my spirit to know that my soul belongs to God.

Decades after I learned my first prayers from my mother, my paternal grandmother and aunts on my father's side of the family encouraged me to claim my calling as a Christian theologian. One year when we were celebrating my Grandma Dot's birthday near the end of her life, my aunts got into a discussion about who in our family should have become a minister. I was attending a Christian seminary at the time, which may have been what led my Aunt Ruby to look in my direction and say, "Maybe it will be you." Grandma Dot, who was unable to speak, nodded and smiled. I laughed at the remark, explaining that I have never felt a call to preach or be ordained. But I knew in that moment that my family supported my active participation in church and my calling to teach, without being concerned that as a woman I should not.

Christianity is patriarchal, often intolerant, and the Baptist tradition in particular has been associated with a type of social conservatism that emphasizes traditional family values, opposition to LGBTQ rights and same-sex marriage, anti-intellectualism, decisions against the ordination of women, and a pro-life political agenda. I do not identify with any of these movements or agendas. I identify with the message of Jesus, the gospel of love and inclusion. I will not give up a faith that has nurtured my spirit and sustained my family for generations because others who also claim my tradition hold views I vehemently oppose. I have felt frustration and anger towards some Christians for their bigotry, hatred, and misogyny, but these Christians do not define what Christianity means to me. Their version of the Christian faith does not compel me to abandon mine.

In my career, I instruct college students about the development of the Christian heritage and guide them through reasoning about complex moral issues from religious grounds. I communicate to my students that there is a vast diversity and range of positions within the Christian tradition. The pluralist character of Christianity helps me to publicly claim the Christian tradition as my own because I do not feel compelled to agree with everyone who claims to be Christian.

I admit, though, that there have been times that I've been hesitant to identify myself as Christian—and more specifically as a Baptist—because of widely-held negative perceptions of us. Gary Javens, my pastor from my teens and twenties, has a favorite Bible verse, Romans 1:16: "For I am not ashamed of the gospel, because it is the power of God that brings salvation to everyone who believes." This verse has encouraged me to stay strong. For me, the Christian gospel is about radical inclusion. It is about God's love and grace for the entire world. God loves us without first requiring us to be something we are not. Jesus associated with women and God tasked women with revealing important messages to the world, as when Jesus teaches the Samaritan woman, and when Mary Magdalene tells the disciples that she spoke with Jesus at his empty tomb.[1] These stories indicate to me that women have an important place in God's paradigm that does not require us to be male. Each of us is included in God's love and has a role in bringing about God's purposes for the world.

I am also strengthened by the knowledge that, despite public perception of Baptists, we have theological doctrines that affirm critical self-examination and renounce blind allegiance to the majority. The two doctrines that are most significant to me are freedom of conscience and autonomy of the local church. At its most basic understanding, freedom of conscience means that each person is responsible for his or her own convictions. While I do believe in the importance of community and relationships, I affirm that every person has their own conscience and that maturity in the life of the mind and the soul is a process of coming to understand and articulate one's own beliefs and motivations. Autonomy of the local church is the Baptist rejection of a particular form of church hierarchy. A local church's association with other churches or denominational bodies is voluntary. This doctrine gives me freedom of identification. I can be a Baptist without being a conservative Baptist. In addition to the well-known conservative Southern Baptist Convention, there are dozens of other organizations that seek to unify local churches and support them. Some are socially conservative, some are progressive, and some are committed to social justice. I do not have to renounce my Baptist identity to have an opportunity to worship with like-minded people.

---

1. Both of these biblical stories are in the Gospel of John. In John 4: 4-40, Jesus encounters a woman from Samaria. Their conversation transgresses cultural and gendered social conventions because Jews and Samaritans would not typically have conversed, nor would single males and females. Jesus reveals to the woman that he is the Messiah. She tells other Samaritans about her meeting with Jesus and many come to believe in him because of her actions. In John 20:1-18, Mary the Magdalene is the first person to notice that Jesus is not in his tomb after being buried there. (He has been resurrected.) While the male disciples are trying to make sense of this, Mary cries at the empty tomb where she then speaks to angels and Jesus himself, who reveals that he is ascending to God. She goes to tell the disciples what she has learned. In both narratives, a woman reveals something important about Jesus' identity and ministry to his followers and others.

You got a right, I got a right,
We all got a right to the tree of life.
TRADITIONAL NEGRO SPIRITUAL

When I have had issues with the agenda or with the male dominance within one particular Baptist church, I've had the freedom to find another Baptist church that resonates with my spirit. Perhaps this is the logic of "church shopping" which so many Christians bemoan as an imposition of consumerist values into the church. But for me, the freedom to change churches has allowed me to find a community where my feminist Christian self belongs. Although churches should be inclusive places, reflecting the values of a loving God, many are not. Finding a place where I can be transparent has been difficult at times, but it has been possible, and the process has been affirming.

By participating in church life, my spiritual well-being is nurtured. Although in my professional life, I seek to make the universal church a more inclusive place, in my church-going practice I seek sanctuary. I seek a community that is already accepting of my place in the family of God so that I can be sustained for my work outside that sanctuary. In the churches I have attended since starting a career centered on feminist Christian practice, I have specifically sought the company of women. While I enjoy worshipping in Sunday worship services with people who are culturally, generationally, and in many other ways diverse, I am intentionally narrow in my pursuit of Bible study and fellowship groups. Many churches have groups for singles, thirty-somethings, forty-somethings, and the like, but I have chosen circles of intelligent, curious, and courageous women to be my closest companions in spiritual practice. Today, it's not only the women in my family who model Christianity for me, but my female friends and peers who pastor churches, attend worship services faithfully, lead ministries, write theology, teach, disciple others, and pray.

My foremothers and my sisters in faith embody for me Jesus' message of love and hope for a just future. They encourage me to keep loving, keep pressing, keep trying, keep walking with Jesus. So I willfully choose to embrace the faith of my mother, my Granny, my Grandma Dot, my Aunt Ruby, and my foremothers too numerous to name. I choose to be a witness for this faith so that others may be sustained by it as we have. Thus, "I don't know where I'd be without Jesus."

# Embracing Feminism in Public to Find God in Private
## by Jennifer Zobair

JENNIFER ZOBAIR is an attorney and a writer. Her debut novel, *Painted Hands*, was published by St. Martin's Press in 2013. She is the founder of the website storyandchai.com, a creative space for readers and writers of Muslim and culturally diverse narratives. Jennifer lives with her husband and three children in the Washington, DC, area. She is currently at work on her second novel. Visit her online at www.jenniferzobair.com.

*My fiancé and I sit before the imam. I'm nervous, but eager. I'm about to convert to Islam, my soon-to-be husband's religion, but I have some questions. Or, more specifically, one question: Verse 4:34 of the Qur'an, which seems to permit the beating of women. My fiancé's family is upstairs, waiting. Everyone assumes this talk with the imam is perfunctory. Even I am certain he'll provide a reassuring explanation—that he'll say of course men cannot hit women—and we'll proceed with my conversion. The imam starts by telling us how often marriages between born-Muslims and converts end in divorce. I'm startled, but determined. I ask my question. He pauses, and then says that yes, that is what that verse means. I say I cannot conceive of a god who would permit such a thing. He tells me that in some parts of the world women are like children and need to be dealt with accordingly. I am certain I look horrified. He shrugs and says I can put something in my marriage contract about it if I want. I look at my fiancé. I think we cannot possibly do this now.*

*He looks back at me, his face not quite a plea, but sort of a plea. It is unthinkable to his family that he would marry me if I didn't convert. It's clear that one of us will have to make a significant sacrifice in this moment. We thank the imam and go upstairs. I convert, but I'm not sure the words reach my heart. Later, in my most private thoughts, which I share with exactly no one, I wonder if my conversion was even valid.*

◆◆◆

To talk about why I stay in Islam as a feminist, I have to talk about all of the times I wanted to go.

These are dangerous words for a convert—both for the skeptics, who didn't trust her conversion in the first place, and for herself, because she knows that if she's left one religion she can leave another. And yet, there are times I have wanted to go, like when my wedding gifts included books mandating subservient gender roles for women, or whenever I was forced to sit in substandard, gender-segregated spaces at mosques. I wanted to go every time someone told me, a grown woman, what to wear, and I especially wanted to go when someone implied that non-Muslim college students are complicit in their own rapes.

I have wanted to go.

I have struggled with the ways many Muslims seem to put more significance on controlling women and their bodies than on true spiritual experience or meaning—actually having a relationship with God. But I converted for marriage—a decision based on sound theological reasons, mostly concerning my inability to fully fathom the Trinity, but also with the motivation to raise children in one faith. It wasn't a course to abandon frivolously.

◆◆◆

Before I converted, my husband and I stood in the vestibule of a Catholic church. Amid the bulletin board notices and holy water fonts, I grew quiet. "Am I just supposed to say goodbye?" I finally asked. My husband said he would give me a moment and closed the double doors gently behind him. At the time, I thought I was saying goodbye to Jesus as God. What I didn't know was that I was also saying goodbye to private sacred space, and that sometimes it would feel as though I'd said goodbye to God altogether.

As a child, I'd been forced to go to church, an approach to religion that can either stick or not, and in my case it didn't until it had meaning for me. I returned to church in my senior year of college, taking refuge from the pressure of exams, some borderline disordered eating, and looming decisions about my future. Soon, I was going every Sunday, sometimes more.

It wasn't the liturgy or the homily that wrapped around me like comfort. It wasn't even the elderly priest who became accustomed to my attendance and sometimes flicked holy water playfully in my direction. Instead, it was the time before Mass when Catholics enter the pews and kneel, engaging in silent prayer. That was where I found God. That blissfully quiet space, the only time my mind stopped racing and planning and worrying. I knew peace there, and it might have been the only place in my young life I had known it.

Islam, with its insistence that no one intercedes with God on a believer's behalf, should have been the perfect place to find a similar peace. Instead, people cajoled and pressured me until I couldn't access the Divine at all.

When I converted, my communion with God became a ridiculously public affair. Suddenly, what I believed, especially about women's rights, and how I behaved, including what I wore, seemed to be everybody's business. (Interestingly, no one in my new Muslim community asked me about my relationship with God during this time.) I've never understood the impulse to be so invested in the spiritual beliefs and behavior of others, but people were invested. Worse, they were in my head. I'd always been an avid reader, but soon that became tainted, too. I told a beloved Muslim professor friend that I couldn't even read novels anymore without wondering what "they" would think of some of the content.

"You've got to get them out of your head," my friend said. She repeated it, as though she knew such a thing had the power to ruin.

◆◆◆

Both Catholicism and Islam suffer from patriarchal exegeses. Both forbid female clergy and place an inordinate emphasis on female chastity. Brilliant scholars in both traditions have carved out sacred feminist space, and, theologically, I believe it is no harder to be a Muslim feminist than a Catholic one. Practically, though, my experience is a different story. I never felt judged for being a Catholic feminist. Not everyone agreed with my opinions, but I felt entitled to have them. I commiserated with nuns who refused to attend church under Pope John Paul II and debated affable priests about women's ordination. I was a feminist, but I was firmly within the fold.

My journey into Islam was much less accepting, as I confronted majority condemnations of women leading prayers, gay rights, and personal choices about one's body. Even though many Muslim Americans believe women should be educated and have careers, it was exponentially more difficult for me to find Muslims who agree to disagree on women's theological issues. It has been a much more conditional space for a feminist like me to inhabit.

The Muslim American community tends to parade *hijabi* (women who wear headscarves) converts around, like proof. But what do they do with a non-covering, feminist convert?

After my conversion, I attended women's *halaqas* (religious talks), primarily led by conservative women. One talk featured a male speaker, who sat behind a screen. It was a surreal moment for me, a practicing lawyer—that women couldn't sit in the presence of a man, even in a large group. To me, it felt like deferring to male authority while admitting female weakness and propensity to be easily corrupted. All I could think was *what am I doing here?*

I already knew, of course: I was pretending. I was routinely honoring the opinions of others over my own opinions. And in pretending to find God on their terms, I lost any real connection to God on my own.

Eventually, I told my husband that I wasn't sure I wanted to stay in Islam. But I didn't know what that meant for my family. We had three small children who we wanted to raise in one faith. My in-laws were highly invested in my being Muslim. I had done the hard work of seeking out feminist interpretations of Catholicism. I had to see if I could do the same with Islam.

That search led me to the work of scholars like Asma Barlas and Amina Wadud and Fatima Mernissi. I inhaled their books and articles. I read interpretations of verse 4:34 that made it clear husbands have no right to hit their wives. For the first time, I felt like I would stay. Still, I missed being able to freely speak my mind on women's issues. The struggle, then, was to join the liberating theology with actual practice. Though intellectually I had carved out a sacred space that felt affirming, in reality, I found being a Muslim feminist isolating and lonely.

Still, I was finding my voice. I had something to say, and I decided to say it in what would become my debut novel, *Painted Hands*. In the book, I engage the assumptions and prejudices of both non-Muslims and conservative Muslims alike. It's fiction, but I am written across the pages of that novel. I am in the woman-led prayer that informs the climax, and Hayden's post-conversion isolation, and Zainab's curse-word-laden rants against the Muslims and non-Muslims who judge her.

The book is fiction. The book is truthful. The book is aspiration. The book is me.

The publication of my novel was, in many ways, my coming out to my fellow Muslims as a feminist. I held my breath on its release, but I had little to worry about. The American Muslim community, in large part, ignored the book. No major Muslim newspaper or magazine reviewed it, though my publicist sent them all copies. A Muslim radio station with a large audience conducted an interview with me but never aired it. There are not many Muslim American novelists. Even so, my book was ignored, and it felt to me like a not-so-subtle reminder that, in mainstream Islam, feminists are decidedly outside of the fold.

But much that matters in life happens in the smaller spaces. After my book released, Muslim women—those who practiced and those who remained secular—contacted me to thank me for writing my novel, saying it was the first time they had ever truly related to characters in fiction. Some of these interactions turned into longer exchanges. Some of them fostered friendships, enough that I started to feel like I'd found what had, up to that point, eluded me: a Muslim feminist community.

And there it is, so ridiculously simple. Speaking our truth leads us to other people who speak their similar truth. When we have the courage to be ourselves, to find our center and hold it proudly and publicly, we find the people who will honor and value us as well.

True acceptance, both self and other, can do remarkable things to quiet the mind. It can make it possible to hear the Divine once again whispering to us: *You have the right to be here, just as you are.*

A few months after my book released, I watched the movie *Life of Pi*. At one point the young main character, Piscine Molitor "Pi" Patel, a Hindu, explores Christianity and Islam in addition to his own faith. To his parents' amusement, he decides to adopt all three faiths. I was charmed by this idea that a person could be more than one thing—that he didn't have to choose. Perhaps, deep down, that is the convert's silent reverie, communing with God by keeping the familiar of the old while trying to find a way in the new. But then, as I watched Pi interact with a Catholic priest and observe the Muslim prayer, there was this: I watched his interaction with the priest as though standing on the outside, as an observer. In contrast, I heard the Muslim prayer—the haunting Arabic recitation—and felt it on the inside, in my heart, in the quietest space, removed from chastising voices. I felt the presence of something greater, something accepting, something peaceful.

In that moment, it seemed possible that God and I had never parted at all, that God had been waiting for me, through the noise and the alienation, the whole time. It seemed possible, blissfully and stunningly possible, that I had been worth waiting for.

It has been my experience that those who judge you, particularly publicly to compel behavior, are not really interested in your relationship with God. Those people cannot be your concern. You will never find sacred space in the cold, judgmental exhortations of others. And they don't really care if you find it anyway. It is never about you, or even about God. It is always about them.

Sometimes faith comes easily, in bursts of marathon reading of empowering texts. Sometimes it is the quiet whisper of a young Indian character in a movie calling you back. As a Muslim feminist, this is what I know: You've got to own your voice in order to protect your sacred space. You've got to boldly and unflinchingly be yourself in public to fully access the Divine in private. This is what I'm doing. This is how I stay.

# Reflections from a Mormon Feminist
## by Caroline Kline

CAROLINE KLINE is a Ph.D. student in religion at Claremont Graduate University with a focus on women's studies in religion. She is editor of *Mormon Women Have Their Say* and co-founder of the Mormon feminist blog, *The Exponent*. Caroline's areas of interest revolve around the intersections of Mormon and feminist theology and the study of contemporary Mormon feminist communities.

In October 2013, I gathered all my courage and flew to Salt Lake City to stand in line with two hundred other Mormon feminists to ask for tickets to the priesthood session of General Conference, a session we were barred from attending because of our sex. Mormon men, who are all ordained to the lay Mormon priesthood, as well as non-Mormon men, blithely walked past us into the session, unimpeded on that cold unwelcoming day.

While our request for tickets to the priesthood session might seem pretty mild to most feminists—no shouting, no signs, and no disruptions—it was a radical act for me and my Mormon feminist friends. To place my body on the line, to ask for entrance where I was not wanted, to transgress norms that pressure me to say that I am fine with the current male-only priesthood structure within Mormonism, took every ounce of bravery I could muster. This action, sponsored by the new Mormon feminist group Ordain Women, was the most confrontational (albeit tame and polite) Mormon feminist activist event since the days of the Equal Rights Amendment (ERA). It was exhilarating and terrifying to stand with my sisters to individually ask the usher for tickets.

As I had expected, we were all turned away. My heart broke as I held my crying friend in my arms after she was rejected, my friend who had prayed in the Mormon temple and had come to an unshakable conviction that this action of ours was affirmed by God. I told her repeatedly that it was women like her, women of faith, hope, and vision, who would show the church that we women were ready for priesthood.

Several months later, an acquaintance in my local Mormon congregation, a kind and conservative woman I had come to know a little through book groups and church attendance, asked me if I was going to go back and stand in line again. "You should go," Ellen said firmly. "It's important to do what you think is right."

I was startled by this exchange—Ellen was no proponent of women's ordination—but on reflection, perhaps I shouldn't have been. While obedience to church authorities (and thus status quo policies) is emphasized in Mormon discourse, other forces at work in Mormonism open up space for non-conformist positions. I had been in this congregation with Ellen for the last eleven years, and we had listened to each other's lessons and talks and comments in church. While she and I didn't agree about women's ordination, she did want to affirm me and support me personally. In Mormonism, community matters. Relationships matter. And learning how to love, support, and see the good in those you disagree with in our geographically determined congregations is a constant imperative.

Ellen's supportive comments to me might have also been sparked by Mormonism's regard for the concept of personal revelation. Mormonism was founded in the nineteenth century by a young man who bypassed clerics and approached God directly with his questions. His revelatory experience as a fourteen-year-old sparked the founding of a church dedicated to the idea that we can all commune directly with God and receive answers to our personal queries. This beloved Mormon concept of personal revelation means that Mormons often give wide space to others' spiritual promptings and convictions, though that inclination toward relativism is tempered by authoritative statements from church leadership giving its members firm directions. Nevertheless, despite this tension, I find in the core Mormon concept of personal revelation an anti-hierarchical tendency that feeds my spirit. My Mormon God can speak to me. My Mormon God can work with individual needs, questions, and circumstances. My Mormon God can lead me to positions and places other Mormons find shocking.

Strong community and personal revelation are concepts and practices I cling to when the going gets rough. Being a Mormon feminist is not easy. I often find myself in a liminal space, too feminist for Mormons and too Mormon for feminists. I am regarded with some degree of wariness from all sides. It's often a lonely place, knowing that I am probably the only person in my congregation struggling mightily with women's institutional invisibility and lack of leadership positions. It hurts to hear concepts taught that subordinate women to their husbands. It hurts to go to church every week and hear the constant androcentrism of our language, which depicts God as male; emphasizes the words, thoughts, and experiences of our male church authorities; and erases me and my sisters and our diverse experiences as women. Every male-focused reference and practice is a paper cut, and I come home from church bleeding and stinging.

And yet I continue on as a church-attending Mormon. After many years of grappling with my place as a feminist in the church, I have come to realize that I can set the terms of my engagement with my tradition. I can set boundaries of what I will and what I won't participate in. I now feel that I have the right and responsibility to reject that which is degrading and limiting within Mormon practice and thought. This rejection gives me the ability to embrace the good, the empowering, and the beautiful within my tradition.

There is indeed goodness and beauty. I love the Mormon concept of Heavenly Mother. She is almost never mentioned in Mormon discourse—Mormon leaders model "Heavenly Father" God-language and discourage the practice of praying to Heavenly Mother—yet she is there in our doctrine, an embodied female divinity, wife of the embodied male Heavenly Father. The silence surrounding her is clearly problematic. I wait for the day when more and more Mormons take the initiative, develop a relationship with the Mother, and incorporate her into their religious discourse. This project of lifting the Mother into the light is essential for Mormon feminists. In our own homes, we have begun to feature her in our religious discussions with our children. I teach my children constantly that God is the combined unit of Heavenly Mother and Heavenly Father. The seeds are there within our tradition to embrace our feminine divine, and thus fully embrace the divine potential of all women.

Concepts of Heavenly Mother bind me to my tradition, as does the Mormon concept of eternal progression. In Mormon cosmology, we humans have divine potential to progress and rise to the level of deity ourselves. Thus the Mormon God works to radically close the gap between human and divine, as he and she reject principles of eternal subordination. The Mormon God is ultimately a god who wants peers.

Peers. I love that concept. It is there, in the cosmology, and it is there in my lived life as a Mormon feminist. My devout Mormon husband, despite contradictory Mormon teachings of male headship and marital equal partnership, fully envisions and treats me as his peer and equal, as I do him. We might cancel out each other's votes every election cycle and embrace different approaches to our faith, but he is utterly committed to our relationship. I know that he constantly wakes up in the morning and asks himself what he can do to make me happy and be a good partner to me. I cannot forget that Mormonism helped form this man. "You wouldn't have wanted to marry me before I served my two-year mission in Wyoming. My mission taught me how to love people," he told me early on in our relationship.

Through Mormon feminist networks I have found peers and companions in the struggle, women who understand and likewise feel every slice and stab I do. Together we lift each other up and give each other the courage to keep pushing, keep trying, and keep raising our voices. A year or two ago, my Mormon feminist friends held me up and sustained me when I decided to raise my voice and push for my inclusion in my infant son's baby blessing. Traditionally, Mormon men gather around the baby in a circle as the father pronounces a blessing during a Sunday worship service. With this child, my last, I knew I wanted something different. I wanted to be in that circle, and not in the audience with the rest of the congregation. My bishop was extremely uncomfortable with the idea, but after months of discussion, agreed to let me hold the baby during the blessing. By that time, however, I was so discouraged by the bishop's negativity that I was ready to give up. That night I emailed my Mormon feminist friends, asking for their advice. Within a couple of hours I had twenty emails encouraging me to move forward, to think of what I would wish I had done when I look back on my life, and to push past my fear and hold my child as I felt so strongly I should. This experience highlights an essential component of my Mormon life—friendship with beloved peers who are there to make me strong when I am weak and discouraged.

I often find peers in surprising places. Last week, Sarah came up to me and asked if I had read Mormon feminist Carol Lynn Pearson's recent essay in a Mormon publication. "You should read it. I think you will like it," she whispered. Like it? I loved it! Pearson called out the homophobia and androcentricism in our Mormon culture and affirmed her own path of claiming her pioneer heritage to create more inclusive practices. How startling that Sarah of all people—who I know is culturally and politically far-right conservative—would want to tell me about it. As I thought about it later, I realized the implications of her brief comment to me. She was trying to give me reasons to stay. She was telling me I wasn't alone. She was telling me there was room for me in the church.

On my good days, I believe there really is room for me. Institutional Mormonism sets up certain roadblocks to women's full participation in the faith, but on my local level, there is some room to push against androcentric structures. As I sing in church, I change the male pronouns in the hymns to female or gender neutral ones. When I read the scriptures out loud in lessons, I read inclusively. When I teach or give sermons, I quote women and lift up women in the scriptures. Occasionally I am vulnerable and reveal my deep struggles with patriarchal beliefs and practices in the church. Afterwards women who don't share my struggles enfold me in their arms or send me loving emails.

Being a Mormon feminist is simultaneously painful and beautiful. It hurts—oh, how it hurts at times. How I despair that meaningful change won't happen in my lifetime, and how anxiety clenches in my gut when I think that I am raising my daughter in a tradition that doesn't want all her gifts. But I cannot deny that Mormonism has also given me an expansive vision of my divine potential and the divine potential of every human. I cannot deny that it has brought profound connection into my life—connection that against all odds transcends ideology and experience. I hold on to these thoughts in the hard moments, and using the words of Mormon feminist Joanna Brooks, I pray, "God, make me brave enough to love my people. How wonderful it is to have a people to love."

# Blessed Are You, Who Has Made Me a Woman

## by Rachel Lieberman

RACHEL LIEBERMAN is the Program Director at JOFA: Jewish Orthodox Feminist Alliance. Rachel graduated from Princeton University with an A.B. in Religion and a certificate in Judaic Studies. Her senior thesis, "Reaching Across the Mechitzah: Feminism's Impact on Orthodox Judaism" was awarded the Isidore and Helen Sacks Memorial Prize in Religion for outstanding work in Judaic Studies. She has studied at Yeshivat Hadar, Yeshivat Chovevei Torah and the Pardes Institute for Jewish Studies.

*"Baruch ata hashem, elokeinu melech haolam, sheasani Yisrael."*
*"Baruch ata hashem, elokeinu melech haolam, sheasani kirtsono."*

Blessed are you, Lord our God, ruler of the Universe, who made me a Jew.

Blessed are you, Lord our God, ruler of the Universe, who made me according to God's will.

These are two of the morning blessings I recite on my walk to the subway. I recite them from memory, these blessings I learned in elementary school. Some mornings I try to figure out the correct order for them—which identity is primary, which one is stronger? My identity as a Jew? Or my identity as a woman? Am I a Jewish woman, or a woman who is a Jew? Is there even a difference?

Some mornings, I even go so far as to recite an additional blessing:

*"Baruch ata hashem, elokeinu melech haolam, **sheasani Isha.**"* Blessed are you, lord our God, ruler of the universe, **who has made me a woman.**[1]

Religion and my gender are my two primary identities, the most significant lenses through which I experience the world.

I see gender everywhere, whether or not I'm in an Orthodox ritual space. I'm always counting—who is up on the bimah, who received which honors in synagogue, who is counted in a minyan, who is wearing a prayer shawl? Who said Kiddush, who stood up to clear the Shabbat table between courses? Is the rabbi a man? A woman? A "woman rabbi?" This reflex extends to the secular spaces too—four girls and twenty-three boys in the advanced high school math class, girls playing varsity softball while boys play varsity baseball, one man who seems to be out of place in an aerobics class, one woman presenting on a single panel during a multi-day conference, no women featured on the masthead of a prominent magazine.

I grew up attending an Orthodox synagogue, which was progressive and modern, but all of my experiences were filtered through my lens as a woman. My bat mitzvah, which was supposed to symbolize my passage into adulthood and the important moment where I would now be required to engage with a new set of responsibilities and obligations, did not mark a point of inclusion for me, but of exclusion. For my bat mitzvah, I was not permitted to do what the boys did. I was not permitted to prove my skills by reading from the Torah and from the Haftorah. I was not permitted to lead the services. My bat mitzvah signaled the beginning of my formal exclusion from organized, ritual, Orthodox Judaism—I would not be counted in the minyan, no matter how early I arrived at synagogue. I would not be permitted to read from the Torah or lead services, no matter how much I practiced or how proficient I was. I was barred due to the simple fact of being a woman. When I approached the rabbis, time and time again, with halakhic (legal) arguments, with social arguments,

---

1. This is the egalitarian alternative to the blessing that men traditionally recite. *"Baruch ata hashem, elokeinu melech haolam, she lo asani isha."* Blessed are you, lord our God, ruler of the universe, for not making me a woman.

with logical arguments, with passion or with tears, I was told that "the community is not ready." The community was not ready for the change that I dreamed of. The community was not ready to count girls like it counted boys. The community was not yet ready for me.

## Egalitarian Experiences

This habit, this reflex, of automatically counting the women and men in the room, and ranking the way women were treated, became a bad habit, blinding and exhausting. There were times when I couldn't focus, when I couldn't sit in synagogue, or in the *beit midrash* (study hall) because I was so furious, hurt, and upset that I needed to leave the room and excuse myself from that community.

As a result, I sought out opportunities in egalitarian communities—nondenominational communities, usually focused on engaging seriously with halakhah (Jewish law) and Jewish tradition and building a space where women and men have equal opportunities and access to texts, rituals, and leadership roles. I thought these environments would allow me to "check my gender issues at the door" and devote my focus to the "core issues" of studying Talmud and halakhah. I wanted to bulk up my ritual skills and take the opportunity to lead all aspects of *davening* (communal prayer) without getting distracted by whether or not I counted, and why I was or wasn't furious at the moment. I incorrectly assumed that an egalitarian space, by definition, would automatically accommodate my feminist beliefs and my gender lens would become a non-issue.

On the most basic level, which I did not take for granted, egalitarian communities count women and men equally in a minyan, and provide opportunities for all interested Jews (regardless of gender) to learn, pray, and to participate in the community. There is equal access to the texts, based on your own ability. But there are still questions, many of which are more difficult to identify, raise, and address, because the gender issues have already been "taken care of" when we enter an egalitarian space. These questions include:

When women are encouraged, but not required, to pray with tefillin, are they being encouraged to pray in traditionally male ritual garb? Or are they being encouraged to pray with ritual objects that all Jewish adults should be required to wear during prayer?

Is the goal of egalitarianism to effectively turn women into men? Is the goal to embrace all ritual obligations and commandments that are required of adult men ("full people" according to tradition), and to extend those obligations to all adult community members, including women? Does this mean that the category of women is still "other" and lesser than, the category that we are trying to erase and move away from?

Is there any way to embrace specifics or particularities of women's experiences and to incorporate them into an egalitarian space? Do we ever encourage the men in egalitarian spaces to embrace and adopt roles or commandments that were traditionally reserved for women, or does it only go one way?

How are women scholars and leaders incorporated as role models? Where are the strong, female, rabbinic role models?

I learned that the gendered struggles were not over, they were just different. Gender was a core lens through which I experienced Judaism, and it did not vanish when I entered an egalitarian space. In Orthodoxy, it is easy to identify the inequalities between women and men. The challenges and the fights are so visible, that it is easier to set a course for change, it is easier to keep the momentum, to struggle, and push against the traditions, searching for ways to incorporate women further. In egalitarian spaces, the differences are often more difficult to identify. Women and men might appear equal, but there is still institutionalized discrimination lurking beneath the surface—differences in pay or benefits, different learning opportunities for men, different ritual expectations for men, male god language, male role models in biblical, Talmudic, and halakhic stories, male as authentic and female as the "other." If the primary objective of egalitarian communities is to create a community where women and men are equals because women have been elevated to the status of men, then perhaps we have failed. If we direct our energy into trying to behave like men, adopt ritual obligations that are required of men, set men up as the goal, then we are still losing. Is it possible to strive for a benchmark of "full adult personhood" without requiring that benchmark to be based on a masculine model?

How can we create a community where we value the traditionally female mitzvot—baking challah, lighting Shabbat candles, visiting the *mikvah* (ritual bath), and observing laws of family purity? We, as a community, and as individuals, must learn to actively value the perspectives that women have developed and earned through experiencing life in our female bodies, through reading stories as an outsider, through combing through texts for a single female role model to emulate or to latch on to. We must figure out what it means to accept and value women as full members of the Jewish community, and that acceptance cannot be dependent on erasing the category of "women."

## Merging Identities

I have found the flexibility to engage with both Orthodox and egalitarian communities incredibly valuable. The Orthodox settings taught me to hone my "counting skills," to develop a hyperawareness of gender, both identifying places where women are not counted, and places where women develop a strong and separate identity outside of the traditional male experience. The egalitarian settings taught me skills, and the immense value of being counted and fully seen. I have learned that neither option is perfect, and neither option allows me to "check my gender at the door." No matter the denomination or the community, women are still the "other" in the Jewish tradition. It is essential for us to learn from the advances and struggles that women have faced, and continue to face, in each denomination, and to incorporate those lessons into our particular brand of Judaism.

The most tangible way I benefitted from this blending of experiences was when I started wearing a tallit (prayer shawl) during prayer. The tallit is traditionally a male garment, worn during morning prayers. It is rooted in a biblical commandment. I opted to start wearing a tallit because I was looking for a more tangible way to connect with God and to connect with morning prayers. I wanted to feel something in my hands, and on my body. I wanted to physically mark the transition into and out of prayer, and the tallit seemed like a perfect solution. However, I was so used to seeing the tallit as a *male* garment, I struggled to make it feel both authentic, and female. I wanted it to look like the *tallitot* (prayer shawls) that I had seen the Orthodox men wear throughout my life. I thought that the end goal was to doctor myself so that I would fit into the traditional, male community. But I still wanted to feel like myself, not like I was wearing my brother's or my father's tallit.

I value the familiarity, tradition, connection, and physical and sensory recognition of the old model—the traditional, Orthodox, male model. For me, the goal is not to shatter the patriarchal tradition with a hammer and walk away. It is much more challenging to use a scalpel, to carefully and reverently scrape away at what doesn't work, to cut away some pieces and open up a sliver that is large enough to insert myself into it. The question for me is: How do I create a new benchmark; a new model of an adult Jewish person who is fully counted by the community, but also has a female gender which contributes to that experience? Sometimes that means transforming a traditionally masculine mitzvah (commandment) so that it fits me, as a Jew who happens to be a woman. Sometimes that means embracing a mitzvah that is traditional for women, transforming it so that it fits me as a modern person.

In the end, I chose a large, white tallit with purple stripes. To me, that felt traditional, yet feminine. It was the appropriate garment to connect me to both pieces of myself—it filled my craving for a bridge between the spiritual and the physical, and it filled my craving to identify strongly as an authentic Jewish woman yearning to merge both pieces of my identity.

*"Baruch ata hashem, elokeinu melech haolam, sheasani kirtsono, sheasani Isha."*

Blessed are you, Lord our God, ruler of the Universe, who has made me according to Your will, who has made me a woman.

# Feminist from Birth
## by Ify Okoye

IFY OKOYE lives in Baltimore, Maryland, saving lives by day as a registered nurse and moonlighting as a storyteller at night. She strives to embody and cultivate the principles of safer and more inclusive spaces.

I think I've been a feminist from birth. One of my earliest memories of eager childlike faith and confusion involved saying my prayers at bedtime. I suppose my mother or Sunday school teacher had taught me to say my evening prayers. As a kid, however, I followed my own script: "Goodnight God and Mrs. God, goodnight Jesus and Mrs. Jesus, and goodnight Holy Spirit and Mrs. Holy Spirit." Theologically speaking, some might say I had misunderstood the lesson, but for me, then as now, acknowledging the equality of women and men in my faith tradition has always been essential.

As a teenager, I drifted away from the non-denominational Christianity I was raised in and lapsed into a relaxed and comfortable agnosticism. Maybe God existed, maybe not, who could say for sure? Saying "I don't know" felt safe. It was around the same time that I began to understand my serious attraction to other girls. My earliest youthful crushes had been on mostly girls and an occasional boy. I didn't have the language to understand my feelings and don't recall hearing anything in church or at home about homosexuality. By middle school, I became familiar with the terms gay and lesbian and all the accompanying vulgar slang. I knew enough to hide my feelings from everyone and I became an expert at being closeted.

The sinister thing nobody tells you about being closeted is how isolating and unhealthy it is for your own sense of self-worth and spiritual connection. I felt as if no one could love me if they truly knew me. How could they? I didn't really love myself. I hated the fact that I liked girls more than boys. I wished and hoped and later in more religious moments tried to pray, fast, deny, and marry my way out of being gay.

My parents immigrated to the United States from Nigeria and raised four kids, three girls and a boy, in a small college town in upstate New York. My siblings and I shared a newspaper route and chores but the chores were divided, in my mind, rather unevenly. The girls were expected to clean around the house, cook, and serve meals while my brother was only expected to vacuum. The task of washing dishes was divided up by day of the week with each daughter getting two days while my brother only had one day, which seemed so unfair and even now still rankles if I think about it. Of course, only my brother had to help my dad take out the trash, mow the lawn, and shovel snow from the driveway. I did not protest too loudly at these latter conditions, out of, I admit, totally unfeminist self-interest. But when my brother went away to college we picked up the slack. I went along quietly with these chores until my teenage rebellion kicked in. One day while my dad, a professor, was away, I posted a message on the refrigerator door, which was the usual place to hang missed phone call messages. My message read, "What do you call a man who teaches about the evils of racism at work while practicing sexism at home? Hypocrite? No, 'Dad.'" That message, my first feminist protest, didn't go over well but it did generate a conversation at home. And to his credit, my dad is one of my biggest supporters even as he struggles to reconcile his traditional views with his unfailing belief in equality of opportunity for his daughters and women in general.

A few months after I graduated from high school, September 11th happened. Those cataclysmic events and their repercussions challenged my agnosticism, and I was left wanting. I desperately wanted to believe in something greater than myself and I wanted to feel connected to a community based on some higher aspiration. I wanted answers, truth informed by tradition, I wanted to feel safe and secure amidst the turmoil of current events. I turned to religion, studying a dozen faith traditions, searching for one that would resonate with my yearning. Judaism seemed familiar and I was drawn to its scholarly tradition characterized by lively debate. The five K's worn by Sikhs—*kesh* (uncut hair), *kara* (steel bracelet), *kanga* (wooden comb), *kachhera* (cotton underwear), and *kirpan* (sword or dagger)—resonated with me on a practical level as a reminder of devotion and because I had just begun to embrace my natural hair. Sikhism and Judaism sounded pretty good but I was neither Punjabi nor Jewish by birth, which limited their appeal for me. Islam then became the most serious contender and after much intense and solitary study, I converted to Islam. The first time I read the Qur'an, I was humbled by the power and beauty of its verses and felt its rhetorical questions were directed at me. There were stories of familiar prophets but the focus was on worshipping God alone through good actions.

Before converting, I read dozens of books and articles on Islam including missionary anti-Islam diatribes; I participated in online religious forums and listened to lectures for and against Islam. In the heady days post-conversion, I drank the agenda-spiked, modern, apologetic Kool-Aid that positioned itself as "true Islam" in a defensive posture against all things I perceived as western or feminist. In a confused bid for authenticity, I began buying conservative Arab-style clothing such as the hijab. Ideas that celebrating birthdays or other cultural holidays was impermissible, or that Muslims should desire to move to and live in a predominantly Muslim country, undermined my own cultural identity as a western Muslim. I put my sexuality on the backburner; I wasn't looking to get married, and I was still struggling to adjust to the newly minted Muslim me.

I knew I believed in God and Islam seemed to be the best way for me to honor that belief. Still, what I read about traditional Muslim marriage—the inequality, the rights, duties, and expectations of obedience, the bride price "gift,"[1] and the need for a Muslim male guardian to contract and negotiate on my behalf to "ensure" my rights—made me uncomfortable. I was scared of entering into a marriage with a man I barely knew (dating was frowned upon) who would have such power over me, which I could only hope would be wielded in a benevolent manner. And I was scared of being in a sexual relationship with a man, particularly because my orientation inclined towards women.

So what's a gay feminist Muslim woman to do? I thought the answer was to get married to a man in quick order to "cure" my gay tendencies. Many Muslims emphasize marriage as a recommended act, so I soon found myself signing up for Muslim dating websites and going to Muslim speed-dating events. I met a Muslim convert who lived in my area and attended the same Islamic classes that I did. We communicated mostly through email, where he told me he was already married with a child and that he didn't want to tell his current wife about us until after the marriage took place. In those early years after my conversion, I was eager to implement every aspect of Islam including marriage, which I had been told was significant. We were soon engaged. Thankfully, that marriage with all its red flags and warning signs didn't happen, but not for a lack of sincere trying.

Some years later, I met another Muslim convert, we became fast friends, and I soon fell in love with her. The trouble was that neither my partner nor I had been exposed to or had matured into an understanding of Islam that would allow us to find affirmation in embracing our identity as gay feminist practicing orthodox Muslims. We loved each other, that we both knew, but we didn't know how to go forward in building a relationship in the face of a religious discourse which told us our love was sinful and contrary to the divine plan.

I contemplated giving up Islam but couldn't do it. So I did my best to try to suppress and ignore my love for her. Even as we repeatedly broke up and got back together again, my love for her remained a constant presence in my heart. Her love for me saved me from believing that I was unlovable, saved me from a life without love and the

---

1. Bride price: Traditionally, money or a gift given by a prospective groom to his wife.

companionship of a life partner to help make me a better person and strengthen my faith in God. Her love helped me to come out to my family and a few close friends. And with that, an immense weight lifted from my shoulders.

I still had to come to terms with Islam. I began to read more widely and critically and started to understand the limitations of the conservative, patriarchal, and at times misogynistic perspective I had bought into as "true Islam." I realized there were other voices; feminist, progressive, and LGBT-affirming scholars and believers equally committed to their faith if not to traditional interpretations of gender relations and sexuality. I'm particularly interested in using religious principles and source texts to queer the tradition. Homophobic religious scholars are no longer my reference point for issues of sex, gender, and sexual orientation. I believe there are solid scriptural and legalistic arguments to be made in support of LGBT affirmation within Islam.

It has taken a long time and a lot of internal questioning and negotiation to see my faith, feminism, and sexual orientation as compatible impulses. I believe in God, prophets and messengers, and divinely revealed scripture. I believe in absolute equality of opportunity for women and men. Feminism for me is encapsulated in this quote by the author, Chimamanda Adichie: "A feminist is a man or woman who says, 'Yes, there is a problem with gender as it exists today, we must fix it, and we must do better.'" My sexual orientation is simply a gift among the many gifts God has given me.

In the early stages of our relationship, I remember talking to my partner about the things we were willing to give up for religion, including each other. We wondered aloud if we would come to the end of our lives or be standing before God only to realize that all the pain and suffering and being apart was unnecessary and not what God wanted from us at all. I now believe that God intended for me to be a gay Muslim feminist; created my partner for me; and wanted us to come together to share our love, to worship and to deepen our faith. I'm utterly humbled and grateful for this love and mercy every day. This is why I stay.

# Confessions
## by Gina Messina-Dysert

GINA MESSINA-DYSERT, Ph.D., is Dean of the School of Graduate and Professional Studies at Ursuline College and is Co-founder of FeminismandReligion. com. She blogs for *The Huffington Post*, is the author of *Rape Culture and Spiritual Violence* (Routledge, 2014), and co-editor of *Feminism and Religion in the 21st Century* (Routledge, 2014). Gina is a widely sought speaker and has presented across the United States at universities, organizations, conferences, and in the national news circuit including appearances on Tavis Smiley and MSNBC. She has also spoken at the Commission on the Status of Women at the United Nations to address matters impacting the lives of women around the globe. Gina can be followed on Twitter @FemTheologian and her website can be accessed at http://ginamessinadysert.com.

I often attempt to uphold the facade that I am above materialism and have no interest in frivolity. However, I must confess that I am obsessed with handbags and like binge watching trash TV whenever I can find "me" time. The HBO series "Big Love" has been a guilty pleasure since it first graced my television screen; but not because of all the sex and drama that comes along with the story of a Mormon polygamous family. Instead, it is the plot of the female characters and their ongoing struggle to remain true to their faith, their family, and themselves that draws me in. Their struggle is one I can identify with, so even though the series ended a few years back and I've seen it from beginning to end, I continue to watch old episodes and empathize with these women who walk the line between faith and feminism.

I most identify with the character of Barbara Hendrickson, the First Wife. She is committed to her faith and her family, although her beliefs conflict with both. Nonetheless, she continually seeks out space to exist as a Mormon, as a member of her family, and as herself. I am most consumed with the final season of Big Love, where Barbara claims a call to the priesthood. Like the Catholic Church, Mormon authorities strongly oppose women priests. To claim such a call is heresy. Each time I watch Barbara's storyline unfold, I feel her struggle and confusion over whether to honor God's call or remain committed to her family and her Church.

During one of the final episodes, Barbara decides to join an LDS community that will honor her call to the priesthood. However, just as she is about to be baptized into this new church, Barbara interrupts the ritual saying, "If my family's not here, then I'm not here." Despite the fact that I have seen this particular episode more times than I can count, each time my reaction is the same. I gasp, I weep, and I long to reach out and embrace Barbara Hendrickson. Although she is a fictional character and I exist in "real life," she is Mormon and I am Catholic, our families are different, and our experiences are distinct, I empathize with Barbara's struggle.

Let me be clear, I have not been called to the priesthood. However, I have considered leaving the Catholic Church on many occasions, and it is my family that keeps me walking the line of faith and feminism. To say my beliefs conflict with my family and my Church would be a gross understatement. Sunday family dinners are never lacking passionate conversation and it was not that long ago that a relative demanded that I leave the Church. I often receive hate mail from other Catholics; recently I was sent a Facebook message assuring me of my place in Hell. Apparently my post denouncing the recent excommunication of Kate Kelly for founding a movement to ordain Mormon women was offensive.[1]

---

1. Kate Kelly is the founder of the Mormon movement "Ordain Women" (http://ordain-women.org). She was excommunicated by the Mormon Church on June 23, 2014.

Claiming a Catholic feminist identity strikes many as an oxymoron. How can Catholicism and feminism coexist? How can one support reproductive justice, same-sex marriage, and women priests while claiming membership in a religion ruled by the Vatican? How can a woman who is rejected by her tradition exist within the patriarchal structure of the Catholic Church? These are fair questions and if I'm offering a true confession, there have not only been many times I have considered leaving the Church, but also many times I have concealed my feminist identity and beliefs.

I first questioned my faith at age thirteen when my parents divorced. Our pastor and fellow parishioners judged our family harshly, and my parents were no longer worthy of receiving communion under Catholic teaching. My mother was too humiliated to step foot into our parish and it seemed that we each bore a scarlet letter on our chests. I felt ashamed, embarrassed, and cast out by God. No longer did my siblings and I have our own identities; instead we were only "those kids from that broken family." In an act of defiance and attempt for control, I rejected Catholicism and believed I would never again step foot inside a church. Of course it was not long before a wedding, a funeral, a baptism occurred and I participated in rituals that were second nature to me. After all Catholicism is more than my faith, it is my culture.

My family is Sicilian and Catholicism is part of our identity. I am a first generation American; my family is from the "old country," home to the Vatican and a place where only God comes before blood. Although I wondered early on why I could not be an altar server like my brother, or why my mother could not be a deacon or priest, I never questioned that I was Catholic. Even in those moments when I believed I was rejecting the Church, I have always known in my heart that I am a Catholic, just as I am a Sicilian, just as I am a Messina , and just as I am a woman. My faith is in my blood and while I disagree with Vatican politics, I have always embraced the rituals, the teachings of Jesus, and the message of social justice.

I am embarrassed to confess that I was in college when I first realized that God is not male. Growing up saying the "Our Father" and making the sign of the cross left me convinced of a patriarchal order.

Throughout college and graduate school I grappled with theology and dogma. By that time, my feminist identity was firmly established and I questioned the beliefs of a Church that placed men above women.

Nonetheless, I chose to be married in the Catholic Church, even after my pastor told me it was my duty as a wife to quit my job and have children; my work in a domestic violence shelter was not of the same importance as raising Catholic children. I confess, I did not quit my job and when I was unable to conceive a child, I wondered if my Church thought I had no value. My pastor reminded me of the biblical matriarchs Sarah and Rachel; both were barren, but eventually God granted each a child. That was not my journey. I never fit the role my faith demanded of me as a woman.

During graduate school I stepped outside of the Catholic Church for the first time. I was in Los Angeles, on the opposite end of the country from my Sicilian family, and I granted myself permission to see what it would be like to go to a church or a temple where I felt welcomed as a woman. I attended Episcopalian and Methodist churches, visited Buddhist temples, and participated in Goddess worship services. In each I found something beautiful that I could never experience in the Catholic Church; but still none were *my Church*. Like Barbara Hendrickson, I could not exist in a community that did not include my family.

Once I completed graduate school, I found that jobs for Catholic feminist theologians were sparse. Desperate for a career in the field I had spent nearly two decades researching, I began to conceal my feminist identity. I confess that I deleted blog posts from the web, adjusted language on my vitae, and avoided mentioning the "f-word" in interviews. Nonetheless, my secret was out; I was a known feminist and it was too late to claim otherwise. In fact, one interviewer asked me, "Can you tone down your talk on women's issues?" And I confess that I responded, "I can be strategic." Interestingly, it was not until I openly claimed my identity as a Catholic feminist in an interview that I found a tenured position in my field at a Catholic women's college. Go figure.

Becoming a mother was a key moment in my ongoing journey as a Catholic feminist. After ten years of infertility, my husband and I decided to adopt. I wanted to be a mother more than anything, and so I prayed to Mary, the mother of Jesus, to bring me a child. Although I grew up praying to "Our Father," I confess it was always Mary in whom I found solace. And it was Mary who heard my prayers. We brought our daughter Sarah home just three weeks after being placed on the adoption waiting list—astonishing given that the average wait is two years. Shortly after, we left Los Angeles and returned to our Catholic Sicilian family in Cleveland, Ohio, to raise our daughter within our traditions.

Motherhood reminded me of what I was missing by being thousands of miles away from my family. It was and *is* important to me that my daughter be raised within my community and with the same rituals, values, and teachings that I learned because of my Catholic culture. Yet, I confess that I fear I am indoctrinating her into a tradition that will abuse her. And so, becoming a mother has led me to many questions about my faith and feminism, and thus, feeling the need for multiple confessions:

> *I confess that I wanted to claim the Spirit of Christ within myself and baptize my daughter.*
>
> *I confess that I didn't.*
>
> *I confess that I want my daughter to embrace our Catholic identity.*
>
> *I confess that I fear being Catholic will make my daughter will feel "less than" because of her gender.*
>
> *I confess that it brings me joy to see my daughter make the sign of the cross.*
>
> *I confess that it brings me sadness to see my daughter make the sign of the cross.*
>
> *I confess that when my daughter talks about God "He" I correct her and tell her it is God "She."*
>
> *I confess that I still imagine God as male.*
>
> *I confess that my daughter told her teacher that Jesus was a woman.*
>
> *I confess that I was embarrassed.*

*I confess that I posted a YouTube video of my daughter singing "Ordain a Lady."*[2]

*I confess that I ignored my daughter when she asked why there were no women priests at our church.*

*I confess that our family attends the same conservative Catholic church I grew up in.*

*I confess that attending the same conservative Catholic church I grew up in brings me comfort.*

*I confess that I enrolled my daughter in Catholic school.*

*I confess that I continue to struggle with having my daughter in Catholic school.*

I confess, I am a Catholic feminist, and though some may not understand how these identities intersect, I cannot separate them. I am not one or the other. I am both. That being so, I am committed to change, to activism, and to giving my daughter both the beauty and comfort of family and tradition, and the empowerment and strength of feminism. With these intentions, I believe she will have a different experience, one that is not damaging or abusive, but that is just.

Catholicism has feminist potential; if it did not, I would never consider sharing my faith with my daughter. The teachings of Jesus and social justice are consistent with feminist practice, whereas patriarchy and the subordination of women are distortions of faith. And so, I confess, I will stay in the struggle, I will work to disrupt the distortions, and I will remain committed to change and transformation.

Although I am not standing on steady ground and at times I feel ambivalent, I refuse to abandon my faith or my feminism. Like Barbara Hendrickson, I will continue to weave each together and celebrate tradition with my family. Doing so, my woman, Catholic, feminist, Sicilian self can be affirmed—can be embraced—can live into full becoming.

---

2. "Ordain a Lady" was produced by the Women's Ordination Conference and lyrics were written by Kate McElwee. It can be viewed on Youtube at: https://www.youtube.com/watch?v=Y0S2WlvNTU8.

# Seeing is Believing
## by Jennifer D. Crumpton

JENNIFER DANIELLE CRUMPTON is an author, media commentator and public speaker on the intersection of religion, politics, popular culture, and women's lives. She blogs for the website Patheos under the title *Femmevangelical: For Women Who Don't Submit*, writes for *The Huffington Post*, and appears on outlets like FOX & Friends and CNN Headline News to support women's rights and interfaith cooperation. After a thirteen-year career as an advertising executive for Fortune 500 companies, she detoured to Union Theological Seminary in the City of New York to earn her Master of Divinity, and in 2011 was ordained in the Christian Church (Disciples of Christ). Raised in the Bible Belt as a fundamentalist Evangelical, Jennifer's complex spiritual and career journey led to a progressive, liberal focus on feminist theology, social and structural ethics, and interreligious justice advocacy. Jennifer lives in New York City with her husband Dave and cat Jezebel. She can be found at Femmevangelical.com and followed on Twitter @JenniDCrumpton.

When I was a little girl, I often told my mother that things looked weird. At any given moment, I would notice that my usual surroundings appeared strange and somehow different. We had not moved from the house where I was born. The furniture arrangement had not changed and the green and gold shag carpeting still rocked the floors. There was no obvious explanation for why I questioned what I saw.

But more often than I admitted, my little soul felt that things were not as they seemed. I would blink my eyes and suddenly everything around me radiated with an intense energy. When I looked up from a coloring book or walked into another room, inanimate objects suddenly seemed alive. The wallpaper patterns possessed an aura of happy or sad, peaceful or mad, depending on the moody noises of the settling house and the subtlest sighs of its human occupants. A crystal chandelier had a sophisticated personality to match its curled, gold-leafed fingers, dramatically spread with mysterious potential to cast both shadows and light, and the benevolence to occasionally shoot rainbows. Potted plants cocked their heads to consider the nature of the universe, their conclusions causing them to either stretch toward sunbeams or droop with sorrow. Their fountains of limbs shrugged in a perpetual wondering of "why?"

All that vivid, vibrating life gestured wildly to me, suggesting that the tiniest nuances mattered tremendously. The world revealed delicately complex layers of being to everything, even—and especially—things we regularly disregard or overlook. It all seemed to be trying to tell me a secret I already knew but was in danger of forgetting.

I instinctually linked these experiences to my innate spirituality, but of course without calling it that, or knowing the names, symbols, or theological restraints that would come later. I distinctly recall playing outside when I was around age five. I stood rapt watching the sun turn the tops of trees into sparklers as the wind rustled the green and gold leaves into a dancing, shimmering, surround-sound symphony of rushing whispers. I knew it was the presence of God, and that it was also part of me, the stuff I was made of. God required no formulaic prayer of salvation, no contrived statement of faith, no blind acceptance of man-made rules. And clearly she had the ability to make absolutely anything imaginable real.

The only description I could muster up during my elementary school years—when I gathered enough about the standard beliefs of others to make me wonder about the validity of my own—was, "Things look weird." By the time I was nine, I had uttered this phrase enough that my mother had my eyes checked. When my sight was declared healthy, she took me to a specialist for tests on my heart and brain. Everything was normal.

Yet I knew I was not just imagining things. Despite my aloneness in trying to name what I saw, I found a curious comfort in the presence of the weirdness. It instilled hope, even though its illusiveness left me with a longing that was at times painful.

In those magical childhood years when we can sense a deeper side of life so viscerally, there exists wide-open possibility. Our trusting confidence in our experiences, innocent belief in ourselves, and innate sense of truth has not yet been admonished or undermined. Even as authority figures teach us there is only one unequivocally established, acceptable reality in which we can function successfully, our wide-open hearts sense another story.

I was born into a born-again home in a born-again town, and in time I lost sight of my special world amidst the towering images of a narrow evangelical Christian worldview as the singular authoritative reality. Christianity clung to my conscience and captured my devotion. But it never lit things on fire like my original God.

I learned that boundaries and expectations for girls were more rigid and judgmental than for boys. Dismissal of the female voice and vision was polite but firm, so kind and smiling one could mistake it for a warm handshake. No women held positions of authoritative decision-making in church business. No female clergy stood before the congregation interpreting the Bible or speaking for God like men did. This was supposedly God's design, and for our own best interest.

I came to expect and even participate in disdain for my gender, and bought into a caricatured weakness and lowliness ascribed to all things "girly." Girls' virginity was property of Jesus and female sexuality was carefully monitored, regulated, shamed, and quashed. Men were silently presupposed to enjoy and consume female bodies without needing permission: "Boys will be boys." I became a shell of the vibrant young woman I had been after being date raped just outside the gates of my small, private Christian college by a boy I had told not long before that I was saving myself for marriage. I told no one since no one would believe me. My religion ensured I implicitly understood that God would no longer protect or bless me. Like so many of the women in the Bible and other cautionary Christian tales, I had unwittingly gotten what I somehow deserved. I was obviously innately a whore, a brazen temptress who aroused my own comeuppance just by being female. Any protest I raised about the transgression would be assumed a malicious attempt at dethroning one of God's ordained, ascending rulers of the kingdom. I suffered deeply, alone.

It was time to accept my place as secondary in the Christian hierarchy and give up any silly ideas I had about who I was, who I could become. My insight into another world of incredible transformations, improbable possibilities, and respect for small, strange beauty was light-years away; at twenty I could not recall it. My sense of destiny, leadership, and vision did not matter; Christian girls were praised for a self-deprecating demeanor, pleasing appearance, good works, good grades, purity, piety, and patience. We were valued most for our resignation to cooperate fully.

Inculcated over two decades with centuries of male-centric God talk, ritual, and doctrine, this became the only reality that seemed to exist. It was not until I moved away another decade later that I realized how seamlessly I had come to accept and energetically worship the submission-centered narrative my brand of Christian girls were allowed to believe about ourselves, the world, and the God that oversees it. And then, from one thousand miles away, I began to take stock of the consequences.

Carlene Bauer wrote, "Because I spent much of my young adulthood trying to figure out what God wanted for me rather than what I did, I came of age—sexually, professionally, and otherwise—rather late…. My struggle to reconcile who I'd become with who I wanted to be took the form of debilitating bouts of self-doubt and sadness."[1] It hit me that the God from whom I had sought my parameters and purpose during the most formative years of my life had actually been the images and perspectives of a series of mortal men.

When I visited my hometown and attended a megachurch service in which a young male pastor assured hundreds of followers that in

---

1. Carlene Bauer, "Someone to Watch Over Me," *Elle* (March 2013): 402.

God's wisdom, women could not be deacons or elders (and hurled 1 Timothy 2:11-15 to boot) I began to understand what this Christianity had stolen from me. My inability to report the rape—and many other timid, ruinous decisions in my life—directly correlated to similar teachings about "God's" view of gender. New generations of girls were hearing male authority claiming to speak for God tell the lie that men are called by God to lead and establish reality for humanity.

Women who challenge this worldview are labeled whiny, angry, crazy, lying heretics. It is so abusive that many women rightly leave Christianity. I went to seminary instead.

I recently learned that I am a "sensitive," a term describing about 70 percent of introverts and 15 to 20 percent of the population. The common trait of sensitives is an inner life of contemplation and exegesis of experiences and observations. Sensitives are almost distractingly intuitive, says Susan Cain in the book *Quiet: The Power of Introverts in a World That Can't Stop Talking*. "Highly sensitive people process information about their environments—both physical and emotional—unusually deeply," she reports. "They tend to notice subtleties that others miss—another person's change in mood, say, or a lightbulb burning a touch too brightly."[2]

Sensitives experience sights, sounds, body language, vocal cues and other data at an elevated pitch, and process them in elaborate, intricate ways. This illuminated why my childhood sensory perceptions seemed weird. The weirdness became intense when I was processing information, attentive, or simply open.

Paying attention, opening up, trusting our intuition, and taking leadership are crucial for Christian women, to ensure girls are no longer damned to self-destructive disempowerment by their faith. Today I practice a form of Christianity that encourages me to serve as a moral voice on behalf of women's equality. I am one of a great force of faithful women who actively imagine things can be different. I stay because following Jesus is all about seeing and accepting another reality.

---

2. Susan Cain, *Quiet: The Power of Introverts in a World That Can't Stop Talking* (New York: Broadway Books, 2013), 136.

Jesus' message at heart was that things are not what they seem. Jesus did nothing if not condemn the pervasive, oppressive world-view of his time and place. If I truly follow Jesus, then I am *called* to question my surroundings, boldly interpret what I see and experience, and act decisively and authoritatively to bring a new vision to reality. Jesus saw what was regularly overlooked and disregarded. He saw another world, where those who hoarded and abused power would be thwarted, the last would be first, the vulnerable would be empowered. The least of these would inherit the realm of God.

When Jesus stood and announced his ministry in the little temple in his hometown of Nazareth in Galilee—a struggling village in the upheaval of Roman-occupied Palestine—he did so purposefully, in a way that would resonate with undervalued people trapped in a world gone wrong. He unrolled the scroll of the prophet Isaiah and carefully chose a few select lines from chapter 61: "The spirit of the Lord is on me, because I have been anointed to proclaim good news to the poor. The Lord has sent me to proclaim freedom for the prisoners and recovery of sight for the blind, to set the oppressed free, to proclaim the year of the Lord's favor." Then he rolled it back up. That is what he came to say; that's the good news. He proposed an alternate reality where all are equal, anyone can lead, justice is served and all are restored.

He said we could enter this new reality, but must risk joining with God in an unpopular desire to bring it into being. Jesus came to release me from the prison of the status quo and help me find freedom by recovering my sight. But I have to envision that world, and believe I have the ability to make absolutely anything imaginable real.

Jesus said we must become like children to enter this realm; perhaps not because of simplicity of mind and heart, but rather complexity of imagination and vision. If I am faithful, I can still see this hopeful other world, even though its illusiveness still leaves me with a longing that is at times painful. Jesus told stories of a world characterized by love, justice and equality that he saw clearly and vividly. Those dependent upon the norm refused to see it, and authorities imagined it would destroy their self-serving system. But he pursued it in spite of the spit in his face, name-calling, bullying, threats, violence and even death. To be Christian means to keep our eyes on Jesus: pursuing a better reality in spite of the one we live in today.

# Beet is the New Orange
## by Amy Levin

AMY LEVIN has an M.A. in Religious Studies from New York University. She worked as a political organizer for J Street as well as Organizing for America, and has written on the intersection of religion, gender, and social justice for publications such as The Revealer and Feminism and Religion. She is currently pursuing her Master's Degree in Social Work at the University of Pennsylvania. In her free time, she works on behalf of Jewish Vegetarians of North America.

I'm not sure which came first for me—the feminist chicken or the Jewish egg. Though I may have identified as a Jew first, it was feminism that birthed the Jew I am today. My commitments to feminism and Judaism grew together, mutually intertwined and actively reinforcing one another. Regardless, neither a chicken nor an egg made it to my Passover seder this year.

Passover has always been my favorite holiday: my sacred space where Judaism, feminism, and activism gracefully intertwine. This happens most materially on the seder plate, where each "food for thought" item signifies and relates to the Jewish struggle for freedom from slavery. In recent years, the seder plate has become its own symbolic site for modern political struggles since Susannah Heschel began the feminist trend of placing an orange on the plate. The practice evolved from its origin at Oberlin, where students placed crusts of bread on the plate in solidarity with lesbians in the Jewish community. Susannah replaced the bread with the orange to symbolize the fruitfulness that occurs when those marginalized in the Jewish community become active participants in Jewish life. Recognizing their own marginalization, feminist Jewish women embraced the practice to support both LGBTQ Jews and women's full inclusion in Judaism. As a young adult, placing the orange on my family's seder plate was the first feminist Jewish ritual I ever performed.

Over the years, my family has gotten used to seeing the orange on our seder plate, but this past year I brought new foods for thought: to make a vegan seder plate we used a beet for the shankbone and a flower for the egg. We also added an olive to signify peace with Palestinians. I've made it a ritual every year to use the theme of slavery and liberation to discuss the many modern slaveries today, and the seder plate offers me a platform to do so.

This large, round plate reflects my identities as a Jew and a feminist, and it represents why I keep coming back to the table. The plate itself represents my Jewish identity; it is a base and structure from which to articulate and fight for the political struggles I care about, in spite of the fact that it contains elements I disagree with. The orange is my feminism, the gift that gives me a voice and reminds me of all the women who struggled before me. It also paves the way for me to articulate and fight for the many other struggles of equality. Indeed, without the orange I would not have known the strength or courage to place beside it the beet, representing my newer struggles of combating suffering and discrimination. Feminism is the faith that inspires and strengthens me to act, and Judaism is the religion that gives me the language, community, and home to do it.

◆◆◆

It was feminism that eventually made me love religion, but it took me a while to get there. Growing up, my parents raised me in a suburban Jewish home. Jewish summer camp, youth group, and religious school were as much a part of my life as my secular, public school education. Judaism was attractive to me insofar as it provided appealing social settings that enriched the surrounding mainstream suburban culture. I was privileged enough to take part in programs and opportunities for Jewish youth, like the eight weeks I spent each summer at a camp in the remote location of Eagle River, Wisconsin. Establishing a home away from home with my Jewish peers who, like me, travelled thousands of miles to be together, offered me the cathartic feeling of belonging and solidarity. For me, Judaism *was* community. And yet, it was a community that didn't feel fully mine, a community I felt alienated from even as I felt tethered to it.

One of the things that distinctly stood out to me as a teenager was my inability to connect to Judaism on a spiritual level in the way I witnessed my closest Jewish male friends doing. I remember *wanting* to feel religious, even if it was just as much to feel the calm that comes from metaphysical certainty as it was my desire to experience Judaism in the way my friends did. I remember countless times sitting in prayer services watching my close male friends, swaying in prayer with their eyes closed, and envying how they seemed to seamlessly connect to Judaism on a deep and esoteric level. Instead, I stared at the ancient Hebrew text in hopes of uncovering its meaning, or closed my eyes, contemplating what exactly it was I was searching for. What was wrong with me? Why couldn't I connect? Was I simply an atheist?

I didn't realize it at the time, but my inability to feel like I fully belonged spiritually arose from a quiet belief that my male friends, and all Jewish men, had a kind of access to holiness I didn't possess. That belief manifested through a repetition of discreet yet powerful moments—during services, looking up at the stage-like bimah at an all-male cast of clergy, or stealing glimpses of my male friends enacting the ritual of kissing their tzitzit (fringes on a tallit, or prayer shawl) during the Shema[1] and craving the comfort they must have felt wrapped in God's holy blanket. Sure, I could have purchased my own tallit, which I thought about many times, but so few women in my synagogue donned either a tallit or a *kippah* (head covering) that I feared I would feel even *more* like an outcast. That large expression of outward piety would have felt incongruous to the wavering piety I felt inside. Would donning male ritual garb have given me the access

---

1. The Shema is considered by many Jews the most important part of the prayer services. During the third paragraph of the Shema, the *tzitzit* are mentioned three times and on each occasion they are kissed as an expression of love and devotion to the mitzvot, or commandments.

to holiness I was missing, or would I have experienced a contrived version of a man's religious experience?

It wasn't until I had my first experience with what I would now call feminist exegesis that Judaism began to feel more inclusive and personal. It was my last couple of years as a high school student and I was one of the few in my class who still attended Hebrew school, when our synagogue hired a new Education Director, the first female rabbi to grace the synagogue. Even though my synagogue was strongly egalitarian, something felt different. Up until that point, I had been a fairly shy, uninterested student both in secular and Jewish educational spaces. It wasn't long after this female rabbi began teaching my classes that the vocal, passionate student in me woke up. I had never interacted with such a strong, intellectual, and confident female Jewish leader. The combination of her modern pedagogy and her role-model attributes slowly but surely made me begin to enjoy reading ancient Jewish texts. I relished offering my opinion, as a woman, on what the Hebrew said about things like abortion. The rabbi listened to me and gave me advice. For the first time I connected to Judaism in a way I hadn't before—as a female with not only a voice, but a canon of experiences to offer.

The act of interpreting Jewish texts through a modern lens with a female rabbi to guide me felt both liberating and exciting. It was like I had been given permission to stop questioning what was wrong with me and shift my judgment to the Jewish tradition. My obsession with comparing myself to Jewish men and reconciling my "crisis of faith" began to slowly wane and I discovered that I had a unique perspective in relationship to the Jewish texts that men didn't have. In vocalizing my opinions and debating with others, I transformed to an engaged academic who loved learning—all because I cared about the subject at hand and felt respected, as a woman, to assert my opinion. I wasn't yet the feminist or the Jew I would become, but I began to relate to both identities in a new and transforming way.

Soon after I entered college, I was a blossoming feminist on the progressive campus of Grinnell College—far from the tiny bud I resembled in high school. Whether I was quoting Simone de Beauvoir or bell hooks, it became my prerogative to apply a feminist lens to everything I was studying. But while I excelled academically in my women's studies courses, a creeping feeling of alienation began to take hold. In learning the various waves and traditions of feminism, I felt empowered in many aspects of my womanhood, and yet uncertain of how other feminists' experiences related to my own. I wasn't sure where I belonged as a feminist or why I was so bothered by this belonging in the first place. I was just as much a wandering feminist as I was a wandering Jew. There was a quiet voice inside me bringing me back to the Jewish table. What had other Jewish women said about feminism? How had they tackled the patriarchal Jewish texts and rituals?

Feminism often draws people away from their religion, but for me, it was the opposite. When I soon discovered the deep, yet relatively recent tradition of Jewish feminism, I fell effortlessly and voraciously into the proverbial laps of women like Judith Plaskow and Laura Levitt. Once again, I felt that these women gave me permission to question the tradition and allowed me to connect to Judaism in a way that felt truly meaningful to me, like I finally belonged, as I had with my first female rabbi. Reading books like *Standing Again at Sinai* and *Jews and Feminism: The Ambivalent Search for Home,* I felt like I could articulate all the shortcomings I felt growing up within my egalitarian, but not quite feminist, Jewish community.

I realized that male God language and the lack of women's stories and experiences in the bible *was* limiting my ability to feel connected and engaged during prayers or study as a teenager. My feminism found a home—it latched on to Judaism and fastened itself through learning and writing about female divine language, feminist kabbalistic art and ritual, and Jewish feminist theology. I grew obsessed with female Jewish divas like Barbra Streisand and intellectual heroines like Hannah Arendt. These women were all part of a powerful feminist Jewish tradition and I began to place myself in that genealogy. I felt my feminist convictions come alive as I witnessed them articulated through a shared language, experience, and community of Jewish women like me, and I found my feminist home from which to build the foundations of my future self as an intellectual, writer, and change-maker.

Just as my feminism latched onto Judaism, so have my other struggles for equality and compassion. The feminist in me aims to change the world, and the Jew in me gives me a voice and connection to do it. These identities have led me on a path with a diverse set of passions: working to promote interfaith dialogue and peace-building, organizing the Jewish community to end the conflict between Israelis and Palestinians through political means, and advocating for animals rights on the basis of Jewish values.

There is no shortage of opportunities and reasons to care about these causes, so why the need to approach them *as a Jew?* In advocating for peace and justice through a Jewish lens within both intrareligious and interreligious settings, I find more meaning, connection, and even spiritual ethos. For example, though I found satisfaction in advocating for animals rights through protest, leafleting, and political advocacy for years, it wasn't until I connected with other Jewish vegans through organizations like Jewish Vegetarians of North America that I felt a more personal home within the vegan community. I even feel more connected to Jewish texts, like the Talmudic principle of *Tza'ar ba'alei chayim,*[2] which means the "suffering of living creatures," and bans inflicting unnecessary pain on animals. These Jewish conflicts and conversations allow me to redefine and deepen both my Jewish and activist selves. I gain strength from others who, like me, learned to love Judaism so much that they want it to be the best it can be.

In *Standing Again at Sinai,* Judith Plaskow argues, "Human beings are fundamentally communal; our individuality is a product of community, and our choices are shaped by our being with others."[3] Thirty years earlier, Hannah Arendt wrote in *The Human Condition,* "Action…is never possible in isolation; to be isolated is to be deprived of the capacity to act."[4] There are many forms of isolation Jewish women have experienced throughout history—including being relegated to a restricting synagogue balcony, silenced in a classroom, shunned for showing interest in clergy positions, or excluded from

---

2. Bava Metzia 32b.

3. Judith Plaskow, *Standing Again at Sinai: Judaism from a Feminist Perspective* (New York, NY: HarperSanFrancisco, pp. 76-81. 1991).

4. Hannah Arendt, *The Human Condition* (Chicago: U of Chicago, p. 188. 1958).

praying collectively at the Western Wall, the holiest site for Jews. And yet, through and despite this isolation, women have organized and fought collectively to act and shape their fate.

It is these historically marginalized women that have allowed me to be brought in to the Jewish community. Now, I take that strength and find myself once again at the margins—this time pushing for compassion and justice for Palestinians, mistreated religious minorities, factory-farmed animals, and soon, through my training in social work, for many populations and individuals in need. Regardless of the cause at hand, this multi-generational Jewish feminist community still guides me. Like the orange that paved the way for the beet on my seder plate, my feminist foremothers empower me to fight new struggles, continuing to repair the world, one beet at a time.

# Shoot the Messenger
## by Rabia Chaudry

RABIA CHAUDRY is an attorney, National Security Fellow at the New America Foundation, and the founder of the Safe Nation Collaborative, a law enforcement training firm. She is a faith contributor to Time Magazine and writes at her blog *Split the Moon*. Rabia has appeared on the podcast *Serial* as an advocate for Adnan Syed, and is the Host and Producer of the podcast *Undisclosed*. She is the mother of two incredible, beautiful daughters and the wife of a man who taught her to never give up. On him or God.

He was calm as he ate his sandwich. His beard was lovely, reds and browns and golds flecked throughout, highlighted in the sun as we sat by the lake.

"It's true, women are like that because they're created from a rib. Ribs are crooked right? And you can't try to bend them to straighten them out, you just have to let them stay crooked or else they'll break."

I blinked, a little confused, a little panicked. I looked hard into his face, searching for a grin, a gleam in his hazel eyes, anything to betray his earnest offering a few minutes earlier that women are by nature *makkaar*: scheming, insincere, untrustworthy. I found nothing.

He continued to eat, looking over the water, occasionally glancing my way and smiling tenderly. Which was natural. We were newlyweds, and these were the first few heady days after I had committed myself to a second marriage. My first marriage was to a non-religious, cultural Muslim from Pakistan. This time I married a madrassa-trained student of Islam, born and raised in Canada.

A couple of years prior, around the time I first met him, I had a dream. A transcendent, glorious dream. Deep in sleep, I saw that I was praying the early evening prayer. Wrapped in a white shawl, I sat by French doors that led out to a circular balcony straight out of Romeo and Juliet. The air was cool and clear and I finished praying, folding my prayer mat as I walked out into the night.

Outside the white doors was a circular stone balcony covered in vines and blooms. I stood there in awe, feet bare, the stone floor cool and firm. The moon, a full fat perfectly circular moon bursting at the seams like a syrupy chum-chum, was descending towards me. It was literally lowering, steadily and slowly, down to the balcony. It stopped in front of me, slightly above eye level, like it was expecting something from me.

Was it breathing? No, but there was life it in. It glowed an indescribable light, warm but without heat. The light wrapped around me like a cocoon and for the first time in a very long time, I felt completely safe. I reached out to touch the inviting orb, but before I could make contact, poof! It disappeared.

I woke up immediately. It was *tahajjud* (night prayer) time, the precious hours right before dawn. The time that Rumi spoke of when he wrote:

*The breeze at dawn has secrets to tell you.*

*Don't go back to sleep.*

*You must ask for what you really want.*

*Don't go back to sleep.*

*People are going back and forth across the doorsill*

*Where the two worlds touch.*

*The door is round and open.*

*Don't go back to sleep.*

That night I didn't go back to sleep. Instead I went downstairs, where my mother was already in prayer. We grew up listening to her wander around at night, whispering God's name on prayer beads. I already knew she would be there. I washed up and joined her to pray. I told her about the dream and she assured me that it held a powerful message, a message that very good things were to come, and that it was a *ruhani* dream, a spiritual communication from the Almighty.

Could it have something to do with this young fellow courting me? Perhaps. She reminded me of the dream she had in Mecca, in which she met a young, fair-colored man with light eyes. Irfan was light-skinned and had hazel eyes. Yes, these dreams were confirmation. He had to be the one.

And so for this and many other reasons I married him. My second husband, a younger man, eager, sweet, devoted, full of faith. My first husband was a secular immigrant, unconcerned with faith and God; my second husband was born in the West, steeped in religion, educated in madrassas across Canada and the United States, and graduated from an Islamic scholarship course in the United Kingdom. Between marriages one and two my priorities had shifted.

Six months before my first marriage ended in a most dramatic yet anticlimactic fashion, I had begun praying the tahajjud prayer. This is the prayer of mystery and majesty, experienced in the darkest hours, when most of us snooze through a nightly miracle. It is said that God the Almighty, may He be Exalted, resides above His Throne in the Seventh Heaven. But in the last portion of the night, in the hours right before dawn, He does something incredible.

God descends in a manner befitting His Glory to the first heaven, to the heaven that encompasses us mere mortals, and asks, "Who will call upon Me, that I may answer him? Who will ask of Me, that I may give him? Who will seek My forgiveness, that I may forgive him?" It is a most extraordinary and loving act of God to come seek us out, to present Himself in a realm closer to us, at a time when, as the mystics have said, lovers are with their beloved.

I wish I could say I began praying in the middle of the night because my heart longed to be with God, but that would be a bald-faced lie. I began praying the tahajjud prayer because I couldn't sleep at night, and during the day I was full of anxiety. I began praying it like a beggar, someone trapped and desperate for a way out. My entire prayer was centered around asking God to correct my situation, or release me from it. Over and over, like a slightly mad person, I repeated the plea.

Over time, as weeks and months went by, something happened. The night prayer became the highlight of my day. I couldn't wait until the house went quiet and it was just me and Him. It took time, but eventually I got it. Or maybe just a hint of it, what Rumi and the pious felt. In the basement of a suburban joint-family home, between a treadmill and a large screen television, I had a nightly appointment with the Divine.

If I am to chart the highs and lows of my spiritual life, that time, those months of miserable days and lovely nights, was the summit. I spoke to Him, often silently, and He listened. He listened, and He also delivered. Months later I was released in the most literal way, pushed out of my home in the middle of the night, from a marriage that had destroyed my faith in people. I emerged, however, with a new faith in God and Islam.

◆◆◆

Years later, as I explored what I really sought in a partner, I knew my paramount priority was faith and spirituality. Little did I know how my faith would be challenged by my new husband, a man who fastidiously, dutifully, and without question absorbed all the lessons he was taught by his Hanafi madrassa teachers.

I had never encountered this world before. In my personal life, no one had used Islam to define or limit my role as a woman. I grew up with cultural expectations, but those expectations included being educated, working, and contributing to society. Feeling triumphant at the power my faith gave me, and having sought out a faithful man the second time around, religion itself was now turning on me.

My husband's reality was that women needed limits, boundaries, set roles, guardians, and permission; existed for the sake of men; had natural limitations; and would be happiest if they observed all of the above. He was taught the biggest cause for pain in marriage and the epidemic of divorce was women not following the rules of nature and Islam. Worlds collided when I entered his reality. I was an independent divorced mother and attorney, compelled to be heard after a marriage in which I mostly kept quiet.

His expectations challenged me and my view of Islam. I never personally knew anyone with a formal Islamic education. What drew me to him made me now question my own faith. At points I thought, if this is Islam, I don't want it. But I remembered the connection to God I made years earlier in those early morning hours, and I couldn't walk away. I dug deeper, seeking context and fuller truths, and finding reinforcement for the dignity and agency of women in scripture, tradition, and history. He opened my eyes to a world where the authentic message got lost in generations of misogyny, and the clerics who forced Islam to conform to their ideas of womanhood were now the prevailing messengers of the faith.

For nearly the past decade, I've worked through the elements of faith that seemed demeaning to women and completely outside the spirit and nature of Islam, while my husband has worked through his education about women and reconciled it with me and with our rambunctious, independent, spirited daughter. We have both been challenged and both risen to meet the challenges, expanding our knowledge and acknowledging the breaches in it. Neither of us is the same person we were a decade ago.

Feminism was never really my thing because I had never felt marginalized, unworthy, or disrespected due to my gender. It had never been necessary until I met the version of Islam that was my husband's reality, an Islam that didn't understand me or accept me. I thought long and hard about whether God, who says He is closer to us than our jugular vein and knows us intimately, would give women intelligence, drive, and compassion, but expect it all to be relinquished in order to be a believer. Impossible.

I've learned that there is a world of difference between what Muslims believe about women, and what Islam teaches about women. For now, feminism is the stopgap to fill this divide. And unless or until Muslims actually begin embodying Islamic and Prophetic attitudes about women, feminism will be necessary. The message of God, meant equally for men and women, was not always understood or faithfully delivered by the messengers, the everyday gatekeepers of the faith. Through my search for answers, my study of strong righteous Muslim women of our past, the many narrations of how the Prophet Muhammad (PBUH)[1] treated women, and how the Qur'an addresses women with dignity, respect, equity and spiritual equality, I came to realize a powerful secret. A secret that men of religion have long kept from us. And that is this: God loves women.

---

1. PHUB stands for "peace be upon him," a statement of respect for the Prophet Muhammad, used anytime his name is mentioned.

# The Sub-Veil: Perversities from the Side with the Seams
## by Tasneem Mandviwala

 TASNEEM MANDVIWALA has studied art history, psychology, and English literature, and has an MA in the latter from the University of Houston. She has taught English in a number of places to a number of ages, including the University of Houston and Madressah tus Saifiyah tul Burhaniyah in Mumbai, India. She is an online editor for academic papers through her website, inkfluence.wordpress.com. Tasneem is also an artist, and her work has been displayed at various venues throughout the Houston, Texas, area including the Jung Center and Matchbox Gallery; it is available for purchase through www.veritasneem.com. Currently a Ph.D. student in the Department of Comparative Human Development at the University of Chicago, Tasneem hopes to foster greater understandings between individuals who are members of diverse populations such as those found in the United States. She believes a willful child-like spirit of curiosity and openness can solve many things in this life, and her laugh sounds like a duck.

The day of the dream, the sun had been a perfect egg yolk, moist and mustardy, surrounded by a pathetic sticky mess of translucent clouds. She can't remember if she has the same name as she sleeps, but she can remember that she is a child, pudgy maybe, and that her hair is still the same foreign blackbrown as it winds frantically against the hot wet air. She also remembers she is completing a kindergarten assignment: What is your mother's name? What is your father's name? And that she replies on the paper, "Jennifer and David," because these are normal names. These names she proudly knows out loud, but she feels ashamed of the real ones inside her curly head. It is an elegant pain to think on it now, because now she feels repulsion toward her honest attempt at mastering her interweaving into the Real People; shame is layered upon previous shame in a bulbous onion of self-regret. Until this moment, she had known she was fine.

I spent many years of my life attempting to pass as a "normal" American. I would insist on my comfort with the most minute of Western norms that I observed my non-Muslim peers engaging in, even though the practice of them definitely caused brainquakes with magnitudes of at least 4.3. Wear shoes inside? Sure. Eat with a fork instead of your hand? Yeah, no problem. Get a Christmas tree? (Or at least pretend to get a Christmas tree?) Of course, what's the big deal? I would rise to these occasions so adamantly that not even a murmur would escape me that hinted to anyone that I was more comfortable if shoes were removed, if food was eaten with fingers rather than forks, and if Christmas trees were kept in the homes of people who actually celebrated Christmas. I'm not sure who I was insisting to harder—others or myself—but I would conscientiously transplant myself into my non-Muslim American peers' mindspaces, believing this was the only way to finally achieve the dream of "normal." I remember experiences from as early as kindergarten, continuing all the way through sophomore year in college.

Enter the saving grace of feminism. I almost don't want to include this clarification here, but because I know there are people who believe feminism is equated with misandry or bras burnt to a crisp (I prefer mine rare), so let me explain which definition of feminism I adhere to:

| Feminism is | Feminism is not |
|---|---|
| Believing in the equal respect and rights of *all* people. | **Hating men.** |
| | **Believing women are superior to men.** |
| This includes people with vaginas, | **A personal attack on privileged individuals.** |
| people with penises, people with neither, | |

people with brown black white red yellow
whatever skin. It is bringing attention to the
previously marginalized ignored rejected
stepped-on individuals who were judged not for
what they were able to contribute to society,
but for what was under their clothes.
And sometimes, their clothes.[1]

So, once again—enter feminism. In some ways, feminism saved my religious identity and, in fact, made it stronger. All my attempts to fit my Indian Islamic heritage on the procrustean bed of Western norms that I saw praised in school and on television as I was growing up I began see for what they were: acts to erase my "abnormality"; my individuality. The norms of the white patriarchal majority that I aspired to as a child—norms I had once thought were definitively Right for being Normal—I began to see for what they actually were: not necessarily wrong, but only one way of being right. There is more than one Normal. Just as second-wave feminism[2] fought for society to acknowledge women's experiences not as an aberrant form of experience but as a different but equally valid form of experience, contemporary feminism bolsters recognition of all marginalized groups, helping kids, adolescents, and women like me to embrace our Abnormal.

You see me, yes? I can let you and not let you. It's just a piece of cloth, it's just a curtain, but which side is the actor and which the audience? This is not opening night, I am not an amateur, I have memorized my lines under your direction but—hey, what's that, my feet are holding the curtain down, even though it's opening night, even though there's a full house? Still, my feet burn from the red velvet friction, my sweaty

---

1. Billowy *hujub* (veils; also "hijabs") have an odd affinity with tight dresses; they are sisters cut from the same cloth. They are both stared at, sometimes with disbelief, sometimes with confusion, sometimes with appreciation for the "exotic."

2. The roughly twenty years of feminist activity between the early 1960s to the early 1980s that began in the United States and spread throughout the Western world. The period coincided with the Civil Rights movement in America and focused on gender inequalities women faced at home and in the workplace.

toes curled against the bottom seam, holding it down holding it down because I will not act when you say Lift the curtain, I will not act when you say Action, I will not act.

His eyes tried picking her, licking her, but she was disappointingly impervious. No matter how much he widened those c'mon-let's-go eyes, she stood there, immobile, unchanged, blinking back. No big deal, he'd won his own Helens many times before, and without the aid of any Trojans at that. Keep going, he says to himself—the challenge will only make the conquering all

the sweeter, sweeter than the tiny droplets of sweat he imagined on her lower back. Eyes so wide, so wide that it felt like his eyelids were peeling away outward from his face, up over his forehead, down over his stubbly cheeks. Surely now I can see! The orbs in his eye sockets began to feel like two peeled grapes, shrinking inexplicably, wrinkling in on themselves. With all his might, he extended tiny, delicate, mangled branches from what remained in the two holes in his face; convinced. Surely now. Surely now. Surely. Blink.

John Berger's *Ways of Seeing* is now old news. His explanation of the dominant male gaze defining the female in Western media from the Renaissance until the twentieth century still shocks me, no matter how many times I read the book. The blatantly systematic methods used throughout the centuries in visual media to remove power from the female body by removing its gaze (e.g., submissive, downturned eyes; or the camera's focus on all possible body parts besides the eyes) and the subsequent threat of not just confrontation, but *assertion* of the female self, seems to me to be full of—pardon the French—merde. It is simultaneously incredulous and logical that the effects of the media could directly shape cultural gender behaviors.

Since Berger wrote, women have asserted power over our own bodies, and we have made many positive strides. And yet, there is still a space and need for books like Ariel Levy's *Female Chauvinist Pigs*, bringing attention to how American culture encourages women to be complicit in their own objectification by rewarding those who laugh at sexist jokes, "playfully" objectify themselves (e.g., *Girls Gone Wild*), or buying into the idea that any sexism that occurs today is "ironic" because second-wave feminism[2] somehow fixed all gender issues in the United States. There is still a need for an ongoing discussion on rape culture and how to eradicate it. There is *still* the male gaze. Its form may have shifted into a more subtle, more slippery one than in years past, but it still rears its ugly head—or rather, eye. And it does not limit its feasting to younger bodies. For example, in the context of her possible run for presidency, former Secretary of State Hillary Clinton was repeatedly criticized in the early months of 2014 by anchors on Fox News for her appearance, down to how many wrinkles she had on her face. I still can think of no rational explanation as to why male politicians would not be subjected to the same aesthetic inspections besides the obvious: they must have discovered a better wrinkle cream than she did. ("Oh my god, Todd, you *have* to try this. It's made from a special fetus extract we gathered from all the clinics we shut down in Texas!" "Oh, wow, thanks, Rick. I really appreciate it. Every baby *does* have a purpose after all!" But I digress—imaginary spa conversations between Perry and Akin will be saved for another time.)

I'm stared at. A *lot*. And I know this is because of my *rida* (a specific style of Indian *hijab*). My chosen "lack" of a body seems to gain much attention, some positive, some negative, but all, by definition, imposed and unasked for. As a recent piece in *The Economist* (April 26, 2014) noted, "Few sartorial choices are scrutinized as closely as those of Muslim women." While this may be true, I feel I need to share the attention—"Scrutiny for all women!"—because from having been perceived only for my clothing choices so many times, I've developed quite a sharp gauge for types of gazes. It is from the experience of being a Muslim woman that I've involuntarily honed a sensitivity to the state and existence of the "other." I am usually the "other" due to my clothing choice, but this "otherness" helps me easily recognize the subtle ways women are still "othered" by men in American culture today. There is not much difference between judging a veiled woman as submissive, mindless, and lacking control than judging a college sophomore wearing a short, low-cut dress as causing her own rape.

My veil frees me from the male gaze. Even though I am still looked at for my clothing, I believe the gaze is met with an abrupt brick wall, a wall that I build when I choose to, and I knock down when I choose to. The act of veiling literally blocks the gaze and subversively puts whatever power and control it may have possessed into *my* power and control. In fact, Islam itself works to remove the power of the male gaze. In the same part of the Qur'an in which women are told to dress modestly, men are told to—in words that are almost unnervingly applicable—"lower their gaze and be modest."

... Because things are not perfect, no, things are always a little out-out-out of sync, there's always an innocent little splatter of sauce that has landed on your lap that everyone pretends is not there, even though you can feel the warmth of the heated, smashed, crashed tomato on your thigh there, through the conversation. There's always a little mess. Believers on both sides, and both sides believe just as religiously in The Way Things Should Be. The way things should be is open and free and various, but The Way Things Should Be is un... shocking. Un-strange. Un-done.

Because things are not perfect, I concede to the inevitable jury of skeptics that will convene now—and who were actually probably already bored in their seats from the beginning, tapping their feet impatiently against the cracked concrete under them—that gender inequality and prejudice still exists within some Muslim communities, and that the one act of *hijab* does not eradicate certain persistent sexist social traditions; these are the splatters we feel we cannot address in polite society. But neither does the West provide a solution for the sexism found at our dining tables, the tried "solutions" more than once having only served to spill even more sauce.

And so it is exactly here, at this mess of a feast, that I find my own solution.

Although feminism as an official social movement may have been coined in the West, I believe if we truly adhere to its tenets, it can be a universal tool for empowering not only women, but any individual who has felt marginalized or disempowered for who she or he inherently is. The problem rarely lies in faith or feminism; it usually can be traced back to individuals misinterpreting, miscommunicating, and misogynying on their own. Rather than further pull apart the two F-words on the spectrum of beliefs, let us find ways to let them fall into one another as they naturally could; let us give enough space.

# Once a Catholic
## by Kate McElwee

KATE MCELWEE is the Co-Director of the Women's Ordination Conference, based in Washington, D.C. Kate earned her Bachelor's degree in Religion from Mount Holyoke College in South Hadley, Massachusetts, with a Five College Certificate in Buddhist Studies. She earned a Masters degree with distinction in International Human Rights Law from the School of Oriental and African Studies (SOAS - University of London). She and her husband relocated to Rome, Italy, in 2014.

As an undergraduate I stopped going to Catholic Mass after my first weekend at school. I had a scheduling conflict my first semester and ended up taking a Buddhist ethics class, which I called "the class that changed my life." Captivated by the content, I became a religion major, studying Tibetan Buddhism, and never looked back. I learned Tibetan, went to India to do ethnographic research, and had private audiences with the Dalai Lama (twice). On campus I ran the Buddhist discussion group, represented Buddhists on the Multi-Faith council, volunteered at the Buddhist Peace Fellowship and the Pluralism Project researching Buddhist communities in the United States, and went on to do a master's dissertation on Tibet and Universal Jurisdiction.

Then I got a full-time job working for a Catholic reform organization. My mom joked at the time, "So now you're Catholic again?"

"Once a Catholic, always a Catholic, mom!" How hard could it be?

I had a lot to learn. Growing up, my parents had wanted to "protect" me from some of their experiences. Both were educated in Catholic schools and raised in Catholic families; they made sure I attended secular schools and went through sacraments at a healthy distance. I heard stories of very scary, abusive nuns and was thankful I didn't know any personally. We went to Mass each week, but my dad timed the homily on his watch (average twenty-one minutes), and complained about Monsignor's obsession with abortion.

Throughout my long Confirmation process as a teenager, I encountered injustices and peculiarities that pushed me even further away. One time the priest had small groups of candidates over for dinner at the rectory and never once spoke to me, but instead spoke to the boys about football. On another occasion during a catechism class we were asked to interview our parents about abortion and report back. My parents were the only parents who said that abortion should be a safe and legal option; my teacher told me to tell my parents that perhaps we should find another church. On a final Confirmation retreat, we were asked to write a private letter to God. I imagined we would burn the letters and let the smoke rise up to the sky, but instead we were asked to read a letter of our peers' and respond back as God. I refused and came home claiming that I was becoming a Buddhist. And eventually I did, except during those "Hail Mary" moments—on a plane, in the emergency room, trying to fall asleep at night—when it was Catholic prayers that ran instinctively in my head. Even though I knew Buddhist chants and sutras, my subconscious filled silence with Catholic prayer.

At first it was easy to create a "moral bricolage" of Buddhist teachings that my therapist would approve of, neutralized affirmations free of words like "Jesus" and "Holy Father" that made me uncomfortable. I read what I liked, safely from the comforts of my liberal women's college, and avoided the more "cultural" forms of Buddhist practice. My relationship with Buddhism was very academic, and I developed strong opinions about casual "bedside Buddhists," or those who simply read feel-good Buddhist-lite books before falling asleep. I went on retreats and had a casual meditation practice myself, but my teacher was always my professor, not a monastic.

However, even equipped with feminist hermeneutics, I found myself doing advanced spiritual acrobatics to explain much of the same sexism I encountered in Catholicism; that worryingly familiar line drawn around sex and gender often felt even more explicit in Buddhism. For instance, the "physiomoral" discourse, which describes the inextricable link between body and morality, illustrated by the belief that a Buddha has thirty-two physical marks of being "a great man," and reflects karmic effects of previous lifetimes.

Furthermore, even if an enlightened being recognizes the worthlessness of the body, he manifests a body that is in the end, always male. Women and other "non-normative" bodies represent a deficit of virtue. Insofar as we are "heart-minds," virtues are always physical *and* moral.[1] The gendered nature of "the ideal" body and spirit brought me right back to the gendered requirements of the Consecration.

Coming back from a study abroad experience in northern India, where I not only encountered theological and moral sexism, but a culture where I felt even less empowered to speak out against what I felt was unjust, I immersed myself in studying Christianity. During a Feminist Theology seminar, Mary Hunt came to visit and I asked her that token, nagging question: Why do you stay? Her response has guided my own Catholic path ever since: "We have a responsibility to speak this language. This is what a Catholic looks like." I understood then that my inheritance of Catholicism came laced with duty to study, to question, and most of all, to refuse to suspend feminism in the name of the sacred. We have a responsibility to speak in the name of Catholicism, as women and as feminists; we cannot be spoken for by patriarchy.

During my first week at the Women's Ordination Conference (WOC), I realized that even though I may speak the language, I had to learn an entirely new vocabulary: I learned everyone was "discerning" something, and "blessings!" was a good way to end an email; the history of the reform movement (a much more fun side of nuns); scores

---

1. Susanne Mrozik, *Virtuous Bodies: The Physical Dimensions of Morality in Buddhist Ethics*, Religion, Culture, and History Series (New York: Oxford University Press , 2007 ).

of Vatican II songs; the acronyms of religious orders and Vatican offices; and the "grave" consequences of working at an organization calling for the ordination of women. I quickly learned that everyone read the *National Catholic Reporter*, and so I bookmarked that, and kept reading over my Feminist Theology course materials.

I also quickly learned that to be fully employed within the Church justice movement is to have a very public voice about a challenging spiritual issue. As I became more familiar with our organization's mission, I realized my personal narrative would also be made very public; storytelling is part of the work. Especially as a young person in the movement, people wanted to ask me questions. What brought me to this work? Why do I love the Church? Am I called to be a priest? The honest answer is that significant spiritual posturing took place. As an employee-activist responsible to a board of directors and a global membership, from my first introduction I had to develop a line, a pitch, an answer.

It wasn't until I went to Rome with Roy Bourgeois, a former Maryknoll priest excommunicated for his vocal support of women's ordination, that I really found my place as a feminist in the Catholic Church. Roy Bourgeois, a Purple Heart veteran, peace activist, and Nobel Prize nominee, has served over four years in prison for passive resistance and social justice work. He worked as a priest for nearly forty years before he started receiving warnings from the Vatican, urging him to recant his public support of women's ordination. Roy joined me and an international delegation of women's ordination advocates in Rome, armed with a petition of over fifteen thousand signatures supporting him, including over two hundred signatures from priests in good standing, supporting their brother's right of conscience[2]. We were able to arrange a meeting between a Vatican official and Roy—the most formal contact that he had with the Vatican since

---

2. Catholic theology understands conscience as an interior space where one can listen to and hear the truth, the good, and the voice of God. This relationship with God helps Catholics understand what is right and just, and guides us forward faithfully in moral decisions. One is called to obey—and never be forced to act against her or his conscience, especially in religious matters. See *Catechism of the Catholic Church* paragraphs 1776-1782.

2008, when he received his first warning letter for giving a homily at a service to ordain women.

Just before the meeting, Roy wore his collar and asked us to pray for him, something he never did before. It was similar to watching a schoolboy go to the principal's office, if the schoolboy really respected the principal. It was clear that the institution had meaning—a revelation to me, as someone who re-entered through the backdoor. While this private meeting took place, some of our group gathered in St. Peter's Square, watching the pomp of Pope Benedict XVI's blessing to crowds of people.

It was in that moment, huddled with the women priests, the former nuns, the canon lawyers, and the "trouble-makers" who have made choices to be anti-sexist in their Catholicism, that I felt most Catholic. With tears in my eyes, I could clearly see the distance between the hierarchy and the people of God. When Roy met us and shared the highlights of their meeting, the consequence of conscience was clear in the treatment of a priest standing for justice. The well-meaning Vatican official ultimately shrugged, said he was doing what he could within a bureaucracy, and told Roy: "You will be made an example of."

Suddenly my time working at the Women's Ordination Conference clicked into place. The Vatican is a vestige of power, filled with fading symbolism and wealth that is desperately trying to rule an empire that no longer exists. Women—and those who expect women to be treated equally—are a threat to this massive power structure simply because we are still here. We are here because we know at the heart of Catholicism is social justice, community, and Eucharistic nourishment. The heart of Catholicism is beating strongly within the trouble-makers, the women priests and their communities, and especially in the tiny WOC office. If being a Catholic means threatening patriarchal power with those who stand up for human rights, sign me up.

By meeting the women and men who are connected to my organization and hearing the stories of those called to the priesthood or called to make decisions, I am able to ask myself the question everyone else asks of me: "Why do you stay?"

I am able to find a way to be Catholic—as far out on the margins as possible, where women are not welcomed, not heard, and not recognized. The best way to be Catholic is through being a feminist. I am Catholic with those who also struggle but have found authentic, meaningful ways to be Catholic, without approval or compromise. I find strength in my religious muscles; in Catholicism I have ground to stand on and space to speak. One thing that I have learned in my Catholic re-education is that the Holy Spirit can be invoked in any situation—in meetings, on conference calls, and to explain the unexplainable. The chance to reexamine my faith, to engage it critically, and to listen to those "Hail Mary moments" has revealed a path greater than I could know. Chance, karma, or the Holy Spirit, I am grateful for the space to be wholly myself: definitely feminist, a little Buddhist, and always a Catholic.

# Music and Prayer: Harmonizing Religious Contradictions
## by Aviva Richman

AVIVA RICHMAN is on the faculty at Yeshivat Hadar in Manhattan where she teaches Talmud. She is also pursuing a Ph.D. in Hebrew and Judaic Studies at New York University, focusing on law and gender in the Babylonian Talmud. She is happy to share a vibrant Jewish home with her spouse Tzemah and their son Boaz.

Some of the most pivotal conversations in life happen at the most inopportune moments. Back in 2008, I was talking with my mom on my cellphone while walking towards the uptown subway in Manhattan. I was on my way home from work at Yeshivat Hadar—an egalitarian yeshiva in Manhattan where I teach Talmud. It was a few months before my wedding ceremony and I was trying to explain to my mom why it was our dream that the officiating rabbi be both Orthodox and female.

As the conversation progressed—in length and intensity—I kept putting off which subway station to enter, assuming we'd have it all figured out in another eight blocks.

"Aviva, you know that it will be very strange for the people in my community if there is a female rabbi."

"I know, mom. But we have to do this in a way that reflects who we are."

Finally, I felt I couldn't delay my trip home any longer and stayed on the phone while I went down into the subway station. The rest of our conversation was punctuated by the periodic clamor of the subways as my mom and I tried to understand how our religious approaches converged and diverged. There was something so appropriate about the chaos that enveloped this conversation; it reflected the chaos of the variety of experiences and choices that have shaped our textured religious lives.

I was born into a liberal, living-room based *havurah* (small, informal prayer group), but soon after my parents divorced, when I was five years old, my mother became Orthodox and half of my life became deeply embedded in the Orthodox community of Baltimore. When I started coming home from public school with uneaten sandwiches because I couldn't find a way to do ritual handwashing before lunch or the time to say grace after meals, my parents decided it was time to consider a Jewish Day School. I was in fourth grade and it was a crucial moment in my own turn towards Orthodox Jewish practice.

For over a decade I vacillated between two communities each Shabbat. There was my mother's "black hat" Orthodox shul, where the community held strict standards of religious observance; only men counted in a prayer quorum and led services, while women sat on the other side of a barrier made of lacy curtain. And there was my father's havurah, where everyone sat in a circle, sometimes in jeans and t-shirts, and took turns leading services weaving together contemporary poetry, stories, and chanting, with some of the traditional prayers. At their surface these communities cherished entirely opposite worldviews—tradition, obligation, and hierarchy versus creativity, autonomy, and a feminist ethic of radical inclusion. This opposition has torn apart Jewish communities in recent decades, and these contradictions could have alienated me from Jewish practice entirely. Yet, even as my own practice came to reflect Orthodox norms, I always felt that at their heart, these two communities were aligned. Both were rooted in a sense of religious life centered around warmth and spirituality. When I reflect on why I have "kept the faith" and stayed inside religious practice rather than being deterred by contradictions and disappointments, I come back to one thing that was at the pulsing heart of these religious communities: the power of music and prayer.

It is hard to describe how powerful it is to grow up with a religious spiritual leader whose musical voice in prayer was as penetrating, sincere, and resonant as that of Rabbi Silverman[1], the rabbi of my mother's Orthodox shul. Born modern Orthodox, in his young twenties he became a hassid[2]. One of the richest parts of this Hassidic turn was the music—both the melodies my rabbi learned and the melodies he came to write. I vividly remember sitting on my mother's lap when I was young, at *seudah shlishit* (the meal that closes Shabbat), where the table was always filled more abundantly with song than with food. Swaying back and forth to the music, I was carried into another world, a world defined by yearning—for truth, for God, and for transformation. Rabbi Silverman's voice and gentle passion was a catalyst, drawing others into a reflective and dynamic religious experience through music. The shul was filled with people who naturally joined into the singing, and spontaneously harmonized. It felt like being awash in a sea of sound made up of the unique intentions of the many individuals in the room, a sea of sound that could in turn hold these prayers and lift them upwards. In retrospect I realize what a blessing it was that this practice was available to and embraced by women of the shul in addition to men. In many Orthodox places I've been since, *seudah shlishit* is almost exclusively a male affair.

Back to the subway conversation in 2008: "Aviva, are you mad at me for exposing you to the Orthodox world? Why did you decide to leave it behind?"

The words sounded chafing to my ears. How was it possible that my mother, who brought me into this beautiful world that I have so

---

1. I have not used the rabbi's real name to protect his privacy.
2. A hassid is a devoted student of a Hassidic rebbe (teacher in one branch of Orthodox Judaism). The Hassidic movement is a Jewish spiritual-devotional popular movement that took root in eighteenth century Poland.

embraced, didn't understand how much it meant to me? Yes, there came a point when I could no longer sincerely believe in approaching God through limitation of women's participation in religious life. There came a point when I felt that Jewish law needed to honestly respond to a world in which gender roles have shifted in dramatic ways. But to me, it was obvious that I loved these two worlds I grew up in and had tried hard to synthesize the powerful elements of both. That was why I was walking home from a yeshiva that was deeply committed to halakhic Jewish practice, rigorous Torah learning, meaningful prayer, and full participation of women in all aspects of Jewish observance.

"Mom, every time I daven (Yiddish for pray), I hear Rabbi Silverman's voice in my head. It is only because of him that I have any sense of what it means to lead *tefilah* (Hebrew for prayer)."

I know it sounded like a paradox. I know that to Rabbi Silverman and his kind of community, women leading prayer is tantamount to transgression. But to me it felt so continuous. If I were male, growing up to lead prayer service would be interpreted wholly as a sign of commitment and observance—taking personal responsibility to embody the practice and values I learned as a kid. Why is it that because I am female this same act can be interpreted in the opposite way, as a sign of rebellion and rejection? My mom's opposition was jarring to me, it made me question if I was deluding myself by thinking that the path I had chosen was a valid observant approach. But, in addition to the hours of study I had committed to examining questions of women and ritual in Jewish legal sources[3], there was another memory of Rabbi Silverman that had become deeply ingrained and anchored my sense of conviction.

After ninth grade, I was considering switching from an Orthodox day school to a pluralistic community day school, where the students came from many different Jewish backgrounds. In part, I thought this would be an environment where I could voice my questions about gender and Jewish practice more openly. I went to talk with Rabbi Silverman, certain that he would dissuade me from moving into a less observant environment.

---

3. For an excellent summary of these Jewish legal sources, see Rabbi Ethan Tucker's article "Gender, Tefilah and Halakhah on One Foot" at mechonhadar.org.

"Aviva, what do you think will change in your religious practice?"

"I might start wearing pants [instead of long skirts, the traditional modest garb for Orthodox women]."

"That's not what I mean. What do you think will *really* change?"

I pause for a minute, trying to imagine if I would stop praying or not keep kosher or stop believing in God.

"Nothing," I say.

"You have to follow your heart."

These last words are probably what any Hassidic rabbi would say as a response to any question. But for me, those words had a profound and lasting impact. With those words, I found the strength to trust my intuition. Following my heart wasn't presented as an option, but as an imperative. The message I got was that to live a true religious life and be in an honest relationship with God, I must be steered by the heart. Anything else would be an act of pretense. This message is so deeply conveyed through the musical tradition I inherited, a tradition of prayer that is rooted in sincere expression of the heart.

The tradition of melodic tefilah that I love so much has a value way beyond aesthetics. I love these melodies for what they are, but also for the metaphor that music represents. Music is a powerful model that combines continuity, mastery, growth, and creativity. Because of these traits, music has the potential to encompass and accompany a religious journey, both for an individual and a community. When I come back to a melody I have known my whole life and incorporate it into my personal morning prayers—whether years ago, in my college dorm room at Oberlin, or now in my living room while my two-year-old plays next to me—I have a sense of passage of time and how my relationship with God has changed over the years with new experiences. When I use this same melody to lead tefilah in a minyan I hear new voices coalescing and creating together an experience that can only exist in this moment and in this space. It is at once an embrace of a tradition and a claiming of a complete sense of ownership.

To me, leading tefilah as a woman with the melodies I learned from Rabbi Silverman represents an orientation of embrace and synthesis. It does not represent a rupture at all—in fact it is the only way I could fully live up to and embody all that I absorbed from my upbringing. My adult Jewish life has centered around striving to synthesize , or more accurately, fulfill, the compelling elements of Judaism I came to know through my multi-layered upbringing.  I continue to feel obligated to observe mitzvot—praying every day, keeping kosher, keeping Shabbat, striving to do acts of kindness, studying Torah—but I also attempt to live this life of mitzvot in a way that adheres to the imperative to respect the dignity of all people made in the image of the divine, in a community where I too can step up to lead. I strive to seek out and create inclusive, feminist communities where people don't feel marginalized, ignored, or stifled, but fully able to participate and grow in all aspects of Torah and mitzvot.

I love the tradition of music I have inherited for what it is, but also for what it represents. It is a model for what it means to stay in religious community in a way that is dynamic. It represents the importance of humbly attempting to master the complexity of a tradition, while also having total respect for the unique voice of the individual. It reflects being deeply embedded in something much larger than myself and allowing this tradition to shape my identity, while being part of preserving, transmitting and shaping this tradition for the next generation.

I know that Rabbi Silverman doesn't officially agree with a number of choices I have made. A few years ago, when I was preparing to lead services for the High Holidays, I called him to ask if he might go over some of the unique once-a-year melodies with me. He declined, but I didn't get a sense that he totally disapproved of me leading services as a woman, just that it would be too much of a stretch of his boundaries. I was disappointed, but not surprised. One can only expect so much from any given person in one lifetime. I feel blessed to have inherited the rare, rich gift of a tradition of prayer rooted in humility, sincerity, joy, and creative expression and I am glad to be able to share this with people who might never step foot in Rabbi Silverman's shul. I can only hope and trust that this is *avodah l'shem shamayim*—an act of serving God.

# I Still May Push a Little
## by Stacy Leeman

 STACY LEEMAN is an abstract oil painter from Columbus, Ohio, and earned her B.A. in studio art from Oberlin and her M.F.A. from Rutgers University. Her studies abroad have included a year in Jerusalem and a semester at Parson's School of Design in Paris. Leeman often takes traditional Jewish texts and creates artworks that use contemporary painting methods. Leeman exhibits extensively throughout the United States and is the author of three books of her own artwork. Leeman is represented by the Sharon Weiss Gallery in Columbus and the Water Street Gallery in Douglas, Michigan.

A feminist, an Orthodox Jew, and an artist walk into a room… It sounds like the start of a bad joke. But the truth is all of them are me, and the vibrancy of each one contains the existential struggles and meaning of my life.

In short, I like to test boundaries and explore contradictions.

If there is one quality that embodies my life it is that I constantly struggle with ideas, values, beliefs, and practices that appear to be so obviously conflicting to the rest of the world. I consider myself to be an Orthodox Jew and a feminist, and in so doing I struggle with melding a patriarchal three thousand year tradition with a twenty-first century college-educated feminist perspective.

As an artist, I find the solitary moments in my studio to be the most profound moments of my life; yet, I seek the tradition and ritual that binds me to a community. I love to study Jewish texts that date back thousands of years and find new insights and ways of reading ambiguities contained within them, and then work through them in the aesthetics of abstract art. I find meaning in the struggle to prove that these qualities can coexist in my life and in my art.

These tensions imbue my paintings and drawings with deeply personal meanings. In them, I explore my religious and philosophical questions and ideas. Often inspired by texts that I've read, I later return to explore these in my oeuvre. One of my most recent series, *Upstream*, evokes these struggles. The artwork is based on a tale found in the Talmud, a book of the Jewish oral tradition, in which a bird is shown to be kosher only if it has the strength to swim upstream. I loved the notion of a tradition heralding an animal for having the strength to go against the stream.

Like most artists today I am a post-modernist. We borrow from tradition and create what Rabbi Joseph B. Soloveitchik, the founder of the Modern Orthodox movement in Judaism, calls *chiddushei* or insights. For Rabbi Soloveitchik these are insights into reading text. For me these insights are for both reading text and creating a new method and language of painting.

Often, in my paintings, I begin with imagery from photographs and use them to develop my own personal symbolism and gestures to turn into abstract artwork. In particular, my *Synagogue Migrations* paintings echo the American narrative of the twentieth and twenty-first centuries by following the path of traditional urban synagogues migrating to suburban areas. I used photos from the synagogue that I grew up in and from a Baptist Church that had been the synagogue when my father was a child. The palette corresponded to the stained glass windows, the stone exterior and the bronze ritual furnishings. In addition to painting with brushes, I painted with drafting tools to allude to the facades of the buildings that house our spiritual lives and communities.

In the past several years, each of my three core identities has come under attack. As an artist, there has been talk about the death of painting in the face of digital media's focus on ephemera. In fact, I find quite the opposite to be true. Paintings are the antidote to a society that is

built on speed and immediate gratification. Making paintings—and viewing them—forces people to be quiet and still. As long as painters find ways to reinvent the language of paint to include contemporary ideas and manners of applying paint, then the medium will continue to be relevant. Art challenges viewers. People sometimes look at figurative or objective work and think they know what the artist intended; often these precursory judgments are not accurate and the works of art are much more complicated than they first appear. The same viewers will often be intimidated by abstract art and refuse even to try and engage with it.

For me, though, abstraction is the attempt to find new ways to explore ideas and stories. Though it may not be readily apparent in the finished product, my art emerges out of a narrative. The more I seek the narrative, the more paradoxical and complicated it seems to become; I don't believe in stories that are simple and straightforward. As these narratives are put into paint, I am forced to be still and consider color, line, composition, and texture, and to contemplate each mark as it impacts the work as a whole.

Abstract artist Barnett Newman wrote in his essay, *The First Man Was an Artist*, "What is the explanation of the seemingly insane drive of man to be painter and poet if it is not an act of defiance against man's fall and an assertion that he return to the Adam of the Garden of Eden?" Thus, the notion of beautifying is a divine act in which the artist sets herself up to mimic the Creator by creating her art.

My commitment to Orthodox Judaism also situates me on the fringe of society. Years ago, I heard a talk by Rabbi Steven Greenberg, the first openly gay Orthodox rabbi. He was asked point blank why he was still Orthodox. He explained that whatever shortcomings Orthodoxy has, it also has a vitality that emerges from the passion with which Orthodox Jews approach Judaism and, in particular, engage in a dialogue with thousands of years of wisdom and experiences through learning ancient texts. Studying these texts is one of the most profound experiences of Jewish life—and one that, unfortunately, many Jews in today's world find unfathomable. The Jewish oral tradition, written down some seventeen hundred years ago, includes conversations and arguments amongst the sages. The stories and arguments have an authenticity that could not have been created.

There are webs to the conversations that are complicated and counterintuitive; yet there is a pursuit of truth and knowledge that is absolutely pure. I love that many of our texts are ambiguous and that there is room for interpretation. It's their ambiguity that speaks to me. On a personal level, I hope that exploring these texts helps me integrate the paradoxes of my being. As an artist, these texts often form the genesis for my art.

For each element of Judaism that I struggle with, I also find something meaningful in it. Observing the Jewish dietary laws can be challenging. It would be easier to eat whatever I wanted, whenever I wanted it. However, being mindful about any morsel that I eat forces me to be conscientious. I like the awareness, too, that I must not only be thoughtful about what I am eating, I must also bless the food both before and after I eat it. I thank G-d for providing the food, but, as Jewish law dictates, when I am satiated and no longer need it, I must pause and express my gratitude.

Finally, as a child of the '80s, feminism became my lens to critically engage with the world. Judaism has carved out gender-specific roles that I may not always be comfortable with. However, I am lucky that over the past twenty or thirty years, exceptional women and men have sought to expand the "Palace of the Torah,"[1] as philosopher Dr. Tamar Ross said.

Gender roles have evolved, albeit not always as quickly or meaningfully as I would like. As a feminist, I struggle with the idea that my husband counts in a minyan (the quorum of ten adult Jewish men needed to pray as a community under Jewish law), but I don't, or that the Jewish practice of wearing something on my head signifies that I am married. It is difficult to practice this law of modesty that, in rabbinic law, is designed to help men control their sexual impulses. On the other hand, I like the symbolism and consciousness; this hat on my head is a sign that I am a woman of faith and that I am part of a community. (The great irony is that most in the art world assume the hat is some artistic eccentricity). I become signified and my hat or head covering becomes my signifier. Similar to painting, the subtle symbolic language is only visible to those who understand my perspective.

For feminists, Western society also has its problems. Women still face glass ceilings and sexism. Women still earn less than men. Women are still often absent from the table when important decisions are made. Sheryl Sandberg's exhortation to women to "lean in" has not changed nearly enough over the past two decades. And society often objectifies women.

As Susannah Heschel says in her essay, *A Little on the Margins*, "My beliefs have put me in an interesting position—a little on the margins of both Judaism and feminism, always looking at things from other perspectives, always seeing tensions and ambiguities. My father used to say, 'Show me a person who has no problems and I'll show you a fool.' I like the struggle and conflicts. I don't want to live in a fool's

---

1. Palace of the Torah is what Dr. Ross calls efforts to address contemporary issues like feminism. Dr. Ross prizes Torah communities as a "palace," but often sees modern critiques of traditional Judaism undermining traditional Judaism. However, Dr. Ross writes that increased public roles and education for Orthodox women has strengthened and "expanded" Jewish traditions rather than undermined them.

paradise." So much of Judaism is about boundaries. Judaism creates a road map for life—from the most mundane aspects of life to the most profound. Which shoe should one put on first in the morning? What are the words one should recite in a blessing over bread? How do we express gratitude to G-d for all that we are able to do? How do we deal with tragedy? I question Jewish law, or halakha. I like to understand the reasons, when there are reasons, and I like to know the bottom line. But I won't disregard the laws.

As an undergraduate student, my challenge in every art assignment was to listen closely and figure out what I must do, but also to ascertain where there was latitude. I never disregarded the boundaries, but I worked within them. This is an apt metaphor for my life. For me there is always this sweet spot in the midst of my boundaries as a feminist Orthodox Jewish artist that I follow (but I still may push a little).

# What Has Remained
## THE TESTIMONY OF A MUJER MESTIZA
### by Erica Granados De La Rosa

ERICA GRANADOS DE LA ROSA, also known as Erica GDLR, is a writer, spoken-word poet, community activist, and scholar of diasporic indigenous descent. She holds a B.A. in social and political philosophy from Loyola University Chicago and an M.A. in Women's Studies from Texas Women's University. She has been invited to share her spoken-word poetry and speak on social justice issues at venues including The Dallas Museum of Art, The Prindle Institute for Ethics, Boston University School of Theology, The Black Academy of Arts and Letters, The General Commission on the Status and Role of Women, and National Public Radio. Erica was born in Baltimore, Maryland, and grew up all over the United States. She currently lives in Denton, Texas, with her partner and her cat.

In the midst of my own identity crisis as a bilingual woman of color born in the Christian faith within the context of the United States, I crave words that are mindful and affirming of my needs and my existence. As a result, I wrote this piece for the Latinas, Chicanas, Mestizas, and Indigenous women who might be lost in overwhelmingly white feminist and conventional Christian discourses. I wrote these words *para la que anda buscando paso* and for the woman who doesn't speak Spanish, isn't Latin American or Indigenous, but is courageous enough to take the extra steps to grow, learn, and understand an experience as told by her multilingual *Mestiza* Indigenous sister. With that stated, throughout this article I use terms that are multilingual and that relate to my reality as a woman of color activist, academic, and writer. In some places I choose to translate or explain terms, and in others, such as the title, I choose to invite the reader to work at creating bridges across culture and comfort zones in order to challenge the ethnocentric forms of expression prevalent in the written word.

It has always been hard to find articles in these types of anthologies that speak to me, instead they often speak to white non-Spanish-speaking people *about me* or my cultural reality. It has been my experience that when people of color do write about their lives or that of their diverse communities, we are often instructed to appease a "general audience" that does not include our own people, as if our people do not read or do not benefit from reading what we have to say. Sadly, I consider how many times throughout my whole life I had to do the extra work to look up or research words, histories, and experiences that are not my own in order to comprehend required Eurocentric literature, theory, and prose. Moreover, if I wish to possibly obtain something useful from reading that might aid my personal growth, I often have to take the extra step to find some sort of connection or resemblance to my own cultural experience. This is the systemic marginalization and silencing of diverse voices and reflections not only in publication but cultural production at large. The violence that ensues from having limited reflections and relevant knowledge production in a globalized world is a form of cultural occupation and genocide. This is the context from which I speak to you today.

A part of my truth begins with the fact that I am a Christian as a direct result of the colonization and genocide of my people. My *mestiza* body is what survived one of the worst atrocities in the history of our species, justified by Christian authorities and their interpretation of the Bible. I am the daughter of indigenous nations who were given the choice of accepting Christianity or death. I am the daughter of women who were baptized by priests before they were raped, in attempts to protect their rapists from eternal condemnation. As I write this, my words are the testimonies of my ancestors. As I walk, my body and my spirit carry the memories of violence that were and are perpetuated through this patriarchal reality. Yet despite the blatantly oppressive legacy of the institutional Church, I stay.

I remain a member of the Christian Church because I was born the daughter of a United Methodist pastor, a small dark-skinned *mujer indígena mestiza* divorced single mother activist who originally came to this country as a migrant farm worker. After abandoning the fields in hopes of continuing her education, she became a part of a generation of immigrant Christian activists who believed they could rediscover a historically violent faith tradition to build healing communities. Consequently, I was born into the breath of revolution ushered by third world liberation theology that spoke of a God who calls us to liberate the oppressed and continue fighting to preserve life in the midst of neoliberal colonization and civil war. I was raised by a new type of faith community that took to the streets on Sunday mornings demanding justice for their neighbors, their communities, and their families while remembering manifestations of Jesus in the examples set forth by political and symbolic icons dedicated to changing oppressive systems, like Che Guevara, Monseñor Oscar Romero, *y La Virgen de Guadalupe.*

As I grew, I honored the struggle of my community and of my mother who was and is a woman of color activist in a time of mass persecution, incarceration, displacement, and violence. I took her lessons seriously. I asked questions and listened humbly to her stories of hurt, anger, and frustration. I grew up inspired by the creative spirit that helped her survive and helped her continue doing things people never expected her to do. My mother taught me that in order to be an agent of change, you must travel and learn different worlds in order to effectively speak across the divides and serve as a bridge for justice and reconciliation for your people. Her life's work in the local church and beyond continues to prove to me time and time again that survival is a creative act. It is a labor of love and care for our community in the midst of our own healing and pain.

It was not until I made the choice to travel into another white male-dominated world called academia that people started calling me a feminist. The term feminist was strange and foreign, served with a side of sarcastic chuckles and looks that said, "She is one of them." I remember being confused, unsure if I should be offended or proud. Mostly I became frustrated. Others' assumptions that I was a feminist quickly taught me that as a woman of color I was not expected to speak for myself. The term feminist erased my identity as a *mujer indígena mestiza* dedicated to carrying on the matriarchal traditions of her mothers, who fought for the dignity of life and the sacred worth of women long before the term "feminist" was conceived.

As I began searching for ways in which to bridge my experience with that of my white feminist sisters and other agents of change, I sifted through lessons that taught me God lives in the complexities of difference. I sought out affirming reflections of women who looked like me and had walked or were walking a similar path. In my search, I found elders who gave me language to align and ground myself while honoring difference and my own particular experiences of systemic and institutional racism and heterosexism. Alice Walker gave me the term *Womanist*, María Isasi-Díaz gave me the term *Mujerista*, Gloria Anzaldúa gave me the terms *Nepantlera* and *Nueva Mestiza*.[1] Their words reminded me of what I knew of interconnectivity and love and affirmed my existence as a person who comes from a woman-centered spiritual legacy of violence and survival, death and rebirth. They conceptually gave me a claim to space as I traveled between Christian spaces, academic circles, and feminist, activist, and indigenous communities. They gave me the strength to sit at the table when no one was there to pull out the chair.

These theologians and writers also remind me of the spiritual strength of my communities; communities rooted in traditions that predate an institution steeped in a legacy of domination and oppression. Yet as I took time to relearn these indigenous traditions, I was brought back full circle to the Christian traditions of my mother. I

---

1. I encourage you to learn more about these terms by seeking out Alice Walker's *In Search of Our Mothers' Gardens: Womanist Prose* (New York: Mariner Books, 2003); María Isasi-Díaz' *Mujerista Theology: A Theology for the Twenty-First Century*, (Maryknoll: Orbis Books, 1996); and Gloria Anzaldúa's *Borderlands/La Frontera: The New Mestiza* (San Francisco: Aunt Lute Books, 2012).

was reminded that as people of color (and speaking more specifically as a person of Latin American descent), Christianity is a fundamental part of what connects us to who we are, who we were, and who we are becoming within a colonial context. The historical encounter of Christianity with an already existing spiritual cosmology and way of life in the Americas resulted in a *mestizaje* or mixture of race, culture, and language, as well as theologies and religious or spiritual rituals (such as La Virgen de Guadalupe, Santeria, and Curanderismo). Consequently, many traditions of our Native American ancestors and our pre-colonial reality creatively survive in the way we pray, the way we worship, the way we speak and give offering. Given the specifics of migrating cultures and colonization, the common experience of indigenous tradition and ritual dressed up as Christianity within Latin American churches makes sense. Our traditions had to be disguised, reshaped, and re-contextualized so that they would survive and be passed on to future generations.

Moreover, my experience watching my mother, the activist pastor, work on the streets and alongside community reminded me of how relevant the Church is in the lives of the colonized and marginalized. As a child, I learned that the Church was the center of life in the 'hood, mostly because the elders made it so. Through prayer petitions and testimonial narratives they updated the congregation on individual and community problems. While they shared meals, they exchanged stories of faith and survival over food that carried our Native American tradition forward to feed the people in more ways than one. There were others in our community who never made it to Sunday service but were loyal to services that left the sanctuary and met them halfway. These services included a free food bank, after school childcare, and an empty seat in the cool sanctuary for those who had no air conditioner at home. Being a part of a congregation also meant sustainable networks and different forms of security, like help finding a job, or the ability to barter services and favors. I later realized that these benefits were necessities for poor and undocumented communities that must continually create alternative economies and enclaves to survive.

Because of these experiences, my life with the church has never manifested in a feminist vs. Christian or Christian vs. activist dichotomy; but rather, my experience of Christianity rests on the ongoing work of women and two-spirited people[2] who took the "master's tools" and were not afraid to transform them into relevant and effective stepping stones for the healing and growth of the human spirit. The Christian faith connects me to my elders, my community, and the painful and hopeful stories of those who walked before me. I find strength in knowing that the seeds, memories, and spiritual stories the context of the Church has given me are ancestral intentions grounded in our survival. To remember the spiritual stories of my people is to remember narratives of political resistance, change, transformation, and rebirth. These stories nourish and reflect our humanity by honoring our ancestors and their legacies. This is particularly important for those like me who are a part of a displaced and marginalized community in the United States that is not offered empowering reflections, or any reflections at all, on our history or our present day reality.

I stay connected to the Church because despite the prevalent violence and erasure we experience as women of color in all facets of our colonial reality, I continue to believe that growth and healing within the wounded spirit can be inspired by formal conversations of love and stories of spiritual legacy within our communities. My faith is grounded in the belief that since birth I have been placed exactly where I need to be in order to play my role in these conversations. Although both Christian and feminist spaces have been the source of much of my woundedness they have also given me language, resource, and strength when I find myself alienated and attacked by a spiritual-phobic and male-dominated culture. Building and maintaining relationships with my white feminist sisters, as well as

---

2. In Native American traditions the concept of gender and sexuality are recognized as more than an oppositional dichotomy (i.e. straight versus gay or woman versus man). We have always recognized and honored the diversity of bodies that simultaneously manifest both feminine and masculine spirits and characteristics. These bodies are referred to as two spirited.

my Christian community, has been vital as I continue to navigate and survive violent and chronic experiences of oppression.

As I continue to walk, I give thanks to my white feminist sisters who have listened with their hearts and minds, selflessly opened doors, and been courageous enough to humbly walk with me in spaces of violence and fear. *Inlakech.* I give thanks to the elders and ancestors for the reflections and stories they provided me, for supplying me with words like *solidaridad* (solidarity) and *el pueblo* (the community). I am grateful for memories of songs, laughter, prayer, and the language of my people. I give thanks for the colors of our indigenous patterns on crosses and pictures of leaders that served to remind us that we must continue to fight for the preservation of life. I give thanks for the women-identified elders, my mother and other spiritual leaders who came together to create sacred feminine spaces that served to protect me and heal me as a young girl within a heterosexist and racist reality. I am humbled by the natural elements that were placed on altars in churches all over this sacred land in order to remind us of our relationship with the natural world, our mother and our creator. These memories are seeds of strength and transformation that live on and spread in my poetry, activism, and spiritual connection with the world. *Tlazocamati. Ometeotl.*

# The Pen Has Been Lifted: You Will Survive

by Samar Kaukab

SAMAR KAUKAB co-leads the University of Chicago's Arete team, an innovative research accelerator program that launches large-scale, complex research initiatives. Prior to joining the University, Samar served as the Executive Director of the Ohio Alliance to End Sexual Violence, Ohio's statewide anti-sexual violence coalition. She is an alumni of the American Muslim Civic Leadership Institute (AMCLI) National Fellowship and a board member of Heart Women and Girls, a nonprofit dedicated to promoting the reproductive health and mental well-being of faith-based communities. When not packing lunches for her children, she enjoys the benefits of having friends and family who cook, laugh, and do nothing, all exceedingly well.

To my three little kittens,

At seven, six, and two years old respectively, this beautiful and tumultuous world has already gripped you, my three babies, and seared in the palms of your hands a mark letting you know that you were born to survive a complicated world. Like cake batter pouring into a baking pan, every day each of your stories continues to unfold, some days in vigorous streams and at other times needing a little coaxing. Given that you are so young, other readers might discount what I've just written as overly dramatic prose. (Who looks for narrative content in the life of a two-year-old?) But this is a letter from a mother to her children and nothing less than the dramatic will suffice.

There is a saying of the Prophet Muhammad (peace be upon him), "The pen has been lifted and the ink has dried." To me, that's a lyrical way to say that all of us are just catching up to what God and the universe already know. As someone who gets to witness so much of your every day, I'm fascinated by all that you already know. You intimately know the sound of my heartbeat and the distinct, subtle tones of my voice. You can recognize the scent of my skin in a crowded room and you know that I'll pack the right amount of blueberries in each of your lunches. You know that I am your Mama. This is intimate and sacred knowledge.

My first years of motherhood were largely a test of physical endurance, with sleepless nights and a need for biceps capable of simultaneously carrying babies born sixteen months apart. Now that there are three of you and you're getting older, I realize that the real test, the one that lies ahead, is one of mental aptitude and psychological endurance. Thankfully, I have the stories of so many others to draw upon, including my mother's.

A physician who graduated from one of the top medical schools in Pakistan, my mother immigrated to the United States along with my father in the era of "send us your brightest" immigration policies. My Ammi, and your Nano, is not one of those people that can be described in a concise sentence. She is the mother who sang *lories* in Punjabi as she tucked me into bed every night until I fell asleep. She is also the mother who worked full-time at her private practice, picking up extra nursing home rounds so that my brother and I could attend private school. As a longtime member of the local *masjid* (mosque) board, Ammi always held her own amongst a group of outspoken uncles at a time when even token spots for women were not a consideration. Through it all, Ammi always found a way to weave together the many parts of her identity, emphasizing what was important to her and discarding what wasn't. Ammi didn't need the world to confirm that traditional gender norms weren't practical. They just weren't. So out they went and somehow everyone else came along, including me, her daughter who otherwise cared so much about what everyone else thought.

There are many more stories to tell—stories about my parents, stories about my grandparents during partition, stories about relatives immigrating to this country carrying the lead weight of family legacies in their suitcases. And, then there are stories about me.

So far, your curiosity has been pretty easy to tame. When I get the "What is your job, Mama?" question, a quick, "I work at the University," suffices. But when you're ready to dig deeper, I might tell you I work with a team of creative, self-effacing, and process-driven superheroes (no capes) who work to accelerate complex research initiatives. When you stare at me glassy eyed and wish that your mom was a veterinarian, I hope that I'll get to make up for it by engaging you in the first of many conversations that we'll have about complexity.

Someday further down the line, you might even start taking some interest in our identity as a family and what it means to belong to the communities we revolve in. Among many other things, I'll tell you that we are Muslims and that we are feminists. If on a stormy Chicago night the power goes out and we are left with nothing to do but talk to each other, we might even get a chance to start pulling apart what it means to be both a Muslim and a feminist *at the same time.*

In that important conversation, I want to get across to you that being a feminist and being a "good Muslim" is not a zero-sum game. At the same time, those who believe in the stark lines of separation are not entirely without good reason. The truth is that it is not easy or simple to be both a Muslim and a feminist.

Many Muslims see feminism as alien and antithetical to Islam. Just like in many other faith communities, it is easy to find those who hide behind the placards of religious tradition as they interpret for others what it means to be a woman or a man of faith. Bring up the concept of gender equality and expect tired, uncompelling diatribes about the biological differences between men and women, the innate nature of men versus that of women, how these differences necessitate different rights for men and women, and, worst of all, how blessed we are as Muslims to understand these differences. What these uninspired justifications don't provide is any context on why so many Muslim women are psychologically, physically, and spiritually disempowered by those who speak for and reinforce religious authority in our communities.

Despite a tradition in which God directly speaks to "the believing men and believing women," (Qur'an, 33:35) current gender norms directly cause women to shrink behind men, making them smaller, less meaningful actors in our spiritual and social communities. Muslim American women are encouraged to uplift their souls and enjoin in communal worship, but too often this is in dingy, curtained off spaces with inadequate sound. Our girls are told to educate themselves, but that they shouldn't be too ambitious—prospective husbands might be threatened.

Our girls grow up believing that in order to engage in the world, survival for a woman entails diminishing herself. In other words, these gender norms minimize girls, shrinking their stature, their psyches, and their connection to the Divine. Yet, God (yes, God!) speaks to us—to women and men—directly and in the exact same sentence. Women are not placed in the footnote or behind a curtain. God has distinctly made a woman's worship, her status, and her spiritual capacity equal to that of a man's. If God has not made gender equality a dirty word, who are we to live in fear of it?

In this cultural minimization of women, their contributions, their worship, and their entire selves, we also do a great disservice to Muslim men. Men are taught that their identity can be threatened by a woman who is of equal or greater size, stature, and status. Our boys are taught that they can be emasculated, that masculinity is a thing that can be taken away. What results is that as a mode of self-preservation, all too many men fear women.

As your mother, I hope you will learn that it is not enough for women and girls to be feminists; it is equally important that men and boys are also self-declared feminists. I want you to know that a strong and intelligent woman does not by her existence reduce the identity of any man. Correspondingly, a woman's identity should never be minimized, and if it is, the best course may be to exit. Until this becomes normalized, I hope that being feminists serves as an act of spiritual worship, as your mode of self-preservation. Remember the marks on your hands; the three of you were meant to survive.

It would be easy to end what I want to say to you on that note, but there are issues with the broader feminist movement to unravel. Finding a community of feminists with adequate space for someone who is not willing to disclaim her Muslim identity has been hard work.

The very idea that a feminist can self-identify as a practicing Muslim can lead to complete cognitive breakdown for many feminists, even when they're your friends.

Similar to the gut-wrenching sense of loss one suffers after the dissolution of a first love, there is a particularly acute pain that floods your body for days when the people that you had hoped you belonged to turn out not to be your people. Several years ago in a previous job, the pursuit of a particular funding opportunity gave me hope for concretely merging my Muslim and feminist identities. In close partnership with a mainstream feminist organization, I worked to develop an innovative, multi-institutional model to provide culturally specific sexual violence services for localized Muslim communities. I felt buoyed by the possibility contained in two of my worlds cohesively forging together. Later, I heard that the same organization that supported this effort also hosted an event featuring a speaker widely known to pull on alarmist chords, asking Americans to wear their savior complexes as she unveiled (pun intended) Islam to be a vile religion that perpetuated gender inequality and violence against women. Eager to elevate a one-size-fits-all, antiviolence against women perspective above all else, the organization overlooked the speaker's blatant agenda to denigrate entire Muslim populations and cultures. Seeing the hypocritical pity in the eyes of women who were my esteemed colleagues as they "otherized" billions of Muslim women, including me, was nothing less than personal heartbreak.

With time, I have come to understand that any willful disregard of intersectionality[1] harms all of us. It splits our identities, our agency, and our ability to survive by telling us that we cannot be both feminist

---

1. A feminist sociological theory first named by Kimberlé Crenshaw in 1989, intersectionality suggests that—and seeks to examine how—various biological, social and cultural categories such as gender, race, class, ability, sexual orientation, caste, and other axes of identity interact on multiple and often simultaneous levels, contributing to systematic injustice and social inequality. Intersectionality holds that the classical conceptualizations of oppression within society, such as racism, sexism, homophobia, transphobia, and belief-based bigotry, do not act independently of one another. Instead, these forms of oppression interrelate, creating a system of oppression that reflects the "intersection" of multiple forms of discrimination. Source: http://en.wikipedia.org/wiki/Intersectionality.

and Muslim. Only through the framework of intersectional feminism have I found a way to stay and survive in the broader feminist movement. I remind myself that violence against women is a universal issue and that my feminist, Muslim, woman of color heart bleeds to speak up about it. From my mother's story, I remember that it's up to me, and not the norms of the mainstream, to keep the parts of my identity that matter intact—everyone else will come along.

What I hope the three of you remember is that making space for complexity allows us to be comfortable with ideas that are sometimes an uneasy fit. Embracing complexity has let me confidently self-identify as both a Muslim and a feminist. More importantly, it has given me a starting point from which to read God's divine attributes. "God is more expansive than all the universe, yet God is closer to you than your jugular vein." (Qur'an, 50:16) As for yourselves, you probably won't be able to fit a circle into a square peg, but in the process of trying you might just be able to carve out a shape that works for you.

My sweet babies, these are complicated discussions that will take a lifetime of conversations to come out, even as I try to force it all out in one overly dramatic letter. At times, you might wish that your Mama was the type to give you a one, two, or even three word answer to a seemingly simple question, but you'll know that the Mama you got is the kind that wants you to know that it is okay to exist in between the lines. So as the pages from your stories continue to unfold, and even if Muslim American feminism is not what matters most in your story, know that there is comfort to be found in complexity. Go forth and make your own choices but know that the ink is already dry.

Love,
Mama

# How Feminism Saved My Faith
## by Emily Maynard

 EMILY MAYNARD is an outgoing introvert from Portland, Oregon. She likes Twitter, mentoring college students, and new information on anything. Emily is passionate about questioning, exploring, and growing healthy faith. Her stories have been featured in various online spaces and she is a monthly contributor to A Deeper Story. Emily is an engaging speaker on topics of culture, faith, and speaking up. Her website can be accessed at emilyisspeakingup.com and she can be found on Twitter @emelina.

I've been caught between faith and feminism since the night I kicked Jared B. in the shin after church youth group.

He had started off joking about women, and when that didn't get a rise, he escalated into mild insults. They hurt. His jabs reinforced all the messages that I'd already picked up in church: girls don't matter as much as boys, God made men to rule over women in life and church, and the things that made me *me* were highly unladylike. I nearly crumbled and walked away.

But I also knew deep down that what he was saying was just plain wrong, so I politely told him to stop. He didn't. Something came over me.

I was angry in the calmest and firmest of ways. I stepped closer and warned him in a low voice that if he didn't stop saying stuff like that, I would kick him. He smiled that easy, mocking smile of someone who knows you won't follow through with a threat.

He didn't stop talking until the toe of my sneaker met his shin. Hard.

As I look back now, I can see that his attempts to engage me were probably an immature but earnest flirtation. He hadn't been shown any other way of interacting with someone he liked, and friendship across gender lines was unacceptable in our group. He tried to capture my attention with patriarchal insults. It didn't go well.

I'm sure my face mirrored the shocked look on his. He muttered and turned away, apologizing and favoring his right leg. I felt a wave of satisfaction. I felt like I mattered.

And now he knew that *I* knew I mattered.

I suddenly had weight, took up space in the world, and had mass and limbs that connected sharply with his. In that moment, I existed. I felt like a human being.

My moment of animation was immediately followed up with a crushing wave of shame. I had overstepped my social and religious bounds and cemented my place in the realm of defiant, angry, ungodly women.

It would be another ten years and a faith crisis before I would actually call myself a feminist.

I grew up on the dotted line between mainstream American Evangelical culture and the strange wilds of Christian fundamentalism. In my early childhood, my parents attended various Evangelical churches. We'd move on frequently because some aspect that I never understood wouldn't be quite good enough. I felt disconnected at any church we attended, because I figured we'd probably be leaving soon anyway. We always did.

About the time that I got my first pair of round glasses at age thirteen, I had four sisters and a brother, and we were one of *those* families. We stood out everywhere in liberal, eco-friendly Portland, Oregon, until we found a church full of people just like us.

The new church was a fun, happy place at first. I made friends with some of the other girls, most of them also from big families and some of them more sheltered than me. Some of them couldn't wear pants except under their dresses, and dating wasn't something we believed in, let alone experienced. We were all homeschooled, so Sundays were the big social outing of the week. The sermons were long and the potluck lunches lasted well into the afternoons. My parents loved the community, the emphasis on family, and the hymns we sang each week. They said this was the answer to their prayers and God had brought us to that church. They were committed.

I wanted to be taken seriously as a young adult, so I committed, too.

Most of the sermons were directed at the men in order to admonish and strengthen them to take on their rightful leadership roles. Nearly every Bible passage we studied was interpreted in light of Calvinistic theology and male headship. I remember feeling a little left out, but I couldn't argue with the Bible. There were occasionally a few cautioning words for wives and daughters, but more often, there was overwhelming public praise for women who exceeded expectations.

I saw women celebrated regularly for their hospitality, creativity in homemaking, submission, generosity, and nurturing children. Girls were encouraged to study theology, too, but only as long as it didn't affect their ability to obey their future husband's spiritual leadership. Motherhood was encouraged and rewarded, and there was a huge outpouring of support for the women who risked their health to birth babies nine, ten, and eleven times, even after a doctor's caution.

All these aspects of femininity were celebrated joyfully, but we criticized and pitied women who had been led astray by feminist ideas and tried to live outside of God's best plan for them. We prayed outside women's health clinics and felt sorry for women who had to work paying jobs outside their homes.

Women in our church didn't exist outside the roles of wife, mother, and daughter. We were promised great power, but only as supporters of the men in our lives. In turn, men were supposed to lead us lovingly, but even if they didn't, it was still our job to respect them. I learned about always respecting a man's leadership. I learned the importance of dressing modestly, rallying conservative voting blocks to bring our nation back to God, and saving my first kiss for my wedding day. The Bible was clear, they said, about all of this. They said we were truly chosen by God when we lived this way.

But sometimes, the weight of being chosen by God made it hard for me to breathe.

The apocalyptic nightmares about the rapture and end of the world started around the time I was seven, but throughout my teenage years, I gained all sorts of new images to fill my dreams. I had one recurring nightmare where I was about to be married, but I tried to back out and couldn't escape. I tried to pass off one of my bridesmaids on the faceless groom and ran and ran and ran. I woke up sweating and panicked. The idea of submitting to a man forever sounded like torture even if I lucked out and got a decent one.

We didn't have a television in my house growing up, but trips to the neighborhood library happened several times a week. It was in that library that I would sneak into the forbidden sections, like Young Adult fiction, and read tales of rebellion. I was drawn to stories of teenage heroines, trapped protagonists breaking free, and pretenders living double lives. I soaked up stories of women taking down the system from the inside.

In those books, I read about people who questioned authority, who felt their emotions deeply, acted on their romantic desires, and who questioned God or had no God at all. I indulged in literary escapism, but those stories and questions were just make-believe to me. The rest of the time, I tried to convince myself that I was chosen by God, and that being a godly woman was a blessing, despite how oppressive it felt.

When I was in high school, I was terrified that I would die and my family would find my journal, so I didn't write about the series of boys that I thought were cute. I didn't confess my sins of thinking about sex or daydreaming about a career instead of motherhood. I definitely didn't write down that I had kicked Jared B. at youth group, and I knew he was too embarrassed at being bested by a girl to tattle on me. Instead, I wrote out agonized prayers begging for more faith. That way, if I died, my family would see how much I cared about pleasing God, and know I was in heaven.

I had flashes of seeking independence, like when I went to a tanning salon with my friend who signed as my guardian because she was over eighteen, but mostly I followed the rules for Christian women. I memorized nearly a thousand Bible verses, read theology books to keep from being led astray by the devil's lies, and pledged my emotional and sexual purity to God on a postcard. I guess it worked, too, because I didn't kiss anyone until I was twenty-one, but I didn't really have any boys interested in me after I kicked Jared B.

After high school, I worked for a conservative Christian youth organization and taught high schoolers about the dangers of multiculturalism, radical feminism, and the liberal agenda. I was only nineteen, but adamant in my knowledge about the dangers facing American culture and Christianity. Feminism was near the top of the list.

It's funny now, when I think about how much I fought against it, that it was actually feminism that saved my faith.

Several years after college, my fervent conservative faith burned out. I finally confronted my doubts about the restrictive theology I was taught, and everything fell apart. I grew up in a world of binaries: if you weren't the right kind of Christian, then you weren't a Christian at all. When I gave up the judgment, fear, and shame that I was raised with, I thought I was giving up on faith forever.

But somehow, I couldn't shake my belief in God. I didn't believe that God was good and I didn't want much to do with God, but I didn't doubt that God was real. I still felt compelled by something about the stories of Jesus recorded in the Bible, so I started collecting pieces from a different kind of belief. I found Christian feminist writing online, and began to get glimpses of a religion of justice and equality.

I found people asking the same sort of questions that I'd stifled for years, and still holding onto faith. I found women and men who believed that being a woman wasn't a liability to any level of leadership, and could support that view with scripture. I discovered feminism, liberation and queer theologies, inclusivism, and pacifism. I learned that there are lots of ways to be a godly woman and plenty of reasons to celebrate women beyond traditional female gender roles.

Feminism freed me from the idea that there is one correct, universal way to experience womanhood. In turn, this gave me the ability to see faith beyond the rigid boxes I was given. I grew to celebrate

Christianity as an incredibly complex, mysterious, and beautiful pursuit instead of a series of rules and recitations. Feminism opened up the door to complexity in my experience of myself and my faith.

So, I remain a Christian, in spite of all the pain that religion has poured out on women.

I stay because other women are showing me how to live and pray and lead and build new pathways in faith traditions that have kept us boxed in for so long.

I stay because feminism taught me to accept my life and personhood, both the doubting and the believing parts of myself.

I stay because I've seen how Christianity can fuel justice, not just for women, but for all marginalized people.

I stay because I believe in regeneration, resurrection, and redemption, even when they exist in abusive patriarchal religious structures.

I am a Christian and a feminist because I'm still driven by that message that compelled my foot to connect sharply with a boy's shin all those years ago. I stay because I know that women matter.

# From Outside In, From Inside Out
## by Tamara R. Cohen

TAMARA R. COHEN is a rabbi, writer, and activist currently working as the Director of Innovation at Moving Traditions, an organization working at the dynamic intersection of gender and Jewish adolescent education. She is a graduate of the Reconstructionist Rabbinical College and has been involved in Middle East peace, social justice, feminist, and interfaith activism.

I am a feminist. I am a lesbian. I am a Jew. I am a rabbi.

I am all these things, and more, because I have learned, over time, to listen to the core of my being; to bring myself into communities that nurture my ability to honor the fullness of who I am; and to work towards a vision of a world that honors the fullness of every human being and living species.

I am a Jew because I was born a Jew, because I was raised to be an educated and proud Jew, and because I have decided to honor this heritage of mine, to value it and to work to perpetuate it. I don't believe that Jews are better than anyone else or that Judaism is God's most cherished religion. I do believe that Jews are a people with a deep and significant and varied history, a history of pain and renewal, and of tradition and transformation. Our history includes externally imposed and internally adopted alienation, sharing and cultural collaboration, and learning from our neighboring and host cultures over time. I believe there is deep value and beauty in Judaism—our texts and rituals, our literature and languages, our material culture and folklore. And I believe it would be a tragedy to lose any of this, because Judaism is among the ancient and long lasting cultures and wisdom traditions that make up the mosaic of world civilizations.

I am a feminist because my mother raised me to be one through her own strong commitments and activism, and also through her heavy sighs and her sometimes swallowed, sometimes bursting expressions of frustration and anger at the way life and family and society are still not fair for women. As I grew up and came into my own feminism, I came to see a wider universe of what's not fair and for whom it's not fair. I read, saw, and learned from friendships and political work about institutional inequities, and intersections such as race, class, and gender. Now, when I identify as a feminist, I mean that I have a vision of, and a commitment to, significant societal transformation based on my feminist critique of the way things are.

Being a feminist and a Jew means I carry the pain of the knowledge that much within Jewish civilization is misogynist and patriarchal. I actively struggle with and challenge these strands of Jewish tradition, along with violence, antipathy to non-Jews, and exclusive claims to the land of Israel and to God's love. Another part of being a feminist and a Jew is drawing strength from the powerful and long standing tradition of midrash (creative exegesis) to interpret and reinterpret sacred texts, their implications, and the way to live out what it means to be Jewish. Thus, as I have felt pain when confronted with historical texts and contemporary manifestations of Jewish misogyny and elitism, I have also felt deeply enriched by historical examples of Jewish creativity and radical transformation. I have felt the power of being in community with other Jewish feminists, courageous and authentic as they forge new paths, ask new questions, and write new theologies and prayers.

It hasn't always been this way.

◆◆◆

My parents were born in 1945 and '46 in Montreal, each to an immigrant father and a first generation mother. They came of age in the sixties, got married young, and were part of the larger circle of young Jews who were taking Judaism into their own hands in a new way.

My mother attended the first Jewish feminist conference in 1973 and was transformed by Jewish feminism and the Havurah movement (a movement of do-it-yourself Judaism, marked by egalitarianism, communalism and a renewed interest in ritual and creative liturgy), which she shared eagerly with her three daughters. Healing the relationship between Jews and Arabs, Israelis and Palestinians was my father's avocation and eventually vocation too. His work became a model for me of what it meant to open oneself to the larger mission of serving the Jewish people, and through that, humanity as well.

After twelve years in various Jewish day schools, I went to Barnard College. In my first semester, I fell in love with a woman I met in the Jewish feminist collective and began the process of coming out. That process shook my foundations. I was afraid I'd lost my chance to be the kind of Jew I was raised to be, the kind of Jew I wanted to be. I would walk into Jewish Studies classes during the first week of every semester and then turn around and walk out because I projected the rejection and erasure I was experiencing into the stares of the students and teacher. I still went to the Conservative minyan for a while but one Friday night the question "Do you count yourself?" (in reference to the minyan, or quorum of ten Jews, traditionally ten men needed for certain prayers) sent me crying into the hallway. This was a question born out of the attempt to equalize the obligation between women and men around prayer. I knew this, but it still felt like a bigger and suddenly preposterous question. The very question was offensive to me on a visceral level, especially in this moment when I was feeling that my entire right to existence and to "count" as a Jew was being called into question.

It was clear to me that God knew I counted and that God could not and would not abandon me because I was finding myself in love with a woman. But what was slowly breaking down was my belief in halakha (Jewish law) as an accurate reflection of God's will. I no longer felt I could trust those who claimed to be its rightful interpreters: the Jewish authority figures in my extended community, almost uniformly men with beards and *kippot* (skullcaps), wielding Talmudic and halakhic sources, whom I experienced as trying to shun me and send me away. They succeeded for a long time in keeping me away, not from Judaism as a whole, but from certain kinds of study and certain dreams for my future.

Later in my college years, the African American lesbian poet and activist Audre Lorde died. At a memorial service for her at the Cathedral of St. John the Divine, I listened to the powerful voices of young lesbian poets of color against the background of the towering eves of the cathedral. There was so much more that was holy than what they were teaching in the Jewish Studies classes I felt increasingly excluded from. I got involved with various protest movements on campus. I went to conferences on the history of the Jewish labor movement. I joined ACT UP protests against police brutality. I marched bare-chested for LGBT equality. I got arrested with Arthur Waskow and others for protesting the verdict in the Amadou Diallou murder case and sat in a cell with Adrienne Cooper, who taught us all Yiddish protest songs. These moments were key in my coming to know the spiritual power of activism and in my reformation of myself as a Jew.

Less than a year after graduating college, I found myself suddenly back in the Jewish world to an extent I wouldn't have imagined. At Ma'yan, The Jewish Feminist Project of the Jewish Community Center in Manhattan, I found women who were the age of my parents but who were totally accepting of all of who I was. They opened the door and I walked back into the Jewish world. Suddenly I was writing a feminist Haggadah, creating posters profiling the lives of Jewish women from American history, and teaching a class on Marcia Falk's new feminist liturgy, *The Book of Blessing*. I had found a new home, a place where all the pieces of myself started to feel like they organically fit together.

After years of living in New York and working at Ma'yan, my partner and I moved to Gainesville, Florida, for her first academic position. In Gainesville, I put together more pieces of my life as a Jewish feminist. As the Director of Multicultural and Diversity Affairs at the University of Florida, I had the incredible opportunity to work with and lead a diverse team of staff and students. We built community together and created experiences to support students' own identity development while also encouraging intercultural and interreligious learning and exploration. Together, we taught hundreds of students to think more deeply about their multiple identities, to take responsibility for their privilege, and to take seriously the role of being an ally to others.

As I taught, I learned. As I listened to my student Adam, the founder of the Native American group on campus, struggle to learn the dying language of his father's tribe, I started to think more about the value and responsibility of saving my own culture. As I worked with Muslim students on campus who were advocating for a simple prayer room on campus, I began to see the large new multi-story Hillel building for Jewish students on campus with different eyes. It became clear to me that as a Jew, I have a responsibility to engage other Jews in conversations about how to responsibly acknowledge and use the historically relatively new and often unacknowledged privileged status we have found ourselves in. As I supported closeted students from various fundamentalist backgrounds struggling with what they were hearing in their places of worship and what they knew about themselves, I realized that I was no longer the hurt college student I had been; I had come to a place of being able to use my own history of alienation and exclusion to help others like me. I also realized that part of what I could share is that LGBT and feminist people from religious communities do not have to choose between staying in a community that is actively hurting them, and leaving and severing all ties with that community. I could share with them that there is a third path.

This is not always an easy path to walk., but for me it has indeed "made all the difference." It is the path of joining with others to actively transform the community and tradition you once called home so that it truly becomes the home you want and believe it could be— for yourself and for future generations of feminists, queer people, and other brave question askers and boundary crossers to come.

Today, I am a queer feminist Jewish mother raising a Jewish family. I am also a rabbi committed to contemporary and future generations of Jewish struggle, life, and innovation, and to working in partnership across religious and ethnic lines in service of social justice. It is with a sense of responsibility and humility that I have chosen a role in defining what it's going to look like, feel like, and be like to be Jewish in the future. I have not abdicated that position of leadership to others. I claim my rightful place as a shaper of Jewish community, experience, literature, and culture—and I invite others who have the wisdom and experience that comes from having been on the margins to do the same.

# Resilience
## by Sabina Khan-Ibarra

SABINA KHAN-IBARRA is a freelance writer and editor. She regularly contributes to her blog, *Ibrahim's Tree*, which she created after the loss of her infant son in 2011. Her other blog is *I Am The Poppy Flower*. She created the website Muslimah Montage as a platform for women to share their stories and inspire others. She is currently working on her novel about Pashtun American sisters growing up in Northern California.

I stood at my parents' front door, unable to knock. With most of my belongings packed into the small trunk of the Toyota Camry my father had bought me years before, I was back at the house where I grew up. I was back but not the same. I was broken. Shattered. I carried most of the pieces that were once me, holding on tightly to them, their edges cutting into me.

The motion sensor porch light turned on and I blinked against its harshness. Warm tears slid down my cheek. Ashamed and angry at myself for crying, I wiped my face and knocked softly on the door. I didn't want to disturb my family, who were probably all sitting in the family room watching *Jeopardy* and drinking tea. Baba opened the door. He took one look at me and pulled me into his warm, familiar arms. I hugged him back, buried my face in his chest and sobbed.

"You don't need anyone. You have Allah," he said. "You have me."

And just like that I felt him take the shards that cut me, open up his chest, and gently put them inside.

He closed his vast chest and shut the door behind us.

My parents raised their four daughters to be independent women by teaching us that that was the way Allah meant for us to be. With patience, they gave us the tools to build our confidence and strength. And slowly that is what I did; I built, deliberately and with care.

My parents are deeply spiritual people. Their love and devotion to God reveals itself in years of faithful obedience and prayer. They wake up before sunrise every morning and pray together. When I was a child, the morning prayer was the only prayer we did together. After prayer, we all sat and read the Qur'an in the family room, my mother's voice the most mesmerizing. Every day, I started off loudly, my voice still scratchy from sleep, and by the end, I would mumble, listening only to Mama.

Mama and Baba talked to us about a loving God, one who had given us so much. They reminded us of how thankful we should be to Him. God would reward us, they said, by granting us heaven. While other children drew hearts and rainbows in my kindergarten class, I drew pictures of heaven with trees and fountains.

During most of our long drives, Baba told us stories. We heard stories from his childhood, and from the Qur'an and the hadith. He taught me much about the strong women in the Qur'an. They were tested, just as the men were, and rewarded just as the men were. They were treated equally. Maryam, Asiya, Khadija, Fatima, Ayesha. Islam gave rights to women—to me—including the right to own property, and the right to my own thoughts and ideas. I never knew otherwise.

Baba often told us a story about a young woman he knew named Halima. When Baba was ten, Halima's father had arranged her marriage with a local farmer. Arranged marriage, my father said, was the only way to marry back then. During the *nikkah*, the signing of the Muslim marriage contract, the imam asked Halima if she accepted the farmer as a husband, and to the surprise of the village, she said no. There was uproar and Halima ran into her room and stood on top of her bed with a gun, demanding to see my grandfather, Babajee, who was the village leader.

Babajee took Baba with him to Halima's home. Halima's parents met with Babajee first and were upset that their daughter was disobeying them by not marrying the man of their choice. Babajee asked to see the bride-to-be.

Halima stood in her red and green wedding dress, a single silver headpiece on her forehead. She told Babajee that she did not want to marry the farmer and that her father was forcing her into the marriage. Babajee asked the imam to come into the room and asked if the Nikkah was valid if the bride was unwilling. The imam said it was not. Babajee then told the imam that Halima did not want to marry the farmer and the wedding was off. Halima's parents were not happy but accepted Babajee's decision. Halima never married, though I don't know if this was her choice or if no one would marry her for being too defiant. I respected her for her strength and courage and hoped I would meet her one day.

Growing up, I didn't know the meaning of "feminism," and when in my teens I found an explanation, it was a deeply political version I could not relate to. The feminism I came across was espoused mostly by women who didn't look like me; mostly white women. And while I wanted to be the one helping myself, the feminism I was exposed to involved mostly white women assisting non-white women. It made me mad that mainstream feminists seemed to view all Muslim women as weak and oppressed when I was clearly neither of these things. It was like I didn't exist. I had other friends of color who also decided that "feminism" wasn't for them. But I knew that I believed that women were as valuable as men in every way and deserved the same rights, treatment, and opportunities; and that I supported any movement that defined, established, and advocated equal political, economic, and social rights for women.

To me, these were God given rights that no human could take away. All humans were created equally and were judged by merits—gender was never part of the equation. When I was in the second grade, my father had me read the Prophet's Last Sermon, the sermon the Prophet Mohammed gave on Mount Arafat shortly before he passed away. The sermon consists of a series of general guidelines for Muslims to follow the teachings that Muhammad set forth in the Qur'an and through his life examples. I read it, memorized it, and loved it. Even as young as I was, I felt that it was all-inclusive and left no one out. I felt as if he were speaking to me personally.

At eighteen, while most of my friends prepared for university, I married a man I barely knew because I had agreed to an arranged marriage with a man my parents chose. I hoped my marriage would be like my parents' or cousins'; their arrangements left them with fulfilling and satisfying marriages. I moved to England where my new husband and his family lived. My dream of a beautiful marriage quickly turned into a nightmare. I was not allowed to be myself—a free spirited young woman who had a love for life and wanted to explore the world. Instead of going to school to pursue my education, I cooked, cleaned, and ironed all day. I spent most of my time in solitude, often forgetting what day it was. On the days I missed my parents the most, I closed my eyes and prayed. I tried not to be bitter and unthankful. I remembered my father's words in those tough times: "God tests only those He loves." God must have really, really loved me.

After years of denying to everyone and myself that I was in an abusive marriage, I finally realized the truth about how unhappy I was. My marriage lacked the love and compassion I saw in my parents' love story. One day, while I listened to my friend tell me about her happily married life, I had an epiphany and decided I would rather die than live so unhappily. I deserved a life where I could be my true self—a life where I knew what happiness was again. After an argument one day that almost got too ugly, I left—wrecked, but free.

I walked back into my old life and to the home I grew up in, unsure of my future, terrified. My parents welcomed me back and did what they could to mend what was left of me. While my friends finished grad school, I prepared paperwork for my divorce.

I wasn't prepared for the backlash of my extended family or the people from the mosque. I was one of the first young women in my community to get a divorce. There were whispers and finger pointing. They didn't care about the pain I had gone through during my marriage. They loudly declared that I shouldn't have gotten a divorce, that it didn't matter that I had been abused, my soul crushed beyond recognition and almost beyond repair. I had aunts who wailed when they heard of my divorce; they couldn't believe what bad fortune I had.

Some saw me as a curse, shunning me from wedding rituals performed at my cousins' weddings. I sat at my table as the rest of the young women my age braided and unbraided the bride's hair and put on henna. My mother came by later after noticing my absence. She tried to take me to the stage, telling me to ignore the women, but I no longer wanted to join. I wanted to go home.

In the Pashtun culture, a girl's reputation is fragile. She takes good care of her reputation, keeping it safe and polishing it by doing what society expects of her. Thinking that my divorce was a crack in my honor, I wanted to not be me: the twenty-four-year-old girl married and divorced while her friends were just starting their lives. I wanted to be someone else, someone without a mark on her reputation. My parents told me to pay no attention to anyone. They wanted to see me happy, but I had forgotten what that word meant. I was still working on finding all of me.

However, in trying to find and reconstruct myself, I no longer knew who I was. After my divorce, I found myself sitting in my parents' family room not laughing at jokes I once found funny. I no longer felt a bond with my old friends. I realized the world had somehow passed me by. I was stuck in a place where no one else existed. My own family was supportive, but I felt disconnected from them. I was in a place no one else had been before. I was divorced. I had lived a life outside of the home I grew up in. A difficult life, one of an abused and lonely woman, and I couldn't pretend anything else. I was no longer the little girl who was protected by her parents from the harsh world. I had lived with harshness and faced it head on and it had left me feeling defeated. Would I ever be the person I used to be—the strong, carefree young woman who dreamed too big and too loud?

I spent a lot of time alone trying to discover who I now was. I went back to praying and reading the Qur'an. It took a lot of time to regain some of the calm I had lost. I felt my heart slowly open and the pieces begin to fall into place, healing as the scars faded. I stayed away from those women who viewed me as a burden and a curse, and once more saw my parents as my friends. It took time, patience from my family, and lots of self-reflection, but I regained my confidence and my strength. I was a divorced woman, but so were the daughters of the Prophet. Divorce was one of my rights. I did not need anyone's approval. I understood that it wasn't me or my divorce that was the problem, but the perception of others. I decided that I had changed, but the old me still lived inside, and it was up to me to acknowledge the change and grow from it.

I began calling myself a Muslim feminist and I learned to love the title, even though, in general, I still hated labels. Feminism within Islam is not a new phenomenon. That is what makes it interesting when some, like my ex-husband and his family, use Islam to deny women rights. Khadija (RA)[1] was a well-known, prosperous businesswoman. She was a widow who approached (via a messenger) Muhammad (PBUH)[2] with a marriage proposal. He was working for her at the time. He was also much younger than she was, and had never married before. He accepted her proposal. Throughout their marriage and even after her death, she was known for her unwavering strength and wisdom.

My compromise is this: Until Muslims and non-Muslims today understand the life of Khadija (RA), I will not drop the word "feminist" when describing who I am. When Islam and Muslims rid themselves of their ugly misogynistic reputation and when Muslims really understand the high and equal position of a Muslim woman, I may stop. The simple fact is that I call myself a Muslim feminist, but I shouldn't have to. My saying that I am a Muslim should be enough.

Life has been tough, breaking and chipping away at me, and I may not be the shiny, unblemished version of me people would prefer. I am okay with that. The beautiful, strong mosaic that is now me is where truth and honor lie, and I wouldn't trade it for anything.

---

1. RA stands for "Radhiallahu anhu" and is used when referring to close companions of the Prophet. It translates into "May Allah be pleased with him or her."
2. PHUB stands for "peace be upon him," a statement of respect for the Prophet Muhammad used after speaking or writing the prophet's name.

# To Be Young, Feminist, Muslimah, and Black

## Nia Malika Dixon

A native of Baltimore, Maryland, NIA MALIKA DIXON is an independent producer with four short films and an award-winning web series under her belt. A former school teacher, she has written professionally for nearly two decades including articles for national magazines, a published novel, short stories, blogs, two volumes of poetry, and several screenplays. She has received awards and recognition for her screenplays and her short films, including several awards for *Chrysalis*, the web series. After completing the short film, *City In the Sea*, shot on location in Venice, California, Nia shot a web series/short film, *Chrysalis*, in her hometown of Baltimore. She is currently in pre-production of her second web series, *Vengeful. Chrysalis* has won awards, including Best Urban Web Series and Best TV/Web Series, in several film festivals. Nia is married to her cinematographer, Antar Hanif, and the mother of two teenagers with special needs, including a son with autism. Visit her online at www.niamalikadixon.com.

Channeling my inner Jay Z , "Please allow me to reintroduce myself."

Music has always been the backdrop of my life. From Roy Ayers singing with me about how everyone loves the sunshine, to The Doors urging me to break on through to the other side, my life's soundtrack refracts the eclectic nature of my life's experiences. All the musical pieces of the puzzle fit together snugly, to create the landscape of me looking out on the horizon of smoky, blue sky meets rippling, dark ocean as the glowing, orange sun dips low. Cue Jason Mraz.

That's me: all poetry and song, and beautiful images, swirling around in a frothy cup of love. I'm not your typical Muslim. I'm not your typical anything, although I've tried my whole life to be "typical." At age eleven, I went to public school for the first time and tried to fit in like everyone else instead of being that one "Moslem girl." At age eighteen, I got married like all "good, Muslim girls" do. At age twenty-three, I got a teaching job, moved to the suburbs, and tried to live with my husband and kids like the Huxtables. Now, at age forty, I see how that whole routine has gotten old. *I* am not old, but the *routine* is old. Forty must be the age people realize stuff like that, because this year was the moment I finally decided to stop playing the game of trying to fit in.

For me, being a Muslim woman has always been a dance of fitting in and playing small. I did not start out that way. I doubt wholeheartedly that any woman is born with the inclination to silence herself, but that is what our society conditions us to do. Being born a girl into a patriarchal society that has become acutely imbalanced means embracing one of two things: feminism or self-loathing. My mother is the blessed reason I choose to champion women instead of participate in self-loathing. And that's because my mother chose Islam.

The thing about being a Muslim that a lot of people who are not Muslim don't know is that you choose to be Muslim. It's not the same to say, "Oh, I was raised Muslim," because to *be* Muslim you hold specific beliefs that directly affect your daily behavior. In other words, the *act of being* Muslim involves not just thinking, but doing. Islam is a blueprint for optimal living as an individual and a community. A critical part of that blueprint, and I imagine what clicked with my mother, is the emphasis on gender equity. Islam is based upon the foundation of balance between men and women: "The believing men and believing women are allies of one another. They enjoin what is right and forbid what is wrong and establish prayer and give charity and obey God and His Messenger. Those, God will have mercy upon them. Indeed, God is Exalted in Might and is Most Wise." (The Noble Qur'an, Chapter 9, Verse 71)

Through the Qur'an, God repeatedly addresses "believing men and believing women" together, especially when referring to what is right and wrong, and the consequences of either choice.

I believe in reincarnation. Before the protests and accusations of me being contradictory begin, let me explain. *Reincarnation* is defined by the Oxford English Dictionary as "to incarnate anew," or "to incarnate again." *Incarnate* is defined as "to give bodily form," or "to personify." Just as Jay Z starts his song, "Public Service Announcement" with a reintroduction on *The Black Album* in 2003, (his latest reincarnation of himself at that time) we are often introducing the world to a different version of ourselves. I believe in our lifetime we each recreate ourselves, personifying who we want to be, over and over again. How many of us have had a "goth" stage, a "geek" stage, or a "tomboy" stage? In our pursuit of an ideal self, we "incarnate anew" through each stage of our life.

After my divorce from my ex-husband in 2002, I took the opportunity to do just that. I experienced a reincarnation. While I have been through a few reincarnations in my lifetime, enough to draft a compelling novel or screenplay, my divorce remains one of the most profound. While married to my ex-husband, I was stifled and made to conform to his expectations of who I was supposed to be. So, after nearly a decade in a controlling and abusive marriage, I decided to stop trying to make something work that was killing me spiritually. It was then that my identity crystallized. I decided to live my life for myself for the first time, instead of living to fulfill someone else's expectations of me.

I took a leave of absence from my teaching job, and packed up and moved to Los Angeles, California, to follow my dream of changing the world through sharing stories. My mother is the one who encouraged me to do it. My imam said definitely not to do it. He warned me that I would lose my soul, because I would be "swallowed up by a morally bankrupt environment and lose my Islam." (I'm paraphrasing, but that's about it.) All the "aunties," the old biddies, and the gossip-girls-in-training weighed in at their clucking circles as to my spiritual status as well as my eventual fate. (The verdict is still out as of yet, but I'll keep them posted.) My mother said, "You've got to live your life, Nia. It's your choice. It's your life." That's what she has been trying to teach me all along. It is all a choice.

I cashed out my 401K, literally giving up financial security, and moved to Los Angeles. I wrote a few screenplays, interned at a production company, and even temped as an agent's assistant. (That was the most harrowing two weeks of my life.) I attended acting classes, was mentored by a few directors, shot several short films, and even acted in a few. I was a fly, Black, Muslim girl, living in Hollywood pursuing my dreams. I did so while staying true to my Islamic beliefs and daily lifestyle. It was my choice. I chose not to drink at the cocktail meetings. I chose to stop and pray my prayers on time throughout the day every day, even when it meant praying in my car. I chose to tell the men with whom I socialized that I did not engage in premarital sex. It was my life, my choices.

My relationship with God is the longest, strongest running relationship I have ever had. My relationship with my mother is a close second. Growing up, it was my solid foundation of Islamic beliefs that created the situation in which I could understand what it means to be a feminist. I was shaped from the girl under the hijab into the Muslim woman I am today, through my mother's guidance. These two relationships are the reason why I am a feminist.

The day I decided to move three thousand miles across the country to pursue my dreams, I truly understood what it means to be a Muslim feminist. I chose to advocate for my own rights by staying true to my beliefs and true to myself as a person, simultaneously. Yet, even after arriving here in Los Angeles, and taking that scary leap to live freely and to my most full potential, I found myself again trying to fit into the standards of the industry under either peer pressure or the "glass ceiling." I am a storyteller, and I arrived bursting with ideas and stories to share with the world. But I was put into a box, and limited. There has always been a singular narrative that gets told the loudest: that of the white, American male. And here in Los Angeles, my stories (along with the diverse stories of others) are ignored, misconstrued, or invalidated. The overarching patriarchal paradigm is set up in such a way that as women we are either ignored, hated, slavishly adored, or exploited. In films and television shows, women are portrayed one dimensionally as vixen or virgin, bitch or bore, princess or bride. Often in stories, a woman is an object or a prize to be won.

Women of color have an even worse fate. They are either ignored, or altogether non-existent; they are almost always portrayed as servants or sidekicks, or not at all. My mission with my film and television productions is to counter this by producing stories on paper, on screen, and behind the scenes that have layered and complex women of many different backgrounds and ethnicities.

As reflected in the way film and television portrays women, our society is in dire need of feminists to speak up and effect change. The Oxford English Dictionary defines "feminism" as "advocacy of the rights of women." Therefore, a feminist is one who advocates for the rights of women. By definition, everyone should be a feminist. Advocating for the rights of women benefits everyone. However, public discourse has come to polarize, politicize, and stereotype feminism. In reality, feminism is a universal truth that does not need a defender, or a promoter. Feminism belongs to anyone who advocates for the rights of women, no matter what their socioeconomic status, ethnicity, nationality, religion, or other identifying label.

We can be allies to each other instead of arguing labels. Yes, I am a *Muslimah* (Muslim woman), and I am Black, and I am also, underneath all the labels, a human being seeking to share stories and change the world for the better. I may just be an optimistic dreamer, a storyteller with a frothy ocean of ideas. Yet, it is clear to me that our lives were created with an innate coding for seeking the balance of gender equity. I believe that it is a part of what it means to be a human being. That is the core of my beliefs. So, when people question how I can as a Muslim ascribe myself to feminism, I ask them, how can I not? It is a part of who I am.

# Say Something. I'm Giving Up on You.
## by Angela Yarber

REV. DR. ANGELA YARBER has a Ph.D. in Art and Religion from the Graduate Theological Union at University of California Berkeley and is author of *Embodying the Feminine in the Dances of the World's Religions; The Gendered Pulpit: Sex, Body, and Desire in Preaching and Worship; Dance in Scripture: How Biblical Dancers can Revolutionize Worship Today;* and *Holy Women Icons.* She has been a clergywoman, professional dancer, and artist since 1999. For more on her research, ministry, dance, or to purchase one of her icons, visit: www.angelayarber.com.

"Say something. I'm giving up on you."[1]

It may seem odd to begin an essay on a topic as serious as why feminists remain involved in their various faith traditions—traditions that often oppress, ignore, and malign women—by alluding to a romantic song from popular culture. I doubt Christina Aguilera and the musical group A Great Big World had the Church in mind when singing "Say Something." Rather, the musicality, lyrics, and music video all point toward love lost, relationships failed, and unrequited romance. Yet, as I consider my own story with the Church, the reasons why I've stayed, and the logic that continues to pull me further and further away, "Say Something" manages to capture the longing, loss, and heartbreak the Church has wrought throughout my ordained life. I committed to follow the Church anywhere at my ordination over

---

1. "Say Something" written by the musical group A Great Big World and sung by A Great Big World and Christina Aguilera.

ten years ago. Like a failed romance, my heart still loved the Church, but said "goodbye" when I resigned from my last pastorate less than one year ago. "Say something, I'm giving up on you," is about all I can muster as I stand on the outside of Eden's walls, my heart and calling coinciding with that of Lilith, the original feminist who opted to go and see what life had in store outside of patriarchy's garden. *Say something. I'm giving up on you.*

I didn't grow up attending church. My family isn't particularly religious. In a poor home, a brave single mother raised me alongside my two younger brothers, instilling in us the values of harmony, acceptance, and kindness. She modeled what it meant to be a feminist, teaching me in word and action that I can be and do anything I want as long as I try my best. I came from a long line of strong women and identified with feminism's cause at an early age. Kindness, harmony, feminism. It was religion at its finest. No dogma. No exclusion. No rules. Yet my heart longed for more. As a teenager I had big plans of dancing my way to Juilliard, dedicating my life to musical theatre and the arts. However, toward the end of high school, I had a conservative religious experience at a non-denominational church that changed everything. Though I condone very little that this particular church stands for today, at the time, the ministers accepted me, even offering me a job as a church janitor. I quickly fell head over heels in love with Jesus.

The Jesus I loved, however, was the Jesus defined by this particular conservative church. I recall my youth minister sitting me down and telling me that I should reconsider attending Juilliard, explaining that the performing arts brought glory to me rather than God. I believed my youth minister. So, in two of the most pivotal years of my adolescence, I changed everything. Gone was the feminism that had brought me this far. Gone was the precocious teen who protested with PETA (People for the Ethical Treatment of Animals). Gone was the very talented dancer and artist, my ballet slippers replaced by a leather-bound bible. I opted to attend a small Baptist liberal arts college and major in religion, assuming I could one day become an assistant youth helper or marry a preacher. I chose Jesus over all of my other desires, gifts, and callings.

I was incredibly fortunate to have wonderful professors in the religion department who taught me that there isn't only one way to be Christian; my talents in the arts and my commitments to feminism and animal rights could coincide with ministry and the academic study of religion. I learned about Jesus the pacifist, Jesus the feminist, Jesus the liberator. My love affair deepened. I took a job as a youth minister at the age of eighteen. I enrolled in a Baptist history course and I began piecing together the parts of my life that had been broken in my initial conservative religious experience.

In the classroom I learned about the core Baptist principles—separation of Church and state, believer's baptism, local Church autonomy, freedom of conscience—along with the radical history of Baptists who stood for equality and justice. I realized that all of these principles, indeed all of Baptist polity, coincided perfectly with the feminism I held dear. There is no hierarchy in Baptist polity. No elder, bishop, board, or pope can dictate what an individual believes. My soul was free, my conscience affirmed. I knew I could not be a part of a tradition that had hierarchical polity or forced members to conform to a particular set of beliefs. Knowing this radical history and understanding that Baptist's egalitarian polity coincided with feminism, I made the decision to become Baptist.

All the while, the church I was serving was undergoing its own transformation. Fundamentalism reared its ugly head and took over the church, once lauded as the most progressive congregation in this small, southern Georgia town. I witnessed deacons shoving one another, hurling insults. The ministers were all told that our ministry was "hampered beyond repair" because of our affiliation with a moderate organization. I shocked myself when I didn't run away screaming. My investment in feminism was more established than my time as a Baptist, after all. I could have taken my boyfriend Jesus and run for the hills, leaving the Church behind and basking in a spiritual love affair unsullied by the patriarchal institution of religion. I am convinced that I stayed because a beloved community surrounded me, affirming a barely twenty-something woman as one of their ministers, and teaching me what it means to "be Church."

The only reason I left that beloved community was to attend seminary, serving yet another Baptist church, and becoming ordained. From seminary, I drove west to pursue a Ph.D. in Art and Religion, finally making the connections my youth minister urged me to sever all those years ago. As cliché as it is for a southern girl to head west and find freedom, it certainly rings true in my experience. I served another Baptist church as an Associate Pastor of Arts and Education. I was finally true to myself and came out as a lesbian. I met my wife. I read more feminist and queer theology and theory. I danced. I painted. I researched. It was religion at its finest.

After the completion of my Ph.D., I accepted a job as Pastor for Preaching and Worship at a flagship progressive Baptist church on the campus of a research university in the Southeast. They had a radical mutual ministry model where co-pastors led the church equally, focusing on their respective gifts and callings. It was yet another way of dismantling hierarchies. I led preaching and worship. The other pastor led pastoral care. Upon hiring me, we became the only Baptist church in the country with two out lesbians as head pastors. My wife and I moved across the country, planted roots, began an adoption process, and celebrated being in a place that affirmed my calling, offering radical hospitality to the LGBTQ community without apology.

But patriarchy and heterosexism have their way of creeping into the most unlikely of places. And the inner workings of power and privilege make dealing with these "isms" ever more difficult. Though the church would not tolerate overt and blatant sexism or homophobia from within the congregation—and spoke out against the overt forms I regularly received in hate mail—microaggressive sexisms and heterosexisms continued to exist, flourishing in spaces we thought were safe, affirming, and progressive. Microaggressions are everyday slights, insults, or invalidations directed at marginalized groups—persons of color, sexual minorities, women, etc—by individuals who typically have good intentions and are decent, moral, thoughtful persons who may not be fully aware of their privileged positions of power. Psychologists who focus on cultural diversity issues claim that microaggressions build up over time, causing stress, pain, and anxiety for marginalized persons in ways similar to minority stress.

After months and months of trying to address these issues with congregational leadership, my health began to decline. I reread Barbara Brown Taylor's *Leaving Church* and I thought a lot about what it would mean to say goodbye. A wonderfully thoughtful congregant penned a poem entitled, "When the Beloved Community Fails." Another congregant screamed in my face and in the face of my assistant. Another threw an offering plate. It was around this time when I began to realize that I may need to give up on the church… possibly even *the Church*.

Not knowing what lay beyond the place I've called "home" for nearly fourteen years, I resigned from my position in a coveted, progressive Baptist pulpit after only two and a half years of service. Since I offered my resignation many have asked me if I think the Church—any Church—can exist *without* sexism and heterosexism. Called, ordained, degreed, and with over a decade dedicated to working to overcome sexism and heterosexism, I'm afraid my answer is a faint, but hopeful, "I don't know." The Garden—the Church—can be a beautiful place. Like Lilith, I must climb over the Garden's walls and find out what's on the other side.

Like many of the feminist authors in this volume, I want to offer a word of hope, rationale for staying inside the Church, a heartfelt admonition to keep the faith. I want to offer these things. But I have to be honest. Ironically, it is the faithful Baptist in me—the Baptist who remains involved in denominational life, works for social justice, teaches religion, and continues to question what exactly she believes—that forces me to stay true to my conscience. And my conscience is telling me—painfully, longingly—that I may be giving up on the Church.

"Say something, I'm giving up on you." A beautiful, beloved community said something thirteen years ago when they included this feminist as a part of their ministry team in the midst of a nasty church split. A beautiful, beloved community said something over ten years ago when they laid hands on my head and ordained this feminist to the ministry. A beautiful, beloved community said something in California when they affirmed me as I came out of the closet, dancing alongside their barefoot pastor in the sanctuary. And while I love and care deeply for the people at my most recent church, I have to conclude that my former congregant was right when he penned that poem claiming that the "beloved community failed." Because not only did that church fail when it condoned the discriminatory ways in which I was treated, but the Church—all Churches—fail when they exclude the voices of the oppressed, when they do not affirm the gendered bodies of women and sexual minorities in the pulpit, when they turn their heads at the sight of black eyes on the faces of queer youth, when they act as though it is acceptable for every face in the congregation to be white, and when they continue to tolerate injustice in the name of tolerating all viewpoints and theologies. While I continue to work for change and justice where I believe the Church has failed, it is with much longing and heartache that I offer these words to the Church: "Say something, I'm giving up on you."

# Staring Down Our Most Troubling Texts
## by Rabbi Danya Ruttenberg

 RABBI DANYA RUTTENBERG is the author of *Surprised By God: How I Learned to Stop Worrying and Love Religion*, which was nominated for the Sami Rohr prize, and editor of *The Passionate Torah: Sex and Judaism,* *Yentl's Revenge: The Next Wave of Jewish Feminism*, and three books on Jewish ethics. She was named by *Newsweek* as one of ten "rabbis to watch," by the *Forward* as one of the top fifty women rabbis, and by the *Jewish Week* as one of thirty-six influential rising Jewish leaders. Her next book, on parenting as a spiritual practice, is due out in spring 2016.

I'm sitting in Talmud class. It's my first year of rabbinical school.

We've already studied the ways in which the High Priest prepared for Yom Kippur and what to do if you find a lost object in the street. It's time to start a new tractate, *Ketubot*. Laws of wedding contracts.

The first chapter of Ketubot opens: "A virgin should get married on a Wednesday, and a widow on a Thursday. For the times of the week which the courts convene in the cities are on Mondays and Thursdays, and if he has a claim about virginity, he can get to the courts [as] early [as possible]."[1] That is, a groom would have put a lot of money into his wedding contract if the bride was specified to be a virgin—double that of a widow. If he didn't see what he understood to be blood from the breaking of a hymen on the wedding night, he could go to the courts right away to complain and perhaps try to get his money back. (Never mind the fact that not every woman has a hymen, and that,

---

1. Talmud Ketubot 2a.

even if she does, she might not bleed the first time she experiences penile intercourse.)[2]

The Talmud then moves into various questions about the extent to which a woman might be considered to be a reliable witness regarding her own virginity status. If she claims that her hymen was broken in a non-sexual way (the old, "riding a horse or doing gymnastics" defense), should we believe her? If she says she was raped, do we believe that she actually didn't consent? If she says that she was held captive but was not raped, do we trust her account? Are we sure she's telling the truth when she says that she was held captive but released before the age of three? There was an ancient belief that if the hymen was destroyed before a child was three years old, it could grow back and she could be listed with the higher dower of a virgin in her wedding contract. So even the age of her release was relevant.

My Talmud instructor explained, very animatedly, about *miggo*, a logical principle in which someone is considered more trustworthy if they're partially incriminating themselves in their confession—she admitted to being a captive, so we can believe her report about how old she was when she was released! He was eager to move us through the various cases so that we could understand how the rabbis understood each situation, financially.

My classmates took attentive notes, engaged, got a little stuck on that one about the woman who was raped by an unknown person when she went to draw water. How should they understand the status of that child? It was a little confusing, a little unclear. Maybe the medieval commentator could clarify.

It was like I had walked into a cocktail party taking place around a freshly dead body. Everyone seemed to think that this was a perfectly reasonable chunk of text to decode, debate, and analyze in a detached, intellectual sort of way.

Finally, after sitting stunned for a few moments, I said something. I observed that this class, full of feeling, caring people who wanted to become clergy, was talking awfully coolly about sexual violence most

2. Needless to say, we know more about human physiology than the ancients did. For more on this, check out *Virgin: The Untouched History* by Hanne Blank.

likely committed against actual real women. And children—there were horrific stories behind these punctured toddler hymens. Even in the most consensual of these situations—the women who weren't raped—we were principally concerned with the ways in which a woman's sexual status might impact the amount of money assigned to her in the event that she becomes divorced or widowed, without male protection. How much, really, was this woman's life worth? It depended on what had happened between her legs.

And people nodded, yes, it's true, thanks for contextualizing. The instructor was a good guy, and he said a bunch of the right things in response to me, to the class. But he hadn't brought this text to talk about rape culture and the treatment of women as property in rabbinic Judaism; he had assigned it in order to show us a great display of a certain kind of logical methodology. The other stuff didn't really occur to him until I—the textual newbie—pointed it out.

The misogyny in Judaism's ancient texts is so pervasive that it's become, in a lot of ways, just absolutely normalized. Once you lose beginner's mind, it's almost hard to see. Almost.

Sure, in ancient societies, virginity was a way of guaranteeing paternity. But the ancients' troubling ideas about women's value and purpose are so much a part of the Jewish background noise that many contemporary rabbis—even those who might self-identify as feminists—still use *ketubah* (Jewish prenuptial agreement) language that refers to a bride that has not been divorced as a *betulah*, virgin. It's become a way of signifying "woman who has never before been married," regardless of her actual sexual history. Needless to say, though, it's a problematic conflation for a lot of reasons.

Also, discussions about normal female bodily processes are filtered, consciously or not, through Talmudic turns of phrase like, "Though a woman be a pot of filth whose mouth is full of blood . . . all chase after her."[3] And while, sure, the laws around women and menstruation and sexual activity (there are some) don't flow *exactly* from that statement, I can show you a thousand places in the Jewish world where you'll find that same fiercely ambivalent mix of contempt and

3. Talmud Shabbat 152a.

desire today. Even the spiritual state, *tameh*, that a person is said to be in while menstruating, is translated as "ritually impure." Consciously or not, this evokes all sorts of ideas about a person being morally bad, icky, nasty, gross.

It's pretty damn depressing. And it is, truly, enough to make a person just give up on her religious heritage altogether. Plenty have—many, many, many ciswomen, to say nothing of "trans," intersex, and gender-nonconforming folks, and queers of all genders—have taken one look at the ways in which the textual and often legal deck seems to be stacked against them, and decided that it's not worth the hassle or the fight. Others decide that the spiritual riches—the thousands of years of actual wisdom crafted and honed by innumerable sages trying to live in communion with the divine and be of service to others—are worth the price of admission, even if they have to put up with some historical sludge creeping in every now and again.

Me, well, I want all the spiritual wisdom. It's there and it's real, though a more thorough articulation of the ways in which the Jewish tradition has—in so many ways—created a framework of holiness and the sacred will probably have to wait for another essay. I want the good stuff. And I can't stand the toxic gender stuff.

Part of how I stay in this tradition is that I'm the very lucky beneficiary of the exhausting, tireless work of the Jewish feminists who came before me. The ones who fought innumerable battles, faced the ire of the male Jewish establishment, suffered all manner of indignities, and blazed all manner of trails in order to change Jewish culture enough that, by the time I was coming of age, I could be counted in a quorum for prayer, I could be "permitted" to say the Mourner's Prayer, I could comfortably don ritual garb and eventually I could be ordained as a rabbi. I can stay in my tradition in large part because other women already did the work to make Judaism a much safer street to walk down at night.

But part of why I stay—besides, sure, the selfishness of wanting all the beauty of this tradition, and being stubborn about not letting the haters win—is a feeling of obligation I have to people of every gender who come after me. There's plenty of work to be done, but we're doing it. Learning Talmud and other Jewish texts gives us the keys to the kingdom—even though, as I learned through Ketubot and elsewhere, the process isn't always easy or comfortable. The reach of feminist work is constantly expanding, influencing and transforming more and more corners of Jewish life. For example, several generations of work on the questions of menstruation and sex have provided sophisticated interpretations, powerful Jewish legal arguments, and a host of new rituals and spiritual connections, as well as smarter ways of thinking. So instead of translating tameh as "ritually impure," some feminists have begun using the language of "everyday state," which much more accurately reflects the Bible's intention.[4]

Queer and trans* Jews can now get ordained and married in the Reform, Reconstructionist, Conservative, and Renewal denominations, and women's ordination has begun to enter the Orthodox world, particularly with the advent of Yeshivat Maharat. A revolution is brewing to face the many problems regarding traditional Jewish marriage and, yes, the language in the marriage contract. Things are moving. They're going to continue to move. And I can help.

I can't, unfortunately, help those girls and women whose lives and fates were so coolly discussed in the ancient Babylonian study houses. I can mourn their suffering—which actually is important feminist work—but their stories have passed. I can make sure that the most troubling aspects of their legacy don't get carried forward into the future.

A male colleague, the senior rabbi of a major synagogue near me, emailed recently with a question. A woman whose wedding he was slated to do had balked at the language of "virgin" in her ketubah. Did I have anything for him? Why, yes, I replied, attaching the egalitarian ketubah (with no mention of anyone's sexual status or financial

---

4. Thanks to the folks at the Mayyim Chayyim Community Mikveh in Newton, MA, for this language. Something that makes you "everyday" is menstruation, miscarriage, any discharge of semen—whether through sex or nocturnal emission or whatever—as well as certain illnesses and contact with a dead body. There's no way to get into a perfectly "elevated state," (way better than "ritually pure," no?) in these post-Temple times. Read Haviva Ner-David's essay in The Passionate Torah: Sex and Judaism (NYU Press) for a smart take on all of this.

worth) that I use when I work with couples, adapted from one crafted by a male feminist Talmud scholar[5] that I use when I work with couples. Some colleagues and I are planning to write a legal paper that would encourage rabbis to look to alternate rituals when they perform betrothal ceremonies, rather than the traditional betrothal, which technically involves the acquisition of the bride by the groom. Little by little, things are getting better. We're doing the work. In order to make change, we have to know our stuff—which means we have to engage with the most troubling of our sacred texts. But when we do so with the intention of enabling people of all genders to connect with God through our tradition, I believe that we sanctify the Holy Name.

---

5. Dr. Aryeh Cohen, always my teacher and an inspiration.

# Finding Feminism Anew
## by Hannah Heinzekehr

HANNAH HEINZEKEHR is a blogger, church worker, and speaker from Newton, Kansas. She completed her Master's degree in theology and religious education at Claremont School of Theology in May 2012, and currently works as the Director of Communications for Mennonite Church USA. She is a lifelong Mennonite who was drawn to studying theology and feminism post-college. Hannah lives with her husband, Justin, and their two children. Hannah's hobbies include reading, playing and watching soccer, cooking, and drinking lots of coffee. She blogs on the intersections of Mennonite identity, theology and feminism at her blog, *The Femonite* (www.femonite.com).

Until I was twenty-two, I thought that feminism was irrelevant to my life. It's not that I had any negative associations with the word or the movement. On the contrary, I admired the feminist movement and all the ways it had advocated for the advancement of women. It's just that it seemed like something that was finished and in the past. The feminist movement was meant for my grandmother and maybe even my mother, but now, in an age where equality was wholeheartedly embraced between people of all genders, there was no need for something like feminism. We had arrived, and with our arrival, feminism became passé.

Truthfully, the fact that I could exist in this unburst bubble for so long is a testament to the feminist movement itself, as well as to the teachers, friends, mentors, and communities where I existed. It also likely speaks to the fact that my own privilege as a white middle class girl growing up in a highly educated community was able to shield me from some of the realities of sexism that likely were driven home to other women at a much younger age. But whatever the reason, I managed to skate through middle school, high school, and even college with my feminine consciousness untroubled. Call it naïve, but I felt warmly embraced by each new community that I entered. I was invited to take up leadership roles regularly, and found both male and female mentors who affirmed my gifts and encouraged me to dream big about where they could take me.

I was not unaware that there were still women who faced some resistance. I had watched my own mother's entry into pastoral ministry within Mennonite Church USA, the Christian denomination I grew up within. Her path to leadership had not been without pushback. There were people who refused to vote in affirmation of her ministry because of their understanding of biblical roles for women. Among those who voted "no" was a beloved youth pastor who sent me a personal letter detailing the scriptural rationale for voting against women in leadership, even though he "deeply loved" both me and my mother. But again, I was able to divorce these experiences from my own. As I saw it, these were the last vestiges of a dying sexist way of life, and they would be long gone by the time I decided to take up whatever my chosen vocation might be.

But all of this idealism came to a grinding halt in 2007, when I entered into my first "real world job," which just so happened to be as a writer and church development person for Mennonite Church USA, my very own denomination. At first, I thought that I might be making things up. Surely my male coworkers just weren't listening carefully enough when they glossed over my ideas. Surely they just heard this same idea differently when it was paraphrased by another male colleague. Perhaps that's why they responded positively the second time. And surely it was just because I liked to cook that I was being fast-tracked onto all of the kitchen and social hour committees, filled to the brim with other women from the office. And probably my coworker who thought I was too aggressive was just having a sensitive day and didn't realize that I was just modeling the same blunt style of communication that he claimed to prize in his team members. And, people probably just didn't realize that I had the same job title as the men they were inviting into special "closed sessions." That must be why I didn't receive an invitation to join the conversation. They just didn't know!

This list could go on. I became a master of rationalization, trying to write off each incident as something isolated or simply borne out of ignorance. However, the longer I worked, the more the nagging sense grew within me that something was simply not right.

After six months on the job, my organization sent me to a week-end antiracism training session, which defined and raised awareness about the systemic nature of forms of oppression like racism. At this training, they talked about the ways that racism can be subtle. It's the sum total of event after event and behavior after behavior that inherently privileges white people and communicates to people of color that they are somehow "less than." As I learned about racism, and the ways that it was still functioning across the Church, I began to better understand my own institutional experiences and to find a name for their cause: sexism.

As I began to understand more about oppressions like racism and sexism, I began to see them at play all around me in the Church. I saw the ways that the Mennonite Church had kept silent about sexualized violence, and implicitly endorsed theologies that glorified self-sacrifice. I learned that out of the twenty-one regional area conferences that make up our national denomination, three still have ambivalence about ordaining women for ministry in the Church.[1] I began to notice the clear lack of women and people of color in upper level leadership

---

1. For some Christian traditions, any ordination of women would be seen as a great stride. But the three Mennonite regional area conferences that still have ambivalence about ordaining women for ministry in the Church explicitly undermine the Mennonite Confession of Faith, adopted in 1995, which emphasizes that God calls both men and women to ordained ministry. And although other area conferences profess an openness to women in ministry roles, many congregations still would not consider a female leader.

across the Church. I chafed at male language for God and began to resist taking communion, which seemed to simply glorify gratuitous suffering.

To say that this realization was painful would be an understatement. I had grown up idealizing the Mennonite Church. As I saw it, unlike so many other groups, we were counter-cultural to our core. For many people who aren't familiar with Mennonites, the first image this name might conjure in their minds are people riding in horse-drawn buggies and wearing plain clothes (an image which actually is more correctly associated with the Amish). For me, being Mennonite had always been about justice. Since their beginnings, Anabaptists, the group from which Mennonites would evolve, have been committed to nonviolence. They believed in the importance of interpreting scripture together in community, and in giving special attention to the narrative of the whole life of Jesus Christ. Following their interpretation of Jesus' example, Anabaptists refused to "pick up the sword" or to defend themselves through violent means. Even while experiencing widespread persecution for their beliefs, many Anabaptists refused to fight back. They engaged in a posture of radical nonresistance; one of the only ways they saw possible to undermine the violent kingdoms of the world.

Since then, in the Mennonite circles that shaped and formed me, this commitment to nonviolence has grown from passive nonresistance to active resistance against unjust systems. As I understood it, we believed that Jesus always sided with those who were radically disempowered by broader society, and our best witness as Christians was to do the same and to actively cry out for justice.[2] So to learn that this community that had raised me to be an activist was actively perpetuating sexism and racism was a huge blow. It shook me to my core.

---

2. As part of our commitment to active resistance and work for justice, Mennonites have been involved in the creation of organizations like Christian Peacemaker Teams, which sends representatives to high conflict areas to bear witness to and raise consciousness about humanitarian violations around the globe. Mennonites started Mennonite Central Committee, one of the largest international religious relief and development organizations, and pioneered techniques for victim and offender reconciliation processes as alternatives to the current criminal justice system. And this list could go on.

There are phases that a person goes through when a seemingly perfect façade gets stripped back to reveal the complex mix of ugly and beautiful that's behind it. First, I was in denial. This could not be right. I was making things up. Then I wanted to learn more. I started to search for the voices of people who had written about faith and feminism. I discovered Rita Nakashima Brock, bell hooks, Rebecca Parker, Rosemary Radford Ruether, Delores Williams, J. Denny Weaver (a beloved professor from my college days), Julia Kasdorf, and many other writers.

The more I read, the more I realized that I was not alone. Sexism is a problem that has plagued (and continues to plague) Christianity from its very inceptions. And then, I got angry. I had to constantly bite my tongue in meetings to keep from "going off" on coworkers who inadvertently triggered something in me. I began to write papers for graduate school that focused on the ways that "female" has been synonymous with "evil" in the Christian tradition; that explored the sociology of people's responses to women in leadership; and that tried to make some sense of what I was experiencing in my day to day reality. Sometimes, this anger even began to spill over into my relationship with my husband and with male friends. My awareness of how much space "men" took up in my life grew, and I started to feel suffocated by this anger.

At this point, the idea of simply cutting and running seemed pretty appealing. On the worst days, the Church seemed to be beyond redemption. There seemed to be nothing there worth saving. Wouldn't it just be easier to walk away?

But you can't stay angry forever. Anger serves its purpose, that's for sure. It galvanized me to learn more. To do more. To reclaim the word feminist as my own. As something that was not only relevant to my life, but vital to the ability of women to thrive. If feminism was, as Rosemary Radford Ruether describes it, simply "the full affirmation of women as human," then why hadn't I always been on board?

But anger can also chew you up inside. It can keep you from having any productive conversations. It can inflate your blood pressure and raise your anxiety levels. And besides, even when I thought about leaving, I couldn't do it. Sometimes I wanted to so badly, but something always held me back.

Truthfully, although it can be dangerous to simply equate religion with any one culture, my Mennonite faith is more than simply that; it's my way of life. It's what I know. It's the food and the songs and the people and the church rhythm that I'm used to, and these memories hold powerful sway. And it's still a source of support and stability in my life.

And it isn't just that. It's a nagging sense that the Church, even in the midst of all its brokenness, still has something powerful to offer. I like to think that Jesus meant it when he called us to "love one another as ourselves." If we listen to his words and watch his actions, the overarching theme in Jesus' speech and life is love, but not just sappy Hallmark card love, rather, love that is about the work of bringing justice. Love that is about the work of unshackling the "isms" that bind us. I couldn't leave while I still held out hope for *this* type of Church.

Now, let me say loud and clear that there are absolutely times when leaving is the right thing to do. Leaving is an individual choice. But it's a choice that I haven't been able to make.

And truthfully, sometimes that makes me sad. I mourn because I can't leave; because I'm bound up in the fate of this Mennonite body, for better or for worse. There are days when I still want to leave. When I wish I could wash my hands and say good riddance. But I love the Church. I love all those people who are striving to be faithful and who believe that Jesus said something that was radically different, changed things, and called us to be better than we are now.

During moments when I want to leave I think on Dr. Martin Luther King Jr.'s reminder that the "arc of the moral universe is long, but it bends towards justice."[3] I want to be part of that slow, steady movement towards justice, no matter how plodding it might seem. So I stay. A feminist and a Mennonite. Both at once.

---

3. Martin Luther King, Jr. "Where do we go from here?" The Southern Christian Leadership Conference, August, 1967.

# Thy Presence is My Stay
## by Marcia W. Mount Shoop

MARCIA W. MOUNT SHOOP is a theologian and Presbyterian minister who lives in West Lafayette, Indiana. Her book *Let the Bones Dance: Embodiment and the Body of Christ* frames much of her work in churches and beyond. She received her Ph.D. in Religious Studies from Emory University and her Master of Divinity from Vanderbilt Divinity School. At www.marciamountshoop.com Marcia blogs on everything from feminism to family to football. Her new book, *Touchdowns for Jesus and Other Signs of Apocalypse: Lifting the Veil on Big-Time Sports*, is now available from Cascade Books.


*How the Church Took Jesus Away*[1]

My son reads books, sometimes comic books, in church
You should see the rough we have every Sunday morning
Just to tell him he's going again
He hates church and won't let up on his protest
The urgency has not dissipated one bit in all the years.
I will not go, he says. He doesn't brush his hair.


The Advent candle didn't light
Not even with matches and candles to burn.
With elegant long new wicks on thin purple candles
Gracefully grounded in fake greenery
No light.

---

1. A poem inspired by an Advent worship service in the Presbyterian Church.

They told a joke about Advent being the season of imagination.
I didn't laugh.

The Music Director in monk cassock
Talent lending itself to concerts
And fine performance
No testimony, does anyone hear testimony?
He's on a campaign to save the church from dumbing down.

A minister, well meaning, well read
Tired and well over any angst about using the words of others
          who believe
Why not… anything for a good sermon
A product of careful preparation, solid scholarship
Propped up by responsible readings of scriptures
It's not personal; it's his claim to fame.

My daughter memorizes "Go Tell It On The Mountain"
She is dutiful in her quiet
She sings and prays now that she can read
She wants to do the right thing
Just show her the way.

I sit there angry, rebuking the demons I see around me
Sad, empty, homesick
The church took Jesus away.
The Jesus I've known forever, who can heal you with a startling
          touch
The Jesus who can show you the way
like a tornado disappearing the whole world we've built
Jesus walks along here from time to time, I am sure of it.
I doubt he'd feel much room to breathe.
I look down at my son's comic book and see the Far Side cartoon
Men at a table. One with a huge head. A man with a gun.
"Ok, who is the brains of this operation," he says.

I start to laugh so hard I can't stop.
Tears come and I hear the monotone of that preacher
Speaking about icons and iconography,
The words of his friend, the one who wrote the sermon for him.

I jot down some notes, some testimony of my own.
I notice how stale the air feels.
And the way the light seems to bounce off the windows
      toward the outside.

I write something about Jesus getting taken away
and wait for the Amen.

*Why do I stay?*

Going to church on Sundays is the easiest thing I do all week. I have always gone to church on Sundays. My family is full of ministers, church builders, elders, Sunday school teachers, and choir members. Going to church is as easy as my knee moving when the doctor tests for reflexes—it is deeply embedded in the habits of my inheritance, in the rhythms of the life I've known.

Going to church on Sundays is the hardest thing I do all week. Unless I am helping to lead worship (now as a guest preacher since I am not serving as a parish pastor anymore) I anticipate the sadness and alienation I will feel. I prepare myself for the flatness, the lack of connection, the going through the motions. I pray for an open heart, for the capacity to let go of judgments and disappointments and expectations. I struggle to get my children ready in time—often against their will. Sitting in the pew feels strange to me, like I am in the wrong place, even though it is familiar territory. Worst-case scenario is I leave angry. Best-case scenario is I leave touched by a moment or a turn of phrase or a melody that struck a chord.

I stay in the church for the same reasons it is hard to be in the church—because I am a Jesus follower. For me, that statement of identity permeates every part of who I am. Being a Jesus follower shapes my social ethic and my commitments to justice. Being a Jesus follower infuses how I interact with people, animals, and creation. Following Jesus means seeking to notice God's generosity and compassion in every moment. Following Jesus means cultivating openness to the way the Spirit moves in my life and in the world. I organize my life around the way Jesus has touched me, the way his presence has taught me how to embrace life even in times when I have tasted death. Jesus shows me the way of healing, the way of love and compassion, the way of truth telling and truth seeking that nourishes vitality and connection. Christ calls me into community and calls me into deep self-understanding. He calls me into difficult conversations and into the soothing rhythms of who I was created to be.

The words of a hymn I know by heart sing to me about why I do not let go of my connections to the communities that say they follow Christ, too. "When I walk through the shades of death, thy presence is my stay. One word of your supporting breath drives all my fears away."[2] When I am laid bare, and when the church is too, I find the abiding presence of a uniquely powerful and mysterious One who seeks to heal and transform in the midst of our worst distortions. While church can seem to seldom embody this kind of edifying connection, it is the institution that gathers those like me, who know this presence and have connected to this lifeline. And even with the complications and deficiencies of my relationship to the church, this institution has entrusted me with the call to ministry, and it has said it recognizes some of the ways God—my creator, redeemer, and sustainer—made me to be pastor, preacher, teacher, healer, and friend.

My experience as a survivor of sexual violence is the tipping point for both my staying and my straining to stay. And it is from this experience that God has called me into an idiosyncratic kind of ministry that finds spaces to serve and minister in both the heart of the institution and along its margins. The hardest part of staying is that many of the church's habits, patterns, and practices are the opposite of what survivors like me need. The easiest part of staying is that I believe the church has the capacity to be a healing space—a space

---

2. From "My Shepherd Will Supply My Need."

that mediates the kind of healing all of us need as human beings. So I move around in this institution that both frustrates me and shows me glimmers of connection. And I listen for ways that I can take up space with a healing intention in the midst of it all. I find a lot of freedom in this liminality—this willingness to wander around the margins and this invitation to be in conversation in the most fraught spaces of institutional maintenance. These different spaces of ministry exist in a symbiotic relationship—I increasingly feel like neither space has integrity without the other.

I stay by practicing modes of connection that fold out of the healing I have known deep within myself. These healing connections give me the eyes to see healing opportunities all around me. The first women who followed Jesus had the courage to receive both things—healing deep within themselves and eyes to see the healing opportunities around them. They found life in their connections with Jesus. And they had the courage to let those connections nourish them even when the institutions and power structures they lived in questioned, diminished, and even sought to erase them. Like Mary Magdalene I seek to stay connected in the midst of being asked to let go of some of the ways I have known, the ways I was told would keep me close to Jesus. I seek proximity through how I find life, from breath, from mercy, from a palpable presence that makes the world a place of more than just suffering. Redemption is why I stay. Redemption is how I stay.

*Mary, Don't Hold Onto Me*[3]
Gentle Jesus
   source of love, friendship
   wisdom, and mercy

---

3. This poem was inspired by a statue of the post-Resurrection appearance that Jesus made to Mary Magdalene as described in the Gospel of John. "Jesus said to her, 'Woman, why are you weeping? Whom are you looking for?' Supposing him to be the gardener, she said to him, 'Sir, if you have carried him away, tell me where you have laid him, and I will take him away.' Jesus said to her, 'Mary!' She turned and said to him in Hebrew, 'Rabbouni!' (which means Teacher). Jesus said to her, 'Do not hold on to me, because I have not yet ascended to the Father. But go to my brothers and say to them, "I am ascending to my Father and your Father, to my God and your God."' Mary Magdalene went and announced to the disciples, 'I have seen the Lord'; and she told them that he had said these things to her." John 20: 15-18 (NRSV).

Mary felt seen by you
  understood, known
  celebrated, loved, and held

She was drawn to you
      a source of love and
      kindness, a safe place
      a place of respect
      and warmth and
      well-being

Your presence in her life
      gave her energy
      hope—a sense of
      herself, as beautifully made
      fiercely held and
      protected by someone
      who would never hurt her

You were a person who
      always understood
      you knew the truth, you
      could be trusted, you
      were a place where
      she could come and
      think aloud and
      be vulnerable and
      not be harmed

You didn't look at her
Like other men did
      Your eyes were not
      cruel or penetrating

in a way that made her feel ill at ease
or restless

Your eyes looked at her
        powerfully, intensely
        with a knowledge that
        was all-encompassing
        and tender.

Your compassion helped her
        find herself—her
        identity as beloved,
        as cared for, as
        protected, as strong
        as able to withstand

And now you tell her not
to hold on to you
        but how can she let you
        go. What will be her
        source of joy, her safe
        place, her reality check,
        her saving grace.

        Of course she wants you
to stay, she wants more
of you—one more minute,
one more touch, one
more breath of release
from worry, one more conversation.

        You are telling her to
let go
        and you do it only

after you let her hear
again how you know her.

You could have gone
without this moment.
But you let her know
that you see her, that
you trust her, and
that you believe in
her courage and
her strength.

She is the one who can
say, "I have seen the LORD."
you have seen her—
so that she can see
You.

# Same Struggle, Different Dogma
## by Amanda Quraishi

AMANDA QURAISHI is a writer, interfaith activist and technology professional living in Austin, Texas. She currently works full time for Mobile Loaves & Fishes, a non-profit organization that addresses the issue of homelessness in the United States. She also leads a populist-based interfaith initiative at InterfaithActivism.org and writes about the American Muslim experience at muslimahMERICAN.com.

Growing up a Jehovah's Witness, I learned from my earliest years what it meant to be a "Christian Woman." Over and over I heard scripture quoted and rhetoric espoused from the pulpit that reiterated my innate weakness and dependence, and my duty to subjugate myself before men in every aspect of my life. "Women are the weaker vessel," and "women must approach God through their husbands," and "women are incapable of religious leadership." I accepted these words without question.

At home my own family dutifully reinforced the same hierarchy we were taught at church. My father was the highest authority in the house, and my mother played a supportive role. This, we were told, was the natural order of things. It was God's loving provision for women to be relieved of the burden of leadership, even within the family. I watched my mother struggle painfully to align with those teachings for years, challenged even further by my father's deep shortcomings as a husband.

My mother chose to leave my father after thirteen years of marriage. Toward the end of their marriage, they tried to address their issues by attending many late night meetings mediated by the congregation elders in our church. The elders reiterated how much God hates divorce, and how important it was for us to put the family unit first. Mom always went alone with my father to these meetings, to sit in a room full of men who gave her their advice about how to be a submissive wife despite my father's irresponsibility, addictions, and infidelity. She tried to do what they insisted was "God's Way" for our family, until she couldn't justify it to her heart and mind anymore.

When she finally made the break, it was from my father and not from our religion. She and my brother and I continued on in our church, but now we were considered an incomplete family without someone—a *man*—to lead us. Our congregation looked at us with a sense of pity and consternation. People who knew little or nothing about the reasons she chose to divorce my dad scorned my mother. The only thing that mattered to them was that she was the one who had chosen to break up our family. She had overstepped the bounds of what it means to be a good Christian wife and mother.

For years after their split, she trudged through life as a single mother in our community. She was damaged goods, a divorced single mother in a religious culture that prized virginity and submission in potential marriage mates. I saw her make painful choices, and live with the repercussions of those choices. She worked to keep us on the straight and narrow path, attending church with us three times a week, holding family Bible study, making sure our grades were good and that we were provided with the best food, clothing, and entertainment she could afford.

As a teenager, I never understood my mom completely. I didn't blame her for my parents' divorce, but I didn't understand what it was she really needed or wanted, either. I assumed that all of the problems she had in her marriage were because of her conflict with my father, and it didn't occur to me until much later than the religion itself played its own role in suffocating her spirit. Throughout my teenage years with my mom, I lived with mixed messages at church and at home about what a woman was supposed to be. At church I learned that a woman is submissive, dependent, and in need of spiritual direction. At home, I watched my mom call all the shots, work and manage our home, lead us in prayer and Bible study and act as an authority figure. The concept of feminism never entered our vernacular, but unbeknownst to me at the time, my mom was living out loud as a feminist. And she was a feminist, not because of but *in spite of* our religious community.

I finally left the church in my late teens. My reasons for leaving were complicated and had to do with some of its teachings that I couldn't resolve within myself. I still very much considered myself a Christian at that time, and the religion of my youth was the only form of Christianity I knew. A lot of indoctrination followed me as I tried to make my way into adulthood on my own. My relationships as a young adult were informed by the kind of role I thought I was going to be expected to play—that of a submissive helpmate. It confused me when the men I met and dated were frustrated by my clinging and my need for constant approval.

After a few years of self-destructive behaviors and bad relationships, I started searching for a new religious community. I began exploring a wide spectrum of religious teachings. My religious "baggage" prevented me from exploring progressive Christianity. While there are many sects of Christianity that welcome female leadership and preach a more egalitarian version of the Christian dogma, I felt as though I needed something entirely new. My understanding of God was deeply scarred by the religious experience I had in male-dominated religious culture growing up, and I was seeking a different way to understand God that didn't include the same doctrinal trappings I'd known as a child. I fell in love with Islam after reading the Qur'an and scores of books on the topic.

As I studied Islam from an intellectual, historical perspective, I was thrilled to learn the stories of early Islamic society and the great social transformation that took place. I learned about an incredibly progressive prophet who cared about women's rights, correcting economic disparities, and even animal rights. Stories of the early

Muslim community included dynamic female characters that were part of the very foundation of this religion. These teachings seemed so forward thinking compared to my Christian upbringing! I found a coworker who was Muslim and began plying him with questions. He wasn't a particularly religious Muslim (in the orthodox sense) but he answered as many questions as he could, and introduced me to some of his friends who also answered my questions and encouraged my ongoing study. My lunchtime conversations with him quickly turned into a relationship. His parents were educated, well-traveled, and forward-thinking people who willingly embraced me when we approached them on the subject of marriage. We were married after I converted in 1999.

It wasn't until I later found myself attending events in the greater Muslim community that I realized that there is a very broad difference between the Islam I learned from books, friends, and my new husband, and the way it is practiced by many in the larger American mosque culture.

The first time I went to the mosque and was directed to a separate door to sit in a room partitioned from my husband, I cried. I could barely hear the prayers or the *khutba* (sermon) because of the partition that divided us, and the chattering on the women's side. Each time I went to the mosque I would cry on the way home and wonder what I'd gotten myself into.

I began hearing from both men and women in the Muslim community about the "Role of Muslim Women," and it sounded a lot like the "Role of Christian Women" I had heard about growing up. The same rhetoric, with different doctrinal window dressing and different religious texts to back it up: women were expected to be mothers and wives; the morality of the community rested upon their shoulders; they were to maintain modesty in all aspects of their lives in order to prevent men from going astray; and they were not qualified to be religious leaders in the community. These were "traditional" scholarly interpretations of the role of Muslim women, some of which directly contradicted the stories I'd learned about the women living in the first Muslim community.

I thought I'd discovered a new way to be a woman of faith when I embraced Islam, but it seemed that I had only found a new style of being the same woman of faith I'd learned about as a girl. The disappointment was crushing. I voiced my concerns to my husband, but he shrugged them off, saying, "You don't have to listen to them. That is their opinion." That sounded good to me, but it was easier said than done. And frankly, it defeated the purpose of me trying to regain a religious community, because my lack of willingness to conform to these gender-specific roles and rules only succeeded in alienating me from many of the women I met at the mosque who embraced them enthusiastically. I didn't have enough self-confidence or experience as a Muslim to stand my own ground, and despite my loving husband and his supportive family, I felt alone as a woman in my new faith.

Eventually, something wonderful started to happen. After a few years I began meeting Muslim women in different places outside the mosque. Sometimes at interfaith events, sometimes at informal women's study groups or social gatherings that I found out about through word of mouth. These women were different from the ones I'd met before. They seemed to stay on the perimeter of the Muslim community, disenfranchised by the mosque culture as much as I was. They were self-possessed—single, married, and divorced. They were professionals. They were mothers, artists, and activists. Slowly, through person to person connections, I continued to meet a collection of seemingly disparate women who were like me: Muslim, and completely unwilling to conform to a single definition of who they should be.

These women, whom I began to count as my sisters, are no longer disparate. We are crowding in from the margins where we've been pushed for so long. As the years have gone by, I've met many more women (and men!) in the Muslim community—locally and nationally—that are challenging male interpretations of male translations of male-authored texts. I've also met Christian and Jewish women who are doing the same thing. We are working from within our faith communities to carry on the tradition of progressive interpretation that our prophets first set in motion when they brought their respective messages.

Like all other aspects of human society, religion is a constantly evolving manifestation of our understanding of the Divine. Many of our religious scholars and teachers are happy to allow our religious interpretations to evolve with the times, but hold back when it comes to including women's roles in that evolution. Those who want to keep God locked in the gilded box of a bygone era are standing in the way of the natural order of the universe. Muslim feminists (and our sisters from other traditions) cannot be defined by societies that failed to evolve.

Every time I see a single Muslim woman struggling to lead her family, or a Muslim woman who is unmarried and dedicated to her cause or her profession, I think about my mom and the years she spent fighting the current in our church. I also think about my daughter growing up, seeing me refuse to kowtow to religious male authority, and I'm happy that she may be able to avoid many of the struggles I went through to find my own feminism. I am honored that *my* partner in life is a Muslim man who does not blindly follow the opinions of religious scholars about women's roles, especially when they contradict what he knows to be true about his wife, his daughter, and his mother.

I've been asked before why I stay in a religion that consistently relegates me to a second-class status, and my answer is simple: I shouldn't have to give up God and my faith community just because religious scholars have failed to recognize my innate worth in their interpretations of Islam. Does that make me stubborn? A trouble-maker? So be it. I'm in good company.

# Exile of a Jewish Woman and How She Comes Home
## by Felicia Sol

RABBI FELICIA SOL serves as a spiritual leader of Congregation B'nai Jeshurun in New York City where she lives with her son and daughter. She is a board and executive committee member of Bend the Arc.

Every March at my synagogue we hold a ritual for children who have just received the date of their bat mitzvah or bar mitzvah and the parasha (the section of the Torah that they will read). The Torah scroll is held up and unrolled around the entire sanctuary to make a large circle. As the rabbi, I have the privilege of inviting the children to each find the section of the Torah that they will read during the ceremony. It's a powerful moment of fifty or so kids running around to find their parasha and to locate their place in the Torah, anticipating that in three years each of them will be standing by that parasha, reading from it as a bar or bat mitzvah. I am always moved by the excitement in the room, the sense of anticipation from parents and kids and the power of literally finding their place. This also symbolizes the process of finding one's place spiritually—of growth and discovery, of not always knowing where to look, the nervousness of not knowing where you belong, and the sense of ownership and pride when there is a moment of arrival.

At the end of the 2013 ceremony, a girl and her mom approached me. The girl looked particularly sad and her mom said that her daughter had just found out that her parasha was Tazria Metzora, a double reading from the Torah all having to do with purity and impurity, menstruation and the origin of the laws for *taharot hamishpah*—family purity. It was clear that following the excitement of finding the actual parasha in the scroll of the Torah, this girl felt that she would not find her spiritual place in this parasha, a deflation for her to say the least.

It took me until adulthood to feel that sense of deflation this girl felt. It took me years to realize that, though my love of and commitment to Jewish life was noticed and honored by so many rabbis and educators, none encouraged me to become a rabbi early on, even though my brother was encouraged to pursue the rabbinate. While internally I had a sense of calling to become a rabbi—I was drawn to prayer, to studying and teaching, to supporting community—I saw no models of women on the pulpit. While I wasn't told I could not be a rabbi, it was never a role in which I imagined I could be actualized. I ultimately decided to pursue the rabbinate without encouragement or role models, and I had faith that I would find my way. But studying for the rabbinate in adulthood, the more I took Judaism seriously the more I had a sense of deflation about the patriarchy and sexism in the tradition that I loved. It was not written for or by women.

What am is a person to do when she feels so at home and so distanced simultaneously? When one prayer or text speaks to the essence of my being and one prayer or text silences me? When for all the progress made to include women—as participants, as rabbis—the structures that are lived day in and day out of Jewish life were built by men and for men?

This tension is the tension I have lived as an adult Jewish woman and as a rabbi. I feel profoundly blessed by the Torah, tradition, faith, and community, but also alienated by its lack of desire to understand me and speak to me as a woman.

Ironically, this very notion of home and exile is at the core of the Jewish religious experience. The Jewish people were exiled from the land of Israel for over two thousand years until the establishment of the State of Israel in 1948. Therefore, there is much that the Jewish textual tradition has to say about exile. I would suggest that there are three core elements of exile that help me understand my experience as a Jewish woman: dislocation, creativity, and return.

## Dislocation

I grew up in a liberal Jewish community in which I felt very much at home and loved my Jewish life. It appeared boys and girls were equal (for the most part), and so I never really questioned the tradition other than in my spiritual searching as a teenager. As I came to study more in rabbinical school and also think more deeply about gender roles and sexism in my life and the world, I had somewhat of a rude awakening. What I had known and loved had a rupture at its essence. Judaism had an injustice at its core. I was objectified as a woman in the very tradition by which I had felt so embraced. I started to see sexism everywhere; it was the frame by which I analyzed texts and experiences. It was a constant critique and I was profoundly influenced by the ideas in Dr. Judith Plaskow's book, *Standing Again at Sinai*. Plaskow explains "the hermeneutics of suspicion" which "takes as its starting point the assumption that biblical texts and their interpretations are androcentric and serve patriarchal functions" and therefore "while mainstream sources may have much to say to women, they cannot be accepted uncritically. All too often, they serve to consolidate or reinforce patriarchal values or to inculcate models of power that are destructive or oppressive."[1]

It was through this suspicion that I experienced heartbreak, for what was once easy and beautiful was now complicated and often distancing. It is important to have the suspicion. It is important to honor the heartbreak. To deny it, apologize for it, or diminish it adds salt to the wound. It's true for women, it's true for LGBTQ people, it's true for people of color. In the Torah, God says to the Jews, "For you

---

1. Judith Plaskow, *Standing Again at Sinai: Judaism from a Feminist Perspective* (New York: HarperOne, 1991), 14.

were strangers in the land of Egypt." Being a stranger is at the essence of the religious experience and it exhorts us to recognize who has been cast out, who has been "othered," who has been treated unjustly, and who has been made invisible.

## Creativity

The exile of the Jewish people from the land of Israel also prompted some of our most creative thinking. The Babylonian Talmud was created in exile, the Hassidic tradition was born in exile, the Reform movement was birthed in exile. And with women's recognition of their "otherness" in Jewish tradition, much has been born—first and foremost a demand for inclusion and justice. Jewish women have birthed creative liturgy and ritual, and the rabbinate has changed because of women's inclusion. The roles rabbis play have broadened beyond the traditional pulpit to pastoral counselors and organizational leaders. How rabbis gain and use their authority plays out differently with women in the rabbinate. Jewish organizations and synagogues are held more accountable to the need for balance between work and life with women in the rabbinate. I would venture to say that the Jewish healing and spirituality movement can in many ways be attributed to Jewish feminism. With questions that Jewish feminists raised and the searching that took place to meet those needs, many new pathways were opened up to respond to a diversity of needs within the Jewish community.

I deeply believe that by distancing from the tradition, there are creative ways to add women's voices to the conversation and create women's spaces in seders, prayer services, and religious texts. Creativity allows us to birth new forms of experience, such as baby naming ceremonies for girls or spirituality groups and ritual ceremonies for divorce, miscarriage, or menopause. As a rabbi, I've been committed to creating spaces for women to find their own voices, to retreat together, to study and celebrate together. These spaces are not only important to heal the invisibility of women in the Jewish tradition, but to also honor the power of women, the unique experience of being together, and the wisdom that emerges in those spaces. Exile demands reformulation, adaption, new definitions of home, and new conversations to address the experience of dislocation.

## Return

The Jewish community and Judaism have been my home all my life. Jewish values animate my being. I live the rhythm of the Jewish year. My faith and relationship with God has supported and guided me through my life, particularly as I try to live out who I am called to be in this world, as a woman, as a mother, and as a rabbi. I don't want to live in constant exile from my religion or my community. I want to feel at home, and so I honor the exile and the creative forces that emerge from that place, and I also return home. I return home not only because so much of what I have learned from my life as a Jew has informed my existence and provided meaning and a moral compass; I return because that home needs to grow and heal and respond and be redeemed with me. I have the power to change it, to help redefine what is authentic and expand the tradition. I have the power to call it to task—to make it more inclusive, more dignified, and more just. Not only so that when women gather, study, or pray we don't feel banished, but also so that we are not enacting injustice and inequality as a blessing of the tradition.

I am still trying to find my way in this place of being at home and exiled at the same time. As a rabbi who is a woman, I feel a deep sense of responsibility to stand up and honor the tension of home and exile and also to transform Jewish community to be an inclusive home that embraces all kinds of diversity: gender, sexual orientation, family structure, and more. Accompanying my dislocation, heartbreak and suspicion is my strong faith that *tikun* (healing) is possible.

There are many texts in the Jewish tradition that I love but there is one that informs my path and challenges and inspires me to fulfill my calling. It comes from a midrash (an interpretation) in the book of Exodus describing the experience of receiving the Torah at Mount Sinai:

Come and see how the voice went forth from each and everyone in Israel, each one according to his strength. The old people according to their strength, the young ones according to their strength, the children according to their strength, the infants according to their strength, the women according to their strength, and even Moses according to his strength, as it says "Moses spoke and God answered in a voice" (Ex. 19:19) that he could bear. And thus it says "The voice of God in strength" (Ps. 29:4); it doesn't say "in *His* strength," but rather "in strength"—in the strength of each and every person, even the pregnant women according to their strength. That's why one can say, "Each one according to his strength."

The essence of the teaching is to recognize that each and every individual has the ability to receive Torah in her own way and that none is like the other. This text inspires me to ask the question: What am I here to learn and teach given the Divine Image that has been implanted in me? And while this text has its own gender bias, it also creates possibility for each and every person to have a role in living out the Torah of their own soul. This text essentially extends that invitation to everyone, despite its construction within a patriarchal tradition. God's voice is available and ready to all those desirous of hearing the call. My role is to hear that voice and stand for the unique human being that I am—mother, daughter, rabbi, Jew, feminist. The Torah will never be whole or complete without the possibility of each and every person being invited in to hear the call. And so, I pray for that young girl who will become bat mitzvah in two years on Tazrai Metzora. This Torah is still your home even when it exiles you. You will find your way because of your humanity and the Divine Image that has been implanted in you. I also hope and pray that in finding ourselves in the Torah, each according to our strength, we will also find a way to see the humanity in the person who we too thought was the other and welcome them home.

# The Life of a Secret Feminist
## by Aisha C. Saeed

AISHA SAEED is a YA (Young Adult) author, attorney, and educator, and one of the founding members of the #WeNeedDiverseBooks campaign. Her debut novel, *Written in the Stars,* will be released in 2015 by Nancy Paulsen Books/Penguin. She lives in Atlanta with her husband and two sons. Visit her online at www.aishasaeed.com.

"What do you do?"

It's a typical question. An innocent initiation of conversation at a playground or dinner party. And yet for so long this simple question struck up the most complicated feelings in me: an assortment of guilt, apprehension, and angst-ridden introspection that sent me into a self-identity tailspin.

It wasn't always that way. Once upon a time in response to "What do you do?" I could proudly answer: a teacher educating underprivileged children—and later, a lawyer working as an Equal Justice Works fellow representing children with disabilities. The question was as simple and uncomplicated as it sounded, and one I happily answered.

What do I do?

Four years ago I turned in my high heels, black suits, and a reliable independent income for changing diapers, planting jalapenos, baking muffins and, most recently, shuttling a little one to and from soccer practice. The transition wasn't easy. I've brought home a paycheck since I turned fifteen years old, but after long conversations with my husband debating every angle of the issue, I crunched the numbers, and it was a choice I made joyfully.

I expected to enjoy snuggling with my newborn in the wee morning hours, and I expected to miss lunches with coworkers and the busy organized schedule I once had. But I did not expect that when I left behind a career I would also leave behind part of my identity. Leaving the traditional working world made me quickly realize that the simple question of what I did involved layers, and one of those layers involved people ascertaining not just what I did, but by association, who I was. And while my entire adult life I identified as both a feminist and a Muslim, what exactly these two identities meant were thrown into an identity crisis upon leaving my job and becoming a stay-at-home mother.

Though seemingly at odds about how they judge a woman's behavior and choices, conservative Muslims and feminists seem unified around the belief that what a woman decides to do regarding certain things like working outside the home defines her. She is either within or outside of the purview of a "good Muslim woman" or within or outside of the purview of a "true feminist," depending on her choice. In doing this, both groups reduce women to what they "do" and not who they are, and they do this in a black and white way with no room for gray. Both of these responses are limiting and inconsistent with the tenets of each group's beliefs. That a woman should have a choice in these matters—and have that choice respected—is both inherently feminist *and* Muslim. While there appears to be no way to be both a feminist and a Muslim on issues like this, it's actually the exact opposite.

While on some level I still knew this, just as I had my entire life, the stark reality of seeing my choices judged through black and white lenses by others was not an easy one to accept.

While most of my friends wholeheartedly supported my decision to stay home with my son, for a few friends, my decision to leave the workforce was a mutiny to the principles of equality and independence, the feminist principles we all valued. "Don't expect to be able to come back," one admonished me. "That resume gap is one no employer will ever be able to look past." Another outright said, "So from a career woman to domestic housewife, huh?"

As disapproving as some were towards my choice, there were others who held just the opposite point of view. The aunties—elders in my religious community—didn't just approve, they were elated. Many of them believe in the traditional Islamic view some conservative Muslims hold: that men and women are equal but inhabit different realms, with men financially providing and deciding for the family while women remain at home, cooking and cleaning and child rearing. In their view, by staying home, I was accepting this point of view.

While my friends' opinions gave me angst, the opinions of my local aunties sent me into a self-identity tailspin. I grew up in a traditional South Asian and Muslim community and many from my community disapproved of my going away to college. In their view, it was unacceptable for a woman to live by herself, and they did not allow their own daughters to go away to college for this reason.

I didn't mind their disapproval. On the contrary, it amused me. My parents had always taught me that all religions were comprised of human beings who often had different views on the same situation, sometimes even within the same religion. This understanding had prevented the disapproval of conservative community members from affecting me. From college to law school to traveling to Brazil with fellow students to keeping my maiden name when I got married, I had always laughed off their pointed observations about how *modern* I was. I knew Islam had many different interpretations and I respected each position while practicing my faith the way I believed, according to my own principles. I understood a certain segment of the Muslim population did not think I was a model Muslim woman, and that was okay. But now? Now that I was staying home with my children, the disapproval I was accustomed to receiving changed. I was getting the wholehearted approval of the women in my community. In their eyes, I was getting back to what I should have been doing all along. I had finally taken my proper "Islamic" place in the home.

It struck me that while my friends and the aunties had different opinions about the choice I made to be home with my children, their ultimate conclusion was the same. When they saw me baking cookies, building Lego towers, or pushing a large green plastic shopping cart through the grocery store with oatmeal stains on my blouse, they all agreed: I was many things, I maintained many identities, but I was no longer a feminist.

The stripping away of this part of my identity was more difficult than I imagined. Just three months after having my son, I found myself holding his sleeping frame against me and perusing job postings. I even went as far as applying and interviewing for a legal job I ultimately, in tears, turned down. While I didn't like the perceptions people had of me, my heart just wasn't as much in going back to work as much as it was in being home with my child.

I decided I would accept the judgments and cohabitate with the uncomfortable reality that by staying home with my children, I could no longer identify with a part of who I was: an independent woman. A feminist. And when the question of what I did arose, I stuttered: *I'm home. For now. But. I will go back. I was a lawyer.* And cringed at the reactions I might receive. There was another part of me that secretly wondered if everyone was right. Maybe by being home I lost the right to the feminist part of my identity.

In the spring of 2013, kids in tow, I met up with a good friend for coffee during her lunch break. We caught up on our lives, current events, and some frustrations she was experiencing at work.

"I want to tell my coworkers exactly what I think but then I worry they'll call me aggressive, but if I don't say anything I'm being a pushover." She shook her head and smiled at me. "Being a feminist is an uphill battle."

"I guess I have no room to say anything on that topic anymore." I laughed and looked down at my napkin.

"Why?" she asked.

"Well, I'm home with the kids and pretty much the picture of a 1950s housewife." I handed my baby a teething biscuit and wiped crumbs from my shoulder.

My friend stared at me like I'd grown a third set of ears. "Why does the fact that you're home change anything?" she asked.

"Well, you don't think of me as a feminist anymore, do you?"

"Why wouldn't I?" she asked.

I stared at her for a moment. I smiled. I shrugged. We continued the conversation.

But that simple moment changed everything for me. It gave me the reminder I needed.

While I did choose to leave my job to clean up spilt milk, kiss bruised knees, and rock little ones to sleep, the key thing, the most important part of it, was one simple word: choice.

I was not home with the kids because society pressured me into it, as it does to many women. I did not do it because my husband felt it was my rightful place, or even because *I* felt it was my rightful place. I did this because it was what I wanted to do and I was lucky enough to be able to afford it.

While feminism can mean different things to different people, the value I place on my belief in choice and equality are why I call myself a feminist. It's no strange coincidence that these are among some of the reasons I have always loved my religion, too.

While some Muslims believe a woman's rightful place is at home, There are many examples of strong, independent Muslim women in my religion. One of the first converts to Islam was Khadijah, Prophet Muhammad's wife. She had her own independent career and was never the prophet's subordinate. Instead, she was his partner and greatest supporter. The ruler Razia Sultan ran an entire kingdom and established schools and libraries across northern India in the 1200s. Lubna of Cordova translated complicated texts for the royal libraries while being a mathematician to boot. While some from outside my faith and even some from within may not believe a Muslim woman is allowed by her religion to work outside the home, history itself quickly dispels this misconception.

Even more important than historic proof, Islamic scripture itself gives women equality and allows women the right to work, going so far as to specifically safeguard her earnings as hers alone to do with as she chooses. While cultural interpretations may find Islam and feminism incompatible with one another, the Islam I follow encourages its followers to use their reason and to define their relationship with God themselves. We use no intermediaries to speak on our behalf to God. Our relationship with God is deeply personal.

My simple coffee break with my friend helped me remember that while my choices may be met with approval or disapproval, ultimately how others see me doesn't matter. Just as I define my relationship with God myself, and just as I believe no one but God has the right to judge me and who I am, both my feminist and religious identities can only be defined by me.

I know many of the aunties who nod approvingly at my stay-at-home status think my current place at home is my rightful place as a Muslim woman. I know many of my friends working in the corporate world think my choice to be home with my kids is ten steps back for feminism. I now know: that's okay.

At the end of the day everyone is allowed their opinions of me, but what matters isn't what they see; what matters is what I see. And what I see is a choice I made. My choice involves deep and long-lasting sacrifices in career growth and financial opportunities, but it's one I made with eyes wide open, knowing the consequences. While many may not see it while I push my kids on the swings, or offer homemade cupcakes, I know who I am: I many things, but among them, I am a proud Muslim and feminist.

# Bane of the Single Muslim Woman
## by Atiya Hasan

ATIYA HASAN is a recent graduate of the International School of Medicine based in Central Asia and is working towards becoming a licensed physician in the United States. She is also the Editor in Chief for *Brown Girl Magazine* and the Social Media Director at *Coming of Faith*. These online publications focus on giving young South Asian and Muslim women in America a platform to voice their opinions and create discussion regarding issues that may be considered taboo or hold cultural stigmas; Atiya strongly believes in bringing these issues to light. In her free time, she enjoys refreshing her medical knowledge and catching up on TV shows.

*A single Muslim woman is a burden to her parents. After a certain point, the only question that her friends and extended family want to know the answer to is, "When are you getting married?"*

*If a single Muslim woman is not married between her prime years of twenty and twenty-five, her chances of marrying become slimmer with each passing year. After twenty-five, she becomes a less appealing stock on the marriage market. The younger, the better.*

*If a single Muslim woman, God forbid, crosses the age of thirty, she is blamed for remaining single. There must be something inherently wrong with her. Or, she must just be too picky. Or, she must be in a relationship with someone not approved by her parents.*

*If a single Muslim woman receives a marriage proposal and refuses it for whatever reason, she is too fussy, conceited, and egocentric. A good single Muslim woman should agree to marry the first "decent" proposal—as defined by the community—she receives.*

*No matter what a single Muslim woman accomplishes in her life, whether it be in her career, her spirituality, her finances, or her intellectuality, none of it matters unless she can find a man and convince him to marry her.*

*A single Muslim woman is unhappy, unstable, and unpredictable.*

◆◆◆

These are some of the stereotypes that single Muslim women have to deal with in the Muslim community. I know because I speak from experience. I can only imagine the additional stigmas divorced women or single mothers have to deal with.

Many single Muslim women can attest to the fact that meetings with prospective partners through arranged marriage processes can be demeaning. Once, I had an initial conversation with a man via text messages that went like this:

"How old are you?"
"How tall are you?"
"Can you send me your pictures?"
"How soon do you want to get married?"
I felt like a car that he wanted to buy.
"How old is it?"
"How big is it?"
"Can you send me its pictures?"
"How soon do you want to get rid of it?"

I know of a mother and son team who came to Houston for a visit and told friends and relatives in the city to spread the word about looking for a wife for the son. They said they would be available to meet with anyone who was interested at a local restaurant, at a specific time. All interested families were welcome to stop by with their daughters, because choosing a wife is no different than choosing an item off the menu for lunch.

More than once, I've overheard my mom speaking to mothers of potential suitors over the phone, saying, "My daughter is dark skinned. I just want to be upfront about that." And every single time the proposal fizzled into nothing. In the South Asian community, having a fairer skin tone often means being a more appealing prospect for marriage. Many times, skin color trumps education, family merit, and age. I always felt a slight pang whenever my mom mentioned my skin color, not at her bluntness, but at the fact that I was considered a less desirable candidate based on my skin color, a quality that Allah had blessed me with and I have no desire to change. There was little regard for my accomplishments or capabilities in the equation.

The worst aspect of the entire ordeal is that these cultural ideals are perpetuated from generation to generation, not by the men looking for their future brides, but by their mothers. Why is it that even though the mothers themselves suffered through such discrimination in the past, they choose to devalue other women by upholding the same unfair standards? Do South Asian Muslim mothers not understand that the cultural intra-racism they are perpetrating holds no weight in Islam, especially when Islam does not differentiate between people based on *any* physical quality?

The heartbreaking story of a girl from my community haunts me as a reminder of how our cultural attitudes towards marriage harm women. This girl was barely past twenty when her parents decided to get her married. She placed her entire trust in her parents' choice. Because of this trust, she didn't get to know the guy prior to their wedding. The day after their wedding, her husband told her he didn't love her and had a girlfriend that he planned on marrying, proof that even Muslim men feel the pressures of the arbitrary rules of marrying the "right" person as defined by the Muslim community. They divorced within a year of their wedding and the girl has been unable to get remarried because of the stigma surrounding divorcees.

When I was twenty-three and teetering on the rocky path of becoming a medical professional, I crossed paths with an amazing physician assistant. She was a devout Christian in her late thirties, who looked not a day over twenty-five. She had never been married despite being intelligent, down to earth, and drop-dead gorgeous. She told me of her Army boyfriend and their plans to be married soon. The giddiness in her eyes when she spoke of him convinced me that true love happens without regard to our socially constructed deadlines, so why stress about something you can't control?

I can understand my parents' point of view, and to be fair, they hold my brothers to a similar standard. To them, marriage means finding a partner who will be a support system through the turbulent journey of life. But this is no longer the social environment that nurtured our parents' marriages through thick and thin. Muslim parents hope to raise daughters who are confident, self-assured, and able to achieve anything they wish without relying on anyone else. Along with self-reliance comes, much to the dismay (I suppose) of the Muslim community, self-worth and the conviction that women should not be desired for marriage based solely on physical appeal.

In the last five years, I have seen more divorces happen in my community and my age group than my parents may have seen throughout the entire length of their marriage. A survey by the nonprofit Sound Vision from 2010 showed that 50 percent of the 405 participants had been divorced once and 25 percent had been divorced twice, with primarily women initiating divorce. It is disheartening to think I might end up being another statistic.

The idealists' response would be, "Then don't get divorced." But you never know what life has in store for you. After growing up in a culture that nurtures individuality and the importance of self-worth, women are not prepared to stay in relationships where their voices aren't heard. It is obvious from the statistics that pressuring girls into marriage doesn't work anymore.

I vividly remember being sixteen and a high school senior, hoping and praying that marriage would be just around the corner for me. When I entered college, it opened my eyes to a bright and alluring new world full of possibilities. It wasn't long before I decided that marriage would happen for me, but not so soon. I wanted to be someone of my own accord first.

But being happy with being single, and unabashedly enjoying success in other areas of your life, gives you "feminist tendencies." This is something the community tends to think no single Muslim woman should have. And what about the single Muslim women, like myself, who actually choose to recognize themselves as feminists? Well, there's just no hope for us; feminists don't make good daughters-in-law, nor good wives, because we are too caught up with wanting to become men.

I think of the Mothers of the Believers as the pioneers of Islamic feminism. It has been popularly touted, by men and women alike, that Islam gave women rights that members of other religions were debating for years after. While this is true, many forget that the years of imperialism that followed the advent of Islam once again stripped women of their rights. This is why feminism is indispensable today.

Khadija, the first wife of the Prophet Muhammad (peace be upon him) and the very first Muslim other than himself, was also a remarkably successful businesswoman. She could have married any man in Mecca. It is said that her trade caravans would equal all the other trade caravans from the Quraysh, the richest tribe of Mecca at the time. When it came time to choose a husband, she sent a marriage proposal to an orphaned man who was younger than she was and below her by all definitions of social status, all based on his reputation for being a trustworthy and honest man. And the rest is history.

Aisha, the youngest wife of the Prophet Muhammad (peace be upon him), lived for over fifty years after his passing. She participated in politics, made public speeches, shared the teachings of the Prophet to men and women widely, and involved herself in matters of war. Also, she chose to never remarry.

In the Qur'an, whenever marriage or wives are mentioned so are the words, "kindness," "justice," or "gentleness," in close proximity. There is a constant emphasis on equality between the genders and the importance of giving each other the rights that Allah has given each and every Muslim. Yet, when it comes to one of the most important decisions of our lives, we have thrown aside all the laws of God and given more importance to the demeaning man-made cultural ones.

So, the question remains, how did we end up here? Where my value as a woman depends on the social standing and abilities of the man I am able to marry. Where a premium is placed on the number and the skin tone of the offspring I am able to produce. There are those who say that there is no place for feminism in Islam. But until the proper gender rights bestowed by Islam are restored, feminism remains relevant for men and women alike.

I desire the fulfilling relationships that many of my friends have been blessed with. They have husbands who encourage them to become better versions of themselves by supporting them through their struggles and triumphs, their familial responsibilities, and their careers. These Muslim men are their equal partners in strengthening each other to establish consistent prayer and embody the Islamic tenets over cultural ones. These Muslim men are shining examples of the Islamic discipline; they realize that their true success is in having wives who help them become better practitioners of Islam.

It is important that we stop seeing Muslim women as reproductive vehicles and start seeing them as what they are: living, breathing humans. Humans capable of awe-inspiring feats, able to cause unfathomable changes in the world and make their own fully informed decisions about what is right for them and what is not. It is time that we begin trusting Muslim women to find and accept fulfilling relationships of their own accord. If the presence of feminism within the Muslim community is deemed as a sickness within our faith, then I ask for the eradication of the stains that cultural stigmas have proliferated. Until that is attained, single, married, divorced, and all other Muslim women need to continue the fight for the rights that Islam conferred upon us fourteen hundred years ago.

As an American Muslim single woman whose market value will soon plummet as I become the dreaded post-twenty-five-year-old single American Muslim woman, I leave you with this: No matter who you are, make *du'a* (prayer) to the All-Knowing to open doors and hearts to all that is right for us when the time is right for us. He is listening. He is watching and will only allow for what is best for us in this life and the Hereafter. In the meantime, I plan on enjoying every bit of success that Allah has deemed me worthy of.

# Sometimes, the Minister is a Girl
## by Kathryn House

KATHRYN HOUSE is a North Carolina native who has made her home in Jamaica Plain, Massachusetts, since 2005. Kathryn is a member of The First Baptist Church in Jamaica Plain, where she is the former Minister of Christian Formation and is in the process of ordination. She completed a B.A. in Religion at Duke University in 2003 and a Master of Divinity at Boston University School of Theology in 2008. She is currently completing doctoral work in Practical Theology at Boston University School of Theology. She is also the co-founder of Bridesmaid Trade, an online bridesmaid dress consignment business. When not studying theology or thinking about alternatives to the wedding industrial complex, she is biking around Boston or tending to tomatoes in her backyard.

As I made my final preparations to preside over the ceremony, Emma, my six-year-old second cousin, bounded up the steps of the gazebo. I was standing at the bottom of the hill while the wedding party prepared themselves a few yards away. She stopped in front of me and asked, "What are you doing?"

I looked down and answered, "I'm getting ready for the ceremony."

"What do you mean?" she continued.

"I'm the minister for your uncle's wedding this afternoon."

Without missing a beat, she countered, "But you're a girl."

Ah… I could see how that was confusing. "That's true, Emma… Well, I guess…sometimes the minister is a girl."

She looked at me for a few moments, turning this over in her mind. "Hmm…OK." Then she ran up the hill, apparently not undone by this scandalous revelation, to find her flower girl basket. My cousin Matthew, her father, had overheard and smiled. "She's never seen a woman minister before." We laughed together for a good long while.

Natalie Watson has written that when it comes to women and church, it is often about "learning to live with ambivalence, to somehow make sense of the reality of oppression and empowerment, of liberation and suffering, of silence and powerful speech at the same time."[1] Certainly this has been my experience: I make sense of the space between laughter with my cousin and realizing the church I grew up in was not one with which I could continue.

It may be that my invitation to be both feminist and Christian in a new way developed over time in the accumulation of many small moments. I am from a place where if you mention feminism in casual conversation, it is more likely to be blamed for "broken homes" and general moral decay than it is to be celebrated as, in bell hooks' words, "a movement to end sexism, sexist exploitation, and oppression."[2] Growing up, my knowledge of feminism wasn't so much a formal definition, movement, or philosophy, as it was a product of looking around my community and family and noting that there wasn't anything women couldn't or didn't do. The women I knew provided for their families, built houses, coached my softball team, worked as trusted health care professionals, and educated others in a variety of capacities. If you had asked me if I were a feminist, I would have said, "Of course! Don't you see all these awesome women? How could I be otherwise?"

No doubt I come from a family of fierce and courageous women. My mother, aunts, grandmothers, and cousins modeled independence, tenacity, and kindness. When I wanted to write or dream or run a marathon and said, "Mom, I think I'll _____," Mom would say, "Sounds great. Get to work." The women in my family are the ones who anchored my confidence and insisted that I find my voice.

---

1. Natalie Watson, *Introducing Feminist Ecclesiology* (Cleveland: Pilgrim Press, 2002), 4.
2. Hooks, Bell, *Feminism is for Everybody: Passionate Politics* (Boston: South End Press, 2000), 1.

Church was a constant for our family. I was christened in a United Methodist Church, but spent most of my life in a Southern Baptist Church in the foothills of North Carolina. I loved Jesus. I loved God, the Bible, quiet times, and praise choruses with predictable narrative arcs and chord structures that induced longing. I couldn't wait for summer mission trips and I chose Bible Study as an extra elective during youth camp. I loved my friends and my youth group and devoured *Brio*, a magazine for teen girls by the nonprofit group Focus on the Family.[3]

At the church I attended, there were (and still are) brilliant, opinionated, funny, and compassionate women who demonstrated thoughtful leadership and devoted discipleship.

There were men too, who mentored me, who spent vacation time chaperoning (and thus being pranked all week) on youth trips, and whose kindness and patience I will never forget. Church was the place where my imagination was cultivated and where my love of poetry, metaphor, and stories were formed. God's family was a weird but beautiful bunch of young people and old people; people who lived in trailers and people who had inground pools; artists, athletes, teachers, and musicians.

I went to Duke to major in religion and become a missionary. I mentioned this a few hours after moving in and a hallmate who would become a lifelong friend raised her eyebrows and said, "God, missionaries are horrible. Why would you want to do that?" I was shocked, although I couldn't tell if my shock was from her use of the Lord's name in vain or my confusion over why anyone would think missionaries were terrible. Much of my theological reconstructing happened during college and in the years that followed. Certainly, classes on other faith traditions broadened my perspectives, but the tradition I learned the most about was my own. In a class on social movements, we read David Halberstam's *The Children*. I was

---

3. The Focus on the Family website, www.focusonthefamily.com, states: "Focus on the Family is a global Christian ministry dedicated to helping families thrive. We provide help and resources for couples to build healthy marriages that reflect God's design, and for parents to raise their children according to morals and values grounded in biblical principles."

floored by the justice-seeking faith of those who participated in the Civil Rights Movement, and I was introduced to the idea that being Christian is not just about "Jesus and me," or jewels in my crown in the sweet by and by. It's about love, justice, and truth in this moment, during these days. My faith was transformed through long conversations and abiding friendships with activists, atheists, poets, Christian anarchists, and recovering-evangelicals turned Episcopalians. I think it is this way: about a decade ago, in a thousand tiny and enormous ways, I ran into questions for which I did not have answers. What did being Christian have to do with race? Economics? War? So much more than I had initially imagined.

When it came to the question of my Christian faith and my gender, I did not wake up one morning and realize that I was a member of a denomination that resisted and discouraged women's ordination. The Baptist tenant of the priesthood of all believers seemed sufficient for my needs. But then I started noticing women's absences. One moment that stands out was the deacon nomination service at my church in early 2000. In my church, the deacon board, a group of twelve men, provided administrative and pastoral support to both pastoral staff and families. After I received the list of nominees, I whispered to the deacon passing them out, a man whom I considered kind and funny: "Where are the women on this list? I'm going to write in my mom and Aunt Martha!" When he scoffed back, "Not in this church," I felt like I'd been punched in the stomach. It was a small moment, but it was one that stayed with me. What sort of church were we, then? How would my questions and observations about what women could and could not do be perceived?

After college, I began to meet women who were ministers. Initially, the very idea of clergywomen made me nervous. Who were these women who thought they could be "preachers" and not just "teachers?" But then I shared meals with them, worked alongside them, watched and learned from them. My world did not end. And yet, it did. Their lives were apocalyptic: their willingness to transform or leave traditions and their persistence in drawing attention to those whom churches excluded were tiny earthquakes that made me ask questions about who I believed God to be and what it meant to love and participate in binding up a broken world. If anything crumbled, it was my fear and hesitation to be open to the gift of their calls. I could not deny the love, justice, mercy, and radical hospitality of their lives.

There were other moments too, other questions and experiences. I began to question why all the women in the Bible seemed to be the happiest when they finally birthed male sons. I wondered what sort of theology could accompany us, my friend and I, as we walked into her apartment for the first time after her rape. I watched my niece, the fiercest girl I know, hop and ribbit like a frog across the living room, wearing a crinoline and fairy wings while I thought, "Get it, girl."

These are some of the stories, some terrible and some beautiful, that make up the life I have known, and contribute to my desire to cross borders between feminism and faith. My church in Boston is also a big reason I keep crossing. I found a church that is taking seriously what it means to be the beloved community. It is not a church full of people who think or pray or read the Bible just like me—far from it—but a church where I am cared for and challenged. These are risk-taking, peacemaking, welcoming, and affirming Baptists. Some are former Southern Baptists (our pastor Ashlee included). Some folks come because the weather is bad on a Sunday morning. Some folks come because we don't care if kids are loud—we are a loud bunch—and some come because we host an awesome slam poetry open mic on Friday nights. It is the place at the crossroads of Centre and Myrtle,[4] where feminists are welcome to break bread and share grape juice, to preach and to pray, to believe or doubt. It is where I learned to breathe again in church, and where I have been given the freedom to speak, to listen, to participate, and to try to live in God's kin-dom.

What does it mean to be a woman who finds herself at the intersections of faith and feminism? It means standing in the midst of contradictions and claiming my right to exist and to remain. I am sometimes accused of trespassing: I am lifting my voice and putting

---

4. The First Baptist Church in Jamaica Plain sits at the crossroads of Centre St. and Myrtle St. in Jamaica Plain.

my body in spaces, places, pulpits, and pews where it doesn't belong. In other contexts, I am doing just about the most old-fashioned and strange thing a person can do. So be it. I see these not as options that cancel one another out but as liminal spaces and permeable borders: as possibilities. It means holding my former community in my heart, with gratitude, but finding the church I need, a community that answers, "Yes. Of course in this church." It involves looking someone in the eye when my presence might trouble the waters. It reminds me that I, too, can take the risk to be undone and remade in the presence of others. It is about staying and leaving, listening deeply, and "couraging" even when I am terrified and the way is not clear. It means standing in front of Emma, saying "Sometimes the minister is a girl," and being open to whatever question comes next.

# Speaking Tradition
## by Leiah Moser

LEIAH MOSER is currently studying at the Reconstructionist Rabbinical College, with a focus on education and congregational life. A passionate believer in the power of traditional texts to speak to the needs and concerns of contemporary life, she is always looking for ways to bring the fruits of Talmud and of Jewish mysticism more fully into conversation with the progressive Jewish communities she calls home. She maintains a blog called *Dag Gadol* ("Big Fish") at http://daggadol.wordpress.com, where she writes about tradition, transformation, and transgender issues in Judaism.

Rabbi Levi bar Hama said that Rabbi Shimon ben Lakish said: "Why is it written, 'And I will give you the stone tablets and the teaching and the commandments which I wrote to instruct them?' (Exodus 24:12) Tablets—these are the Ten Commandments. Teaching—this is the Torah. Commandments—this is the Mishnah. That I wrote - these are the prophets and the writings. To instruct them—this is study. This is to teach that all of them were given to Moses at Mount Sinai." (Babylonian Talmud, Berachot 8a)

What does it mean to speak within a tradition? When is it we ourselves who are speaking and when it is the tradition speaking through us? According to Rabbi Shimon's teaching, all sacred speech—from the Bible itself, to the rabbinic commentaries on the Bible, to our own insights into the meaning of these texts—is somehow contained within the words spoken by God to Moses at Mount Sinai. If at first glance this statement seems paradoxical, the reality Rabbi Shimon is trying to present should be familiar to all of us who try to build our lives within a framework delineated by the texts and rituals of Jewish religion. The confusion we feel upon reading it is at least a homely confusion.

If we take Rabbi Shimon's proposition at face value, then to speak words of Torah is to presume to speak in the name of God. But it is also true that we never encounter the word of God except as mediated through the words and actions of human beings. This is what we mean by "tradition"—the word of God as it lives and breathes within the particular life experience of a community. This means that, while Torah is theoretically all-encompassing, in practice its scope is limited to those experiences we are willing to recognize and address within our communities. At the same time, what we are willing to address is frequently limited by the models we find within the tradition, as well as the language available to us. When we find concepts and experiences playing a central role in our lives for which there is no corresponding language within the tradition, the result is often a crisis of authenticity which, if not addressed, can seriously undermine our sense of connection either to the tradition or to our own truest selves.

I can't help but think of the period immediately before and after my conversion. It's still hard to put into words what it felt like for me to discover Judaism. For what seemed like forever I had struggled with the conflict between the part of me that felt a deep need for the grounding of a critical worldview and the part of me that longed for some sort of spiritual connection with the divine. What I found in Judaism, with its mystics and its sages, its rhapsodic psalms and its exacting chains of Talmudic reasoning, was a place where both these parts of me could finally feel at home. Intoxicated with the tradition within which I had found a home and a language with which to express a hitherto hidden part of my soul, I dove in with abandon. I sought to make myself a mirror, to be totally receptive and reflect back the kind of person I imagined the tradition expected me to be. If following the patterns available to me sometimes meant quietly editing out parts of my identity and pretending they didn't exist, it didn't occur to me at first to be bothered very much by this. After all, I had been editing and pretending all my life, with very little sense that any other possibility was available. It was comforting, at least for a while, to have any sort of pattern on which I could rely as I navigated my developing Jewish identity. I was learning to speak the language of Jewish tradition. Concerning those parts of myself for which no words existed in Judaism, I felt myself bound to remain silent.

The most significant of these zones of silence had to do with the problem of my own gender. Long before converting to Judaism I had been grappling with the problem of reconciling the gender I had been assigned at birth with the lived reality of how I felt and perceived myself in the world. While the problem of my gender did not begin with my conversion to Judaism, it was certainly intensified by the fact that the tradition in which I had found my spiritual home lacked the language to address a conflict that formed a central part of my inner life. Gender is one of the most basic categories of Jewish life, and yet Judaism has no word for "transgender"—or "lesbian" or "gay," for that matter. The modern Hebrew equivalents for these words are adapted directly from English, a fact which has often caused me (and quite a few other religiously engaged LGBT Jews I have known) to feel curiously bifurcated in my identity, struggling to find the queerness in my Jewishness, and the Jewishness in my queerness.

The binary distinction of male and female is built into the language itself, and the assumptions that all Jews are either male or female, that these identities carry with them distinct social roles, and that the relationships between them are patterned according to a heterosexual norm are found throughout Jewish tradition. From the Bible to the rabbis and so on down to our own communities, these assumptions persist. Even as many of us strive to make room within our communities for members who do not fit into the binary, heterosexual norm, we still find it difficult to do so in a way that fits comfortably into the tradition. For most of Jewish history the authority to speak in the name of the tradition was almost exclusively the domain of heterosexual men. When it came to women, a combination of religious law and social custom effectively created a situation in which they have traditionally been seen but not heard, lacking the authority to dictate the terms in which their experience would be described. When it comes to individuals with non-normative gender and sexual identities, an enforced invisibility prevails. We cannot be sure which of our sages fell outside of prevailing gender and sexual norms, but it is clear that, for those who did, the authority to speak in the name of the tradition was only theirs to the extent that these parts of themselves remained safely hidden away.

If there is as yet no authentically Jewish language with which to describe my gender and sexuality, I can at least take comfort in the knowledge that my experience is not all that different from that of Jews throughout history, who faced situations that the tradition as they had received it had not prepared them for. As a Reconstructionist, I am concerned not only with the ways in which the tradition is passed on unchanged from generation to generation but also in which it has grown and changed in order to survive and thrive within a constantly changing historical reality. Just as the sages of the Mishnah and Gemara assumed responsibility for transforming Jewish practice in light of the destruction of the second Temple and dispersion of the community, so too is it the responsibility of every generation to take the tradition in hand and work to make it adequately address the needs of the community. This, for me, is the power of working within a shared tradition—nothing is lost, and the language and concepts of previous generations are shaped and adapted to fit the circumstances in which we find ourselves.

For us, as for Rabbi Shimon, I see the path to transformation as ultimately springing from the creative re-appropriation of language found within the tradition itself. Just as the rabbis turned to the Bible for texts that could be creatively read to provide the basis for a new, post-Temple Jewish society, so too are we free to make use of terms and concepts from the tradition to meet the needs of our own lived experience. Here it seems that in terms of transgender identities the Jewish tradition is singularly blessed. Though adhering to the normative binary of male and female, the sages recognized a number of intermediate or indeterminate categories that challenge this binary while at the same time upholding it.

It is true that these categories, as understood by the rabbis, relate to anatomical characteristics observable upon the body and thus have more to do with an externally imposed system of classification than with the self-understanding of the individual. Nevertheless, it is equally clear that the conditions described by the rabbis under the terms *androgynos* (an individual displaying a combination of male and female characteristics), *saris* (a male who takes on feminine characteristics), *aylonit* (a female who takes on male characteristics), and *tumtum* (an individual whose sex is unknowable because of covered or "hidden" genitalia), do not always clearly or easily map onto real intersex conditions as understood by modern medical science. The rabbis may have been aware of the existence of particular intersex individuals, but the categories they constructed had more to do with exploring the theoretical limits of Jewish practice as it applies to gender than they do with accurately describing individual bodies. It is precisely for this reason that the terms in question are so ripe for re-interpretation in light of the very real need for authentically Jewish language for talking about the full range of gender diversity.

The truth is that in Judaism, the authority to speak has always been manufactured to cope with the matter at hand and then retroactively read back into the framework of what came before. Given the high degree of emphasis placed on continuity within Judaism, successful revolutionary groups (such as the sages of the Talmud) have always found some way to place themselves in the camp of traditional authority and paint their opponents as dangerous innovators. The value of this approach is that it has allowed us to creatively re-appropriate aspects of the tradition that might otherwise have faded into irrelevance. The danger is the tendency to forget that there are moments when the continuity of the tradition can only be preserved through a sincere and open-hearted discontinuity.

What I am concerned with is the difficulty of creating truly new language within Judaism, language capable of giving expression to a fuller range of human experience and bringing it within the bounds of the tradition. If the revelation of the Torah at Mount Sinai truly embraces God's Creation in its entirety, the realization of this ideal is conditional on our ability to make it speak in and through the life of the community, all of it, without exception. According to Rabbi Shimon, *talmud* (study), is an essential part of revelation. As long as some voices are silent, unable, or unwilling to reveal the Torah that they alone are uniquely able to teach, this revelation can only be partial and fragmented. This understanding keeps me embedded even as I struggle to find myself within my tradition. I recognize that as much as I need my tradition and my community to help shape and define myself as an ethical and spiritual human being, so too do they need my own particular contribution in order to become more fully like the transcendent Torah, which shines forth from Sinai without ever fully revealing itself.

# Finding my Faith through Feminist Jewish Values

## by Christine Stone

CHRISTINE STONE is a community activist who champions women's rights and social justice. She current serves on the Board of Directors of the National Council of Jewish Women as the Assistant Treasurer. Christine chairs the National Council of Jewish Women's BenchMark Judicial Nominations Campaign, which focuses on ensuring a fair and independent judiciary.

My chosen Hebrew name is Tzedakah, a Hebrew word literally meaning justice or righteousness. I chose it right after my conversion to Judaism, because it was working for justice that brought me to my Jewish faith.

As an officer on the Board of Directors with the National Council of Jewish Women, I often have the opportunity to live out my Jewish values in public by speaking out on behalf of women, children, and families. Whether invited to the Roosevelt Room of the West Wing, meeting with a senator's staff in their regional office, or working in a coalition with other Jewish social justice organizations, social justice is a part of my daily life. It has been social justice rather than ritual, prayer, or ceremony that has been the ongoing inspiration for my commitment to Judaism.

You could say I took an unlikely path.

I am the oldest of four children. Aside from Christmas trees and Easter egg hunts, religion was almost non-existent.

By the time I reached tenth grade, I was distracted from my AP algebra and physics homework by the television broadcasting the news of the day: the Rodney King beating, the William Kennedy Smith rape trial, and Clarence Thomas's confirmation to the Supreme Court. At the age of fifteen, I could feel the pressure on Anita Hill as I watched highlights of her testimony before the Senate Judiciary Committee on the evening news. I sat on the family couch in the living room, with my homework scattered across the coffee table, I was overcome by a sense of unfairness over how she was repudiated. It just wasn't fair.

It wasn't until I was juggling college courses and seeking a full-time job that I started to connect my strongly opinionated views on issues impacting women with speaking out to make a difference. I was hired to work for an attorney, who happened to be very involved on the national level with the National Jewish Community Relations Advisory Council, known around our office as NJCRAC (pronounced nack-rack). I was intrigued by his work and found a similarity between their mission and my own personal values.

While I was listening in on the attorney's numerous telephone conferences for NJCRAC, members of the law firm were quick to invite me to events at their synagogue or to talk about rituals and routines of Judaism. Starting with the contrast and comparison of Hanukkah and Christmas, the conversations would turn to *Yahrzeits* (Jewish tradition of honoring the deceased), bar mitzvahs, and mohels (professionals who performs ritual circumcisions).

When I met my husband a few years later and he told me he was Jewish, I felt like I already had an Intro to Judaism course under my belt. Despite the pleas from my mother-in-law for me to convert, my soon-to-be husband and I didn't feel it was necessary at the time and a local judge presided over our vows. Knowing that my husband embraced his Judaism in a cultural way—preferring Passover dinners to Shabbat services in the pews—I was very open to learning how to make brisket, recite some basic prayers, and learn a few Yiddish phrases from my father-in-law. And, when our first daughter was born, there was no doubt she would have a *brit bat*, a ritual naming ceremony.

The spring of 2001, my husband and I welcomed our second daughter. 2002 brought politics, faith, and an outlet to speak out publicly. We were in the throes of parenthood, breastfeeding, and wrangling two children in diapers. I was using a contraceptive patch until, as I soon found out, it failed. We did not second-guess our thoughtful yet prompt decision to terminate the pregnancy. Locating a doctor to perform the abortion was quite another story.

By the time I found a physician willing to do the procedure, I was exasperated by the lack of access to my reproductive health care needs. Just a few years earlier, an obstetrician who specialized in high-risk pregnancies like mine was much easier to find. Now, I was calling doctors' offices, explaining how I got their number ("Yes, Dr. So-and-So gave me your number. Oh, you don't perform them anymore? Do you know who does?") while thinking to myself, *the last time I checked, Roe v. Wade was still the law of the land.* I was beyond frustrated.

A few weeks later, I found myself invited to a friend's new home to hear about a Jewish women's non-profit volunteer organization called the National Council of Jewish Women. The local sections of the NCJW are chapters of a national umbrella organization, and there were nearly seventy other young women in attendance. I knew the host from my book club group and I listened attentively to her and the volunteer leaders. After they described a few community service projects, someone mentioned their advocacy efforts and I about fell out of my chair—reproductive rights were at the top of the issues on their list.

After the event started to wind down, I went over to introduce myself to some of the volunteer leaders. While some appeared to be old enough to be my grandmother, I saw their social change work as inspiration for me to act on my recent feeling that "the personal is political."

Soon, I became a member of the NCJW and started getting involved. I initially volunteered for one of the section's community service projects benefitting children and I found out what many of my friends already knew: the NCJW embraces women of diverse backgrounds and temperaments; thinkers and doers who want to play a part at the local, national, and global level. I easily found a community for my feminist values, especially those focused on reproductive choice and advancing the well-being of women.

The NCJW was an early supporter of abortion rights and access to a full range of family planning options. Today, the organization continues to advocate for reproductive health and rights at the local, state, national, and international levels. For the NCJW, ensuring that women and young people have access to reproductive health care, information, and options is a moral imperative and is essential to preserving religious liberty. While opponents of these rights are often motivated by their religious beliefs and seek to codify those views through legislation and public policy, the NCJW believes no religious belief should be imposed on us all. To do so threatens the nation's commitment to religious liberty. The NCJW is committed to the protection of every woman's right to reproductive choices.

As I started using my voice to speak out for reproductive choice, stop domestic violence, and expose the issues of sexual assault and harassment, something very interesting happened. My own commitment to Judaism began to take root. I started to pen op-eds, encourage other members to submit their own Letters to the Editor, and participate in lobby visits.

When speaking with legislators and decision-making bodies, it wasn't enough for me to merely speak in a feminist voice. I knew that through a Jewish lens, the core values central to Reform Judaism gave my voice much more power to effect change. These values allow me to understand *why* I should act to change my world. And as a member of the NCJW, I'm part of a community of women who are inspired by Jewish values to take action when the issues of the day are urgent.

As an advocate for reproductive justice, Judaism informs me that while all life is sacred, the life and well-being of the mother is paramount. When asked by elected officials why the NCJW takes a position on Choice, I can point to our shared values and the textual validation behind them: Judaism places a higher value on existing life than on potential life, and there are even instances when Judaism actually mandates abortions so that women care for their own health above all else.

For example, as we read in Mishnah Ohalot 7:6[1], a woman is forbidden from sacrificing her own life for that of the fetus, and if her life is threatened, the text permits her no other option but abortion. In addition, the Mishnah permits a woman to terminate a pregnancy if the mental health, sanity, or self-esteem of the woman (such as in the case of rape or incest) is at risk due to the pregnancy itself. The need for medically accurate sexuality education and family planning methods would fall under this Mishnah as well.

And, when I spoke out on behalf of the NCJW against City of Pittsburgh police officers who were promoted in the police force despite histories of domestic violence, it was my commitment to Judaism that compelled me to work in coalition with our women's groups to demand an end to this city policy.

The *Sefer Nashim* (Book of Women) includes several passages relevant to the topic of wife abuse. The text reads: "And thus the sages commanded that a man should honor his wife more than he honors himself, and love her as he loves himself. And if he has money, he should increase her benefits according to his wealth. He should not intimidate her too much; he should speak with her gently, and should be neither saddened nor angry."[2]

With so many instances of my Jewish values strengthening my feminist beliefs, I made the decision a few years ago to formally start the process to convert to Judaism. Those who knew of my social justice work with the NCJW knew this commitment was long in the process. For me, it seemed both right and inevitable. It wasn't merely feeling a need to share the religion of my spouse or have a common religion for our family. Judaism led me to live a life where I am able to advocate for my feminist beliefs in a meaningful, rooted way. After a year of classes, study, writing, and meeting with my rabbi, it was time.

---

1. While the Torah is the first five books of Moses and is written on the scrolls that Jews read from in a synagogue, the Mishnah is the first recorded written oral Torah; it is a compilation organized by subject matter.

2. (Mishnah Torah, *Sefer Nashim* 15:19).

I'll never forget the day of the conversion. I was a little nervous as I went before the *Bet Din* (religious court). The three rabbis peppered me with questions, covering such topics as holidays, prayers, and how my husband and I were raising our children. An hour later, I was in the bathroom of a small, nondescript house. Removing my makeup, jewelry, and the dirt from underneath my nails, I was ushered into a room unlike any I had ever seen. The old woman who lived in the house removed a plastic cover from a pool of water. I disrobed and climbed down the steps. She pointed to the prayers taped to the side of the wall. After saying aloud each prayer, I immersed myself three times in the *mikvah* (ritual bath). Each time, she would yell out "Kosher!"

Later that evening, during Shabbat services, I was on the bimah for a public ceremony for my conversion. Behind me on the Ark (a cabinet) sat the beautiful Torah scroll, containing the words that make my values more sacred. As a social activist, I'm reminded daily that in those scrolls are the words that give power to my voice as a Jew and as a feminist. As a Jew, I know there is a spiritual connection between my Hebrew name (Tzedakah) and my soul, providing a path in life.

# Blind Faith Has No Reward
## by Zareen Jaffery

ZAREEN JAFFERY is a writer and editor who lives in New York City.

The first time I was hit on by a man, I was twelve years old. One Friday night, my mother asked me to run in to the A&P to get laundry detergent while she waited in the car. In the checkout line behind me was a group of guys—I remember at least three—who were buying cases of beer. I assumed they were in college. Clearly, at least one of them was over twenty-one. They struck up a conversation with me about the size of the laundry detergent container I was buying (I was one of five kids, so my family did a lot of laundry). They just seemed silly.

Then one of them said they were on their way to a party, and that I should come with them. I don't remember exactly what I said beyond a version of "no thanks," but I remember clearly the way my heart sped up. I was afraid, suddenly, of these men, and their interest in me. I continued smiling and being polite. I don't know how old I looked to them. I do remember they followed me out of the supermarket, trying to convince me to join them, and how I ran to my mom's car. Worst of all, I remember getting on the phone with my best friend that night, and telling her what happened, leaving out my reaction.

Why? Because, in the safety of my home I felt like something good had happened to me. On the precipice of adolescence, I had been deemed worthy of male attention.

I suppose it is no surprise I felt this way. Whether a boy, or boys, liked you was what most of the girls I knew talked about, and judged one other by. The magazines I read featured articles like "Clothes guys love" and "What guys think of girls who have sex." Even though dating was off-limits for me as a Muslim, this belief that "what guys think" mattered most had been drummed into my subconscious.

Being Muslim has come easy to me, in the way that religion does when you are born into it. My parents are from Pakistan (officially the Islamic Republic of Pakistan), and immigrated to the United States in the 1970s. My siblings and I were born and raised in Connecticut and attended Catholic school. This forced my parents to teach us Islam by comparison, and our religious education was marked by active discussions. This ethos allowed for doubt. Only by asking questions can we arrive at the truth. My parents of course didn't always have the answers, and as we got older we had to seek them out on our own—from scholars, from books, from debates with other Muslims. Intellectual curiosity is encouraged for both sexes, not just in my family, but in Islam.

Muslims make up nearly a quarter of the world's population, and we practice Islam in various ways. Owning a Muslim identity simply requires belief in one God and the teachings of the Prophet Muhammad (PBUH). Everything else is subject to individual interpretation—be it through personal reading of text, reliance on a certain scholar, or via familial or cultural filters. Islam is not a monolith, despite what the media would have people believe. We do, however, need to work on being more accepting within the Muslim community. Certainly, how one practices her religion should be a private matter, but too often, as it happens in religious and social communities, deviations from the established majority leads to judgment and gossip. Muslims are as human and flawed as everyone else.

Becoming a feminist was difficult. Or rather, claiming my feminism was difficult.

When I was a kid, I thought being a feminist meant shouting at men and having lax attitudes about personal grooming. I had no interest in joining that club.

The aversion I felt was transitive. What young heterosexual girl wants to align herself with a group that is proudly unattractive to men? We were told, explicitly and implicitly, that girls who were worthy of love were the sweet ones, the beautiful ones. (Add to that the ideals of my parent's Pakistani culture: the shy and modest ones). To identify myself as a feminist was to make myself unlovable. In short, I had internalized the male gaze.

What I didn't know was that I had feminism wrong. This realization has come to me later in life, and was sparked by seeing the damage being done to women around the world under the guise of "protecting" them. This form of "protection" is seen via practices such as forced marriage (Pakistan), or denying women agency over their own body's reproductive health (United States). All that is required to claim feminism is the support of women's liberation. To borrow a definition from bell hooks, "Feminism is a movement to end sexism, sexist exploitation and oppression." Who wouldn't stand in support of that?

In order to talk about being a Muslim feminist, I need to dispense with a few misconceptions.

Contrary to what some feminists believe, being a Muslim feminist is not an oxymoron. Islam is not a misogynist religion. The hijab is not inherently a form of oppression. In fact, it can be a source of liberation in that for some women it is a way to make public their desire to please God before their desire to please man. (While the hijab doesn't protect women from harassment, it can be a way for women to reject the male gaze, and therefore a feminist act in itself.) Muslim women do not need to be saved from themselves. Telling women how to think is a form of oppression, and some feminists are guilty of this.

Contrary to what some Muslims believe, being a Muslim feminist is not a misguided attempt to be more like men. Nor is it an admission that Muslims require feminism because Islam doesn't provide these rights. Islam has granted women equal rights with men, and was progressive in doing so.

So what does being a Muslim feminist actually mean? I define a Muslim feminist as someone who acknowledges that Islam accords humans equal rights, but sees that society the world over is not following suit, and fights to gain those rights back. It requires action, not simply belief. (To use maybe a bad analogy, just because I buy organic, sustainable foods, I am not automatically a food activist.) Men can be feminists, too, because it's not about gender, but how you behave, and whose voices you promote.

It is impossible to escape sexism in the world we currently live in. Like all women I know, I have been sexually harassed more times than I can count—in the United States, in Pakistan, on my travels through Europe and South America. There is literally no place on Earth that feels safe from the unwanted attention of men. This has nothing to do with perceived attractiveness, and everything to do with power dynamics. Men who act this way behave badly because they can get away with it. Women will be blamed for inciting the unwanted attention (What was she wearing? Why was she alone? Was she asking for it?)

I know that I have been lucky. There are too many women and girls who suffer not only verbal abuse, but physical violence on a daily basis. They are denied an education, access to healthcare, the dignity of having their thoughts and opinions heard.

Now that I have nieces, I think about the society they are inheriting. In 2014, women are still accessories in a male-dominated world.

When it comes to marriage, it seems true partnerships are rare, and that many women (Muslim and non-) turn to marriage to ensure their own financial or physical safety. Women get harassed when they are alone or with other women, socially enforcing the belief that we need men to be safe. In the workplace, we pay men significantly more than women, providing a reason for women to stay dependent on men. Wouldn't it be better to join in marriage as equal partners?

Islam grants women a say in all matters, control of their own finances, and the freedom to choose their profession. How can we accept the status quo knowing this?

Women deserve respect even in the absence of marriage. Women are human beings with a full spectrum of emotions and desires and aspirations. We should be given the opportunity to seek an education, to make full use of our intellect, to make our own choices. Why should we let a patriarchal society take away what God has granted?

Dismantling this male-dominated system does not require the denigration of men. There are men who are advocates of justice; feminists in actions, even if they don't label themselves as such. Muslims look to the Prophet Muhammad (PBUH) for guidance on how to live. We have an incredible example of marriage and female leadership in his wife, Khadija (RA). Despite the fiercely patriarchal society she lived in, Khadija was a successful and well-respected businesswoman. Our beloved prophet's love for his strong, successful wife runs contrary to my younger self's internalized belief that strong women were unattractive to men. Their example is a worthy one.

There are Muslims who twist Islam to promote the oppression of women, and this is a terrible perversion. The Qur'an calls for Muslims to treat every human with dignity. I question anyone who suggests we treat each other otherwise.

We are all at different points in our journey, and for this reason it's important not to judge others. We must share our stories, resist and speak out against oppression, and lend a hand to those who need it. Since I make my living as a children's books editor, I am keenly aware of the impact sharing stories can have. Being an advocate for diverse voices and stories is an important part of my life as a Muslim and a feminist. Additionally, as someone who works with and appreciates literature, I know this for sure: There is a reason for all that God does, and the fact that the Qur'an is written in lyrical poetry is no mistake. Art is a bridge between people, making us feel less alone. Art speaks directly to our soul, and the Qur'an is no exception. It is the highest form of art. What better proof that Muslims are meant to find comfort in their own creative endeavors? Art has the power to change minds, and I am thrilled whenever I see Muslim feminists owning their voices and telling their stories.

In the most basic sense, I am Muslim because I love God. And Islam requires Muslims be advocates of justice, which includes the fight against gendered inequality.

I will not pretend to be a scholar of either Islam or feminist ideology. I am imperfect in both respects. I am imperfect because God has made us imperfect, and there is beauty in this. There will never be a point in life where we've learned everything we need to learn. To experience the blessing of every new day is an opportunity for growth and enlightenment.

I pray that God increases my knowledge with each year, gifts me with an open mind and an open heart, and the strength to stand up against injustice, including harm done to women. My faith is not passive, it is dynamic, rising to meet me for strength and comfort wherever my life leads.

In the end, perhaps it would be truer to say: I am a Muslim, therefore I am a feminist.

# Tilling the Soil of Faith
## by Mihee Kim-Kort

MIHEE KIM-KORT is an ordained minister in the Presbyterian Church. She is the staff person for the Presbyterian campus ministry at Indiana University in Bloomington, Indiana. You can connect with Mihee on her website http://miheekimkort.com or on Twitter @MiheeKimKort.

"That same day Jesus went out of the house and sat beside the lake. Such great crowds gathered around him that he got into a boat and sat there, while the whole crowd stood on the beach. And he told them many things in parables, saying: 'Listen! A sower went out to sow. And as he sowed, some seeds fell on the path, and the birds came and ate them up. Other seeds fell on rocky ground, where they did not have much soil, and they sprang up quickly, since they had no depth of soil. But when the sun rose, they were scorched; and since they had no root, they withered away. Other seeds fell among thorns, and the thorns grew up and choked them. Other seeds fell on good soil and brought forth grain, some a hundredfold, some sixty, some thirty. Let anyone with ears listen!'" (Matthew 13: 1-9, NRSV).

The lectionary for today was on the parable of the sower.

As an ordained minister and associate pastor at two churches for seven years, I often preached monthly, sometimes twice during the summers, and I would prepare sermons the night before with a ferocious urgency. Even though I had a whole month to lay down seeds for the sermon, I felt desperation was good for the creative process.

Like a refining fire, it helped to eliminate the unnecessary dross and dribble from over-thinking the twelve-minute proclamation that would likely go over the heads of many of the listeners.

While I'm not currently serving a church, I try to keep up with the Revised Common Lectionary, which many pastors across denominations use as inspiration for their weekly sermons. This includes my husband, Andy, who is the senior minister of a church where he preaches every week. We have conversations about his sermon before and after, and I often tweet my reflections during his preaching of it Sunday morning.

I missed this morning's service. However, I did read his sermon the previous night, and I recall seeing tweets about it a couple of weeks ago. A few of us got caught up in #3wordsermons, and it was a lovely exercise in engaging the passage. My favorites include:

> Always dig deeper.
> Rocky soil abounds.
> Throw seeds irresponsibly.
> Green thumb unnecessary.
> Sun, water, darkness.
> God loves dirt.

I'm no master gardener. But I do dabble a little in coaxing vegetable plants to yield Korean peppers, cherry tomatoes, and the hardier herbs. It's in my blood. We've always grown up with makeshift gardens, and my parents continue to do so today. They love to give me updates on just how big their harvests are week by week.

I love it, too.

While we talk about the plants and the size of the vegetables, we also talk a lot about soil—what it means when the ground is hard like clay, the kind of fertilizer to use, and how much water and attention is needed in those cases. What it means when there are a lot of weeds, and how much work it is to safeguard the nutrients essential for the plants. What it means when some plants grow quickly, and some never make it. What it means to till the soil each year, and how preparing the soil is a part of each new season. I think of my own faith, and how much the soil has changed over the years, and particularly in the last ten to fifteen years with seminary, marriage, ministry, and raising a family. I think of what it means that God loves dirt, and is in it right there with me.

Growing up in a traditional Korean home and being Korean meant just as much as being Christian. The roles for men and women were rigid, as they are in the church. Being a woman, and a young one, put me barely above infants. But, my conversations with my father were often quite open. Oddly, it was my father—the ultimate symbol of Asian patriarchy—who would make the biggest impact on me concerning my life's work, and in the most surprising way.

When I started my undergraduate studies, I had planned on going pre-med, but I fell in love with the humanities courses. I would never have considered actually pursuing ordained ministry until I had a late-night conversation with my father. He was attending Princeton Seminary at the time and enjoying the classes and community with numerous women who were also studying to become ordained ministers. "Ministers? You mean, preaching in the pulpit? But the Bible says that women are supposed to submit to men…and church leaders are supposed to only be men; I can't imagine a woman being able to do it! That just sounds wrong," I said.

I argued with him over the phone and we went back and forth.

With conviction he told me stories of how women had been leaders of the church for a long time, and many were elders in the Presbyterian Church, and were becoming pastors all around him—they had a voice. He admired and respected them, and in fact, he supported them. He reminded me that the first people to preach the gospel after Jesus' resurrection were women. He was even taking a class on feminist and womanist theologies—the same class that would impact me deeply some years later during my own seminary coursework.

Later I would encounter the work of one of my favorite feminist theologians, Serene Jones. She tells the story of sitting on a search committee that was debating whether a woman should be called as the church's next pastor. Some members said women are more nurturing than men, therefore more pastoral and better listeners. Some thought a woman minister would be better with the children in the congregation. Others said having a woman as a minister would make a difference in a negative way, although they couldn't really articulate how. One member said, "It's just not the same."[1]

I started to see the kind of struggle I would face in pursuing this vocation. While my father was hopeful and optimistic, as a pastor's wife, my mother did not hesitate to share the countless hardships she experienced alongside my father. Unlike my father, she had no say in church matters. My mother never minced words when it came to talking about the difficulties of ministry as she watched my father enter into it as a second career. Still, I knew I wouldn't be alone, and that she would be supportive.

My father encouraged me: "And, you can be a leader, too, an elder, a pastor, anything you believe God is calling you to be in your own life," he said to me. "God can speak to you through your dreams. Sometimes those dreams will surprise you. But, don't let anyone tell you what you can or cannot do for God's kingdom." I think of his words often, and how much they changed my life. My father spoke of his Christian faith, his belief in God's provision and will, that led him to pursue the vocation of ministry, and to feel convicted to support my pursuit of ministry. This conversation not only shaped my faith, but my life, my ambitions, and my dreams. As I thought about the kind of parent I longed to be to my own children, I thought of the soil that needs to be laid down for them, and of the changing soil in my own life.

After a struggle with infertility that shook but strengthened my faith, we had twins. Becoming a mother, once again I had to till the soil of my faith. What was there needed to be broken up and loosened in order to plant new seeds for the season of life I entered: a mother, a pastor, and a writer. I became a mostly stay-at-home mother, and it was much different from what I envisioned my life would be as a minister and parent. Yet, even throughout the haze of new babies, lost sleep, and the physical grind of raising children, I found that

1. Serene Jones, *Feminist Theory and Christian Theology* (Minneapolis, Minnesota: Augsburg Fortress, 2011), 22-23.

this time was rich with meaning for me as a woman seeking to work for social justice and bring God's kingdom to bear in this hurting, hungry world. At every turn I slowly began to see the ways this time would contribute to my development as a pastor, and as a person of faith. It was in the soil of my Christian faith that I felt the ability to struggle and question what it meant to be a woman, a clergywoman, and a person of faith. The soil was never perfect, never free of rocks or weeds, but it was enough to allow seeds of hope and joy, goodness and faith, to take root and cultivate a spirit of resilience in me. It was and is enough to continue to give me what I need in terms of community and a gathering of people to work towards justice and equality, love and peace. It is enough for me to press on, and to lay soil down for my children to also plant seeds to grow a faith that will hopefully help them in their own lives, ambitions, and dreams; but more importantly to live and love fully in the world.

# Do You See What I See?
## by Mariam Williams

MARIAM WILLIAMS is a writer born and raised in Louisville, Kentucky. When not working in the field of social justice research and taking graduate courses in women, gender, and Pan-African studies, she blogs at RedboneAfropuff. com. She can be followed on Twitter @ missmariamw.

I was a twenty-year-old college student the first time I documented my thoughts about feminism and Christianity. At a campus-based women's prayer group primarily made up of African American women, we discussed submission in Christian marriage. Some members advocated for women to remain in abusive marriages, and I ran to my journal fuming.

*What twentieth-century, college-educated woman could think this way?* I asked my pages. Why were my peers applying gender expectations from four thousand years ago to modern times and not seeing the Christian man's duty *not* to be violent in the first place? *Obviously they haven't seen what I've seen,* I thought.

I became a feminist the day my Aunt Grace came running to our house barefoot and bleeding from cuts her husband had etched into her face with a knife moments before. My mother and I, plus Aunt Grace's fifteen-year-old daughter, who didn't get along with her stepfather, lived with my maternal grandparents then. My grandfather wasn't home at the time, and knowing his extremely peaceful nature, I doubt the scene would have unfolded and shaped me as it did if he had been home. I watched my grandmother pick up the phone; instead of dialing 9-1-1 she called Aunt Grace's home number and unleashed curses upon Aunt Grace's husband. My grandmother said words I did not think she knew and that no eight-year-old should hear. My mother grabbed her car keys and ran out the door, saying she was going to get her sister's shoes and some clothes. My grandmother dropped the phone, ran to the door and called out, "You can't go over there! He's crazy!"

My mother stood sternly in her five-foot frame and responded, "I ain't scared of no man." My cousin, who was seven inches taller than my mom and weighed a hundred pounds soaking wet, ran past my grandmother and said, "I'm going, too!"

The situation terrified me, but the strength of these women was staggering. Their united audacity to think that their daughter/sister/mother had a right to be free from abuse—and their fearlessness in defending her—awed me. My mother and cousin returned with the clothes, they tended to my aunt's wounds, and my lifetime of fascination with women's empowerment began.

Now thirty-something, I know that I was also inspired by the immediate shift I saw in my mother and grandmother from church women to cursing, badass superheroes. My mother was the Sunday school secretary in our small, family church; as a child, I would mimic her as she took minutes each week. Her earrings, shoes, and hat always coordinated perfectly with her dress, and she looked poised and beautiful as she stood to read attendance and treasury figures. I loved to watch my grandmother arrange wafers and grape juice on the silver trays she and the rest of the deaconesses passed in front of us children as we knelt at the altar for communion. Like a reflection of their crisp, starched white uniforms, the deaconesses were precise when arranging the trays, but they seemed gentle and loving during the communion ritual, undoubtedly feeling a sense of peace as they watched their descendants symbolically ingest the body and blood of their beloved Jesus. At home I saw my grandmother read from her tattered black leather Bible every day and I frequently heard my mother sing over gospel records. My grandmother and mother weren't perfect, but they were both women of faith who held high level lay positions in our church—and they never demonstrated the meekness and submissiveness many of my peers thought were necessary to be a good Christian wife.

I grew up churched while being raised by fearless, independent women who possessed high moral character and a keen sense of justice and morality. Despite disagreement with some of my college peers over model Christian womanhood, I don't think my experience is uncommon for African American women. We live with and often willingly perpetuate the "Strong Black Woman" myth. The archetypal Black matriarch can rear her children, keep up her home, work long hours outside the home, endure the daily stresses and indignities of racism, and fight injustice alongside men—all while singing a gospel song. Yet, there is also a cultural expectation that Black women endure sexism rather than acknowledge, fight, or even recognize it. And in every city I've lived in and every predominantly or historically African American church I've been to, I find Black American women enduring gender-based oppression from what they are most devoted to: their Christian faith and its institutions.

I see patriarchy at work in the story of Hagar in Genesis 16. My notes from a sermon I recently heard on the subject tell me what I *should* see. As descendants of Africans sold into enslavement, I and all African American women ought to feel a bond with Hagar because she is an enslaved Black woman sexually exploited and abused by those in power over her. Although she escapes, an angel tells Hagar to return to her owners. The angel also tells her that she will have a son. Hagar's story should encourage me because it shows that you must face your adversity; God hears our cries; and God knows our future. During the sermon, I could hear the chimes of "Amen," and see the waving of hands among members of the congregation in agreement with the words spoken from the pulpit and written in my notebook; but I thought, *Do you see what I see?* No one else seemed to notice that the angel also told Hagar the world would be against her son and that he would always have to fight. At a time when sons were valued far above daughters, and women had no hope without a husband or son to take care of them, Hagar rejoiced at the gender of her child, nothing more.

In Mary the mother of Jesus, the congregation celebrating the Advent season with me is inspired by the message that God will do miraculous, world-changing things through anyone. For Black women, who are often as demonized now as someone in Mary's position was then, this is a powerful message. God bestowed the highest honor—the carrying of the divine seed, the germination of the salvation of the world—on a poor, unmarried, teenage girl. Most pastors will tell you Mary accepted or even obeyed God with little, if any, doubt or hesitation. "What exemplary faith," other Christians say. But I think, *Hmmm. How convenient that God would choose someone who was not in a position to say no to any authority figure.* "Let it be done to me according to what you have said," says Mary to Gabriel (Luke 1:38, AMP). *The passive voice of an obedient girl*, I say to myself.

Christian peers and friends see God's protection—meaning generous warnings to stay away from what God knows will harm you—and God's requirements for holiness in the marriage and sexual behavior laws in Leviticus and Deuteronomy. They see an opportunity for faithful acts of sacrifice and exercises in self-control when the Apostle Paul implores believers to "flee sexual immorality." *I see* a strict morality code that reduces women's value to their virginity status, breeds secrecy, and contributes to rape culture, unplanned pregnancy, and disease. Purity culture has left me with so much shame about healthy sexual desire that at the time when I should be reaching my sexual peak, I watch otherwise good relationships disintegrate because of a religiosity-induced discomfort with my own body that I have never been able to shake and fear I never will.

Having grown up in the African Methodist Episcopal Zion church, a denomination where there are no restrictions on women's ordination, I didn't encounter sexism the way many women and girls do: by never seeing women at the pulpit or by being banned from preaching in church when called by God. As an adult, I've joined Baptist churches whose pastors supported and encouraged women preachers. My positive experiences notwithstanding, I'm well aware that institutionalized sexism exists within the Black church. Across denominations, female followers support a disproportionately male leadership with their faithful attendance, prayers, and money. Ministries outside of normal service hours push women into traditional roles as wives and mothers, presuming those are their primary desires. Women's bodies are policed routinely; skirts and dresses must be of a certain length for women sitting in the choir stand or on the front pews. If not, an usher will kindly bring her a scarf to drape over her exposed legs.

Although I wrestle with the blatant sexism in the churches I grew up in and attend, I learned something about "the struggle" from the badass women in my family. In the moments after Aunt Grace fled from her husband, my grandmother and mother demonstrated a biblical sense of justice that African Americans have used to push their causes since abolition. Just as I can't forget the shame that strict interpretations of the Word produced, I also can't forget its calls to fight sexism and racism through radical love that shifts priorities from self-importance to servanthood and that equalizes everyone. And as problematic as the image of a strong Black woman singing a gospel song is, I draw strength from knowing I have God and all God's power on my side when I'm doing slow and often thankless social justice work.

I continue to practice Christianity because I still believe. I periodically recite the Apostle's Creed to myself, and I ask myself after each point of doctrine, "Do you really believe that?" And I always answer, "Yes." Singing "Near the Cross" or "The Blood Will Never Lose Its Power" on communion Sunday still moves me to tears because in spite of everything, I still long to be with Jesus.

This said, my practice has changed in recent months. I'm less enthusiastic about Christianity now than I was in my teens and twenties, but it's not a result of biblical misogyny, the church's sexism, or some Christians' racism. It's because joy is elusive in an adult life full of disappointments. Without the joy, the patriarchy is easier to spot and peace is harder to achieve. Since I haven't found like minds in the pews, I work out my issues in my writing and in my independent studies. I boycott my "progressive" church's annual True Love Waits ceremony. I keep my resistance on the low, but express my thoughts through social media. I embrace as truth the parts of the Bible where I find salvation, good advice for living, or liberation theology. I see the rest as a collection of stories of people living in a particular historical time—and I accept that I may need new interpretations to help today's world make sense. Heretical? Maybe, but I acknowledge that reconciliation may be impossible without a little heresy, for to take the Bible literally would mean I was less important than a man, but to abandon it completely would be too great a loss.

# #realtalk
## by Jafreen M. Uddin

JAFREEN M. UDDIN has a habit of turning her hobbies into multiple full-time jobs. She is currently the Events Manager of the Brennan Center for Justice at New York University School of Law; Book Salon Editor for Aslan Media (aslanmedia.com), and Editor-in-Chief of the website Shaadi Belles (shaadibelles.com). She earned her B.A. in Political Economics from Barnard College and Columbia University, and her M.A. in Global Histories from New York University's Graduate School of Arts and Sciences. In her rare moments of spare time, she can be found reading a book, watching an old movie, or dancing along to a Bollywood music video.

As a woman who listens more than I speak, and lives entire lives in the course of a three-minute daydream, the idea of saying *out loud* exactly what is on my mind has always felt strangely foreign. Somewhere between my mind and my mouth, words and thoughts get lost. It's why novels and stories appealed to me from practically the minute I was born. Books were more than words on a page; they were descriptions of settings I'd transport myself to. Characters in each story were people I imagined having my own conversations with—from friends to foes to love interests, putting myself in the story was as much fun as reading the book itself.

And then came the Internet. Somewhere between cat videos and selfies lies a surprisingly thoughtful corner of the virtual world where there are insightful conversations between people from all corners of the planet. Twitter has transformed into a global town hall where a

New York City writer can share thoughts with a photographer from Delhi at the click of a hashtag.

While there is a cloak of invisibility that comes with participating in these online discussions, it's still not enough to take me out of my comfortable and familiar role as an observer. Instead of listening to the words people say, I read the ones that they write, and I craft hilarious and intelligent responses in my head, but I never find the courage to put my own thoughts down for the world to see.

Early in 2014, a Twitter discussion, signaled by the hashtag #IfKhadijaCanDoIt, was as fascinating as it was fast-paced. With a slightly provocative premise and a globe full of articulate Muslim women ready to take it on, the conversation took on a life of its own in no time, with hundreds of women chiming in and participating. As I kept up with the tweets from women all over the world staking their claim on the First Lady of Islam, and looking to her for inspiration rooted in the divine but applicable to a contemporary context, I was struck by how so many of the tweets reflected my own thoughts.

Reality collided with imaginary as the words of these women from around the world easily turned into a script of things I wish I could have said, things I wish I would have thought to say, and things I could only dream of having the courage to say:

To the community leaders who designate the darkest corner of the mosque for the women, *did you know the first believer of Islam was a woman, the Prophet's wife?* #IfKhadijaCanDoIt

To the journalists who devote countless hours of news to the stories of oppressed Muslim women who need saving, *did you know that long before her marriage to the Prophet, Khadija was regarded as a powerful and independent member of society?* #IfKhadijaCanDoIt

To the extended family members whose intentions are good but who can't hide their cringes of disappointment at learning about a woman nearly thirty years old who is still unmarried, *did you know Khadija was nearly forty years old when she married the Prophet?* #IfKhadijaCanDoIt

To the chauvinistic man who believes a woman's place is only at home in the kitchen, *did you know Khadija's business was one of the most prosperous in the region?* #IfKhadijaCanDoIt

To the well-meaning liberal who looks down on a woman who chooses to make her place at home in the kitchen, *did you know that along with managing a successful business, Khadija was also a loving mother to nine children?* #IfKhadijaCanDoIt

As the tweets scrolled in, it dawned on me that in a world where some Muslim women face oppressive hardship every day, I've been blessed with a bubble of privilege, along with a painful awareness of how many people across the world don't share that privilege.

The truth is, my personal feminism doesn't come from my religion. It comes from a set of loving parents who never differentiated between boys and girls. It comes from attending Barnard College, where I met some of the strongest, smartest women I know. The liberation of feminism was ingrained in me from birth, and continues to be a defining piece of my personality and perspective.

Islam has served as a separate safe haven for me, unrelated to my personal feminism. My religion is inextricably linked to the warmth of family traditions and the richness of cultural customs. Growing up in a Bengali family where religion was closely connected to the culture of my parents' homeland meant that in my faith, I found a path that always brought me home.

One of the most enduringly beautiful aspects of Islam is how it guides each of its believers in different ways. Each of the women responding on Twitter from a different corner of the globe had a context and perspective on religion that was unlike the woman tweeting before her. I may not have found my personal feminism within the context of Islam, but as I quickly learned from Twitter, there were plenty of women across the world that had. And that's just the tip of the iceberg when it comes to the interpretation and perspective of Islam each believer chooses for herself.

The lessons I've learned from my faith are likely to be entirely different from those learned by another woman in another place. My lessons were learned in the only way I've ever really known. By listening. By watching. By observing.

And so the imaginary scenarios continued to play out in my head. Strong Muslim women from across the world were writing out a script of responses I would always have at my fingertips, so that if I did find myself in the middle of a conversation about feminism and faith that suddenly took a politically hostile turn, I would have an arsenal of articulate responses.

And then reality woke me up.

Just as fast as the empowering discussion about the role of women in Islam had cropped up, so did the backlash. Commenters chimed in with their thoughts on putting Khadija on a pedestal. Others saw it as an opportunity to draw unfair comparisons between modern Muslim women of today and the leading female figure they were finding inspiration from. The commenters did not mince words, twisting the discussion from #IfKhadijaCanDoIt to #KhadijaCanYouCan't. The women participating were publicly reprimanded, accused of having the arrogant audacity to compare themselves to Khadija, and told that the pious pedestal built by our Prophet's wife was not one for them to reach. It was astounding how quickly reverence for the Prophet's wife was misconstrued as something shallow and ill-intentioned. What started as a dynamic and thoughtful conversation quickly devolved into a nasty exchange of barbs.

The thing is, when you make up conversations in your mind, you tend to leave out the bad parts.

The same cloak of invisibility that empowers smart and insightful people to write words they might otherwise be unable to say out loud also allows hateful and negative people to retort and insult at will. Unlike the safe haven of the imaginary conversations in my mind, the real world (even the virtual one) is filled with as many people who frustrate and denigrate as ones who inspire and uplift. The power that came with a global group of Muslim women staking claim on an empowering hashtag was unfortunately tied closely to the risk of being open to criticism and negative commentary from people less informed and more hateful. Watching the discussion unfold, from its inception, to the backlash, to a dialogue that engaged as much as it enraged, was a real-time tutorial in the consequences—both good and bad—of turning Twitter into a global town hall.

And then, as quickly as the whole thing had started, it died down. That's the other thing about the Internet—you're only interesting and topical until you aren't. Another discussion, another hashtag, and suddenly, an emotionally-charged conversation abruptly comes to an end.

But when you're in your head as much as I am, the conversation lingers. And this one certainly did, as it reaffirmed what I subconsciously already knew about my beliefs as a Muslim feminist.

Whether it's an ignorant journalist on Fox News or a chauvinist cleric misguiding the community, Muslim women are often talked more *about* than talked *to*. For a community of Muslim women craving to have their voices heard, an open forum becomes more than an invitation—the chance to speak out becomes salvation. The isolation that comes from not being heard can be suffocating, making the empowerment found on the Internet particularly potent for Muslim women.

Some people think being a feminist means being the loudest person in the room. But what about the women who don't want our voices to be the ones heard? What about the women who believe that other women say it a lot better than we ever could?

If hashtags like #IfKhadijaCanDoIt teach anything, it's that there is space in Islam for Muslim women to make their mark in the world—starting with the Twitterverse and working our way out to the wider universe. It means there's also space for Muslim women to take the risk of being confronted by commentary that isn't pretty, and face it head-on. But perhaps more significantly, with role models from Khadija to my new favorite *Muslimah* (Muslim woman) on Twitter, the inherent nature of online discussions teaches that not every feminist necessarily needs to be heard. And that's not a bad thing. A dynamic and diverse Muslimah community online means that there is space for women who jump at the chance to speak out, and there is space for women who choose to stay out of the limelight. We're all still connected.

For better or worse, there are a lot of things that have been born out of the Internet. One thing that I never expected to find is a Muslim girls' club filled with women I learn from, and with, every day. Women who empower and inspire. Women who are as brilliant as they are hilarious. It's a club where the girl who imagines her response to a bully has a standing membership right alongside the one in combat during a Twitter discussion. It's unequivocally one of the reasons I stay.

# Owning My Voice
## by Rabbi Rebecca W. Sirbu

RABBI REBECCA W. SIRBU is the Director of Rabbis Without Borders at CLAL – The National Jewish Center for Learning and Leadership. Rabbis Without Borders stimulates and supports innovation in the rabbinate. In 2013, Rabbi Sirbu was named as one of the most inspirational rabbis in America by *The Jewish Daily Forward* newspaper. She speaks and writes about Jewish life, health, healing and spirituality. A Phi Beta Kappa graduate of Vassar College, she holds a master's degree and ordination from The Jewish Theological Seminary of America.

Entering rabbinical school when I was twenty-two, I quickly learned that I was not just like every other rabbinical school student; rather, I was a "female" rabbinical school student. This colored everything. Though clearly female, I had not been labeled a "female" anything before.

I grew up in a setting where I was encouraged to do whatever I wanted. There were no doors closed to me and nothing I could not achieve if I set my mind to it. My undergraduate experience at Vassar College deepened this approach to the world. Formerly a women's college, Vassar had a proud feminist history. As students, we quickly learned to refer to ourselves as "women" instead of "girls" and to use our own voices and power.

In this atmosphere, I took several Women's Studies classes, and initially focused my history major on African American studies. By sophomore year, however, I realized that while these courses were interesting, I wanted to learn more about my own people, the Jews. I soon discovered Jewish feminism and read everything written by the first wave of Jewish feminists, Judith Plaskow, Paula Hyman, and Rachel Adler, to name a few. I fell in love. I connected to the passion these women had for Judaism, their love of the inherited tradition, and their desire to make it better by including women's voices in the vast array of literature, prayers, and legal arguments.

Like these women, I felt inextricably bound to Judaism. Having grown up Jewish in a very Christian environment in Texas, I was often in the position of having to explain my religion to others, and answering questions about Judaism became second nature to me. While my family's observances were considered strange by others, I loved Hanukah, Passover, and the other holiday celebrations. They were warm family gatherings. By observing them, I felt connected not just to my family, but to a larger group of people spread around the world. I also had a deeply personal relationship with God, though I did not have the language to explain it at the time. When I read the work of the women who were applying feminist thought to Judaism, I immediately identified with their questions, struggles, and ideas. I loved the idea of inventing new rituals and practices that were geared towards women. I loved the idea of reclaiming the stories of the matriarchs, not as minor figures but as pivotal characters in the Bible. I was so moved by what I was reading that I began to consider becoming a rabbi. I wanted to be like these women. I wanted to be at the forefront of reinterpreting Judaism for a new generation.

After writing my undergraduate thesis on the history of Jewish feminism, I naively thought the transition to rabbinical school would be an easy one. I expected to enter a world where I would be embraced as an equal partner in exploring the richness of Jewish tradition and making it come alive for a new generation. The school I was attending had been ordaining women rabbis for almost ten years when I arrived. Because I was so immersed in my own world where I took feminist thought for granted, I forgot that ten years in the history of a religion like Judaism was like the blink of an eye. I was ready to be a rabbi, but the world I was entering was still getting used to the idea.

Reality hit like a slap in the face in September of 1994 on my first day of rabbinical school. At orientation, a rabbi, who was one of our teachers, stated that, "More important than anything you learn here is that you get married and have babies." Though this was said to the entire gathering, male and female, my jaw dropped. Marriage? Babies? They were the furthest things from my mind. I was there to learn, to study, and to start my professional life. I would soon learn that the pressure to marry and procreate while still in rabbinical school is huge, particularly for a female student. Who would want to hire an unmarried rabbi? Furthermore, who would want to date a female rabbi? We were odd creatures, somehow outside the natural order of things. My independent feminist sensibilities were out of sync with this new religious world I had just joined, where marriage and family were paramount.

Then, in my very first Talmud class, a student asked the professor how long our term paper should be. He replied, "Like a woman's skirt, long enough to cover the subject, but short enough to be interesting." Again, my jaw dropped. It was clear I was not at Vassar anymore, where a comment like that would get a professor fired. No one said a word. In fact, some students even laughed along with the teacher.

My mind could not stop whirling. I had arrived at rabbinical school ready to study a tradition I loved, and from the first day I felt alienated and different because I was a woman. This feeling continued when I applied for a job teaching afternoon Religious School. In the interview, the male principal told me I was wasting my time in rabbinical school. "Just get a master's of education," he said. "You are only going to want to work part time teaching in a Hebrew school once you have children anyway." I felt like I was in a time warp and had landed in 1950. On top of all of this, as I delved more deeply into Jewish texts, their patriarchal structure and misogyny only became more clear and frustrating to me.

By the beginning of the second semester, I seriously considered leaving rabbinical school. After confiding my thoughts to a professor, things went from bad to worse. His reaction to my wanting to leave school was to shower me with attention, and not the good kind of attention. The kind where he showed that he thought so highly of me, he wanted to sleep with me. I was horrified, and had no idea how to react. Luckily a male student heard an exchange and told me that I should tell the professor to stop. Thankfully, the student's words kicked me into gear. I told the professor to stop. He denied any wrongdoing, and told me I was crazy to think he was out of line.

Emotionally and spiritually, I hit bottom. I was so conflicted. I spent hours crying in my room. I couldn't eat because my stomach was constantly in knots. Entering rabbinical school, I had such high hopes. I wanted to feel close to God, to learn the sacred texts of my tradition, to learn how to be a good leader. Instead I felt debased. My worth as a woman centered on my physical appearance and my marriageability. Somehow my brain and my identity as a full, complex person had gotten lost in the span of six months. If this was what it meant to be part of a religiously observant world, to be a rabbi, then I wanted no part of it.

And yet . . . and yet . . . the desire to learn more about Judaism was still there. The idea of creating new Jewish rituals still thrilled me. The urge to bring new life to an ancient tradition captivated my imagination. Despite everything, I was not ready to walk away. I still wanted to be a rabbi. The question then became, if I was committed to the end goal, how was I going to get through five more years of rabbinical school? First, I decided to transfer schools. There was no way I was going to remain where I was. Next, I sought out support from other female rabbis. This was far harder than I anticipated. Unlike the female bonding I experienced in college, the first generation of women rabbis were not a sisterhood. There was no network set up in my movement for women to support each other. I did find an online listserv open to students and joined that. I also reconnected with friends I had lost touch with over the years. Then, I kept my eyes on the prize and kept moving forward.

At my new school, I quickly organized a monthly gathering for female students. While some of the women did not share my feminist consciousness, and left the group because of it, I did manage to create a small but supportive group for myself. Having other women to share the struggle with meant the world to me. I don't think I would have made it through school without them. This group alone made the environment more bearable, but the new school was far from perfect.

When I organized a special morning prayer service which used female God language, I was told by several professors after the service, "That was interesting, but don't do it again. You can't stray that far from the tradition." I was disappointed, but not crushed. I was learning the limits of what I could do in the seminary community, and was beginning to understand that my creativity would have to unfold elsewhere. I spent my time outside of class exploring Jewish life in New York, which was rich and varied. I experimented with different pedagogic methods while teaching Hebrew School and tutoring, and discovered that God came alive for me when I worked as a hospital chaplain. In a hospital room, I could freely pray with patients using words that were current, meaningful, and chosen for the present moment. Here, I could finally be the kind of rabbi I dreamt of being.

With each passing year, I spent less and less time at the seminary. I learned that I needed to take the education the seminary offered, but nurture myself and my ideas in other settings. Luckily the more time I spent working and exploring the kind of rabbi I wanted to be, the less my being a woman seemed an issue. While I still encountered sexist comments from time to time, I realized that if someone did not want a "woman rabbi" then I was not the rabbi for them. There are more than enough people out there for whom my being a woman and a rabbi was not an issue. These are the people that I want to serve.

I have stayed deeply entrenched in the Jewish world despite the hardships I encountered because I fully believe that there is room for me and my beliefs in Judaism. Judaism is an expansive religion that has continued to evolve over thousands of years. It is meant to be lived, challenged, and adapted. It is not static. Throughout my journey in the rabbinate, I have always felt that God was with me. God created me as a woman, and does not see me as any less than a man. I fully believe that the gender inequality that exists in our tradition is because of patriarchal systems created by men, not God. We are at a point in our history where we are correcting these systems by adding women's voices and leadership. I continue to want to be a part of these new voices.

# Finding My Identity in Solitude
## by Laila Alawa

LAILA ALAWA is the founder and president of Coming of Faith LLC, a social enterprise devoted to redefining the faith narrative of Muslim American women through storytelling and community engagement. She is a jewelry designer and owner of Lilla Stjarna, a handmade jewelry business that sells internationally. Laila also works as a Communications Associate at KARAMAH: Muslim Women Lawyers for Human Rights, an educational nonprofit focused on working for human rights issues both domestically and internationally. She writes regularly for the *Huffington Post*, Religion Dispatches, AltMuslim, PolicyMic and *The Islamic Monthly*, among others. Laila is also an associate editor at *The Islamic Monthly*. She previously worked at Princeton University, conducting a study on Muslim American perceptions of belonging. Laila is also a Fellow with the American Muslim Civic Leadership Institute. A Wellesley College alumna, Laila is based in Washington, DC, and works toward bettering the Muslim American experience for both Muslims and Americans at large.

I am the product of two traveling souls who were not really accepted by the communities they called their own: my Danish mother grew up fierce, agnostic, and popular until the moment she accepted Islam, at which point she was promptly alienated from her high school community. My Syrian father left his family and home because he chose to study engineering, a career path that was punished by his dictatorial government with forced enlistment and service in the army. My parents found each other through a family falling apart and another coming together: My mother's Syrian father divorced his wife and brought my mother along with him to find him a new one in Syria—where she found my father at the same meeting my grandfather found his wife. After a courtship of many years, my parents married and moved to Japan. I was born shortly thereafter.

My parents believed in the power of community. That didn't always mean that community believed in them. This sense of standing alone—of being without community—would profoundly impact my life as a Muslim woman as well.

The bonds my family formed amidst the scattered groups of Muslim immigrants and students in our town in Japan were tenuous, slipping softly apart upon graduation or inevitable job offers. Losing community members was an unspoken understanding, one I couldn't truly fathom until at age five I lost my best friend to his family's career change and move. So when a few months later, in 1997, my mother broke the news to me that we were moving to America, I was wracked with sadness at losing the chance to become a part of the developing kindergarten community but enveloped in resignation that change was natural.

I spent two years in the public school system. Being Muslim was a source of fierce pride for me, expressed through my careful explanations of Ramadan to my friends and my frequent prayers in the corner of the classroom. One day, my friends stopped speaking with me, which led to my being taken out of the school and homeschooled.

I thought this sudden alienation was my fault, and internalized the need to please people until, years later, my Mama revealed that my friends stopped talking to me because they had found out what Muslim really meant: a Danish woman wearing a white headscarf, picking up her loud, big-haired daughter from school. Their parents told them not to talk to someone like me. My mother failed to tell me for as many years as she did because she thought it simply wasn't relevant to the life knowledge I needed to know—a thought that was further from the truth than she could have realized.

Instead I looked for community elsewhere. I tasted pieces of it in the occasional neighbor or homeschool friend, people who had space for me to be myself. These tastes were never truly enough, and I never grew comfortable with the notion that I would remain lonely amidst all the friendships in the world.

With homeschooling, my parents set out to instill in us a deep Muslim identity. Every night, my Baba would come to my room, and my sister and I would recite passages from the Qur'an before we could go to bed. I craved a deeper connection with God, beyond the simple melodic recitations, and began making prayers to him in the best way I knew how—through quickly muttered conversational requests. It became a nightly routine for me to ask Him, "Dear God, please keep me on the straight path, keep my family on the straight path, give us friends and happiness and enter us all into paradise please please please *ameen*."

If I said please enough, I deeply believed that He would say yes.

Fast forward to September of 2001. Mama had just had my twin sisters earlier that year. I now had five younger siblings and my father was traveling for a new job. I felt like the patriarch in his stead, fiercely protective of my family. One day, we were in the supermarket and ran into my first grade teacher. She cooed at my twin sisters.

"If you ever need me to help you out," she said to Mama, "I'm here!"

Then 9/11 happened. I remember the alienation, crushing loneliness, and most of all, thinking that my teacher would never want to associate herself with a bunch of "others" like us.

That week, my mother took me and each of my siblings by the shoulders and told us we were the ambassadors of Islam.

I talked to God a lot those days.

I put on my hijab at ten years old, on a bet with my mother I wasn't willing to lose. It was an interaction that was seemingly simple, but was layered with meanings I am still discovering now. My mother, leaning towards me as she pulled the car out following a playdate with my recently hijabbed best friend, said, "I bet you can't cover like Ayonna." Straightforward as the challenge seemed, my stubborn insistence at taking her up on it represented an identity and struggle with being covered that I, at times, cannot truly fathom myself.

So ingrained is my covered identity, that I wonder sometimes who would be left if I were ever to unveil. Yet in that decision, there rests a part of my ten-year-old adamant self, brazen and firm in her under-standing of choice. The decision had been mine to make, and it was made in front of authorities who doubted my capabilities. It remains, at its dusty core, the first expression of my feminism.

Prayer, however, was something that I couldn't truly do for many years.

It was a struggle. In the familial enforcement I found myself re-belling. I didn't want to have my relationship with my Best Friend policed. So I fought back in the best way I knew how: within myself. I went through the obligatory motions of prayer to please my family, but inside I stood up, defiant to the definition of worship they had imposed upon me.

That didn't mean I didn't feel guilty. I knew I owed Him a lot of prayers. Every night, I took the *shahadah,* the Muslim profession of faith, and prayed I would start observing the required prayers soon.

As a young teenager, I began devouring stories of the men and women that lived, breathed and struggled during the time of the Prophet Muhammad (SAW).[1] It was in the raw truths of their stories that I drew my beliefs and principles; truths that I found on my own, not through interpretations colored by the opinions of others.

Having the chance to discover the world of the Prophet for myself was a gift, tenderly handed down in spite of the hubris of "experts" and without the pressure that comes with wrapping stories of his life in principles and propaganda.

My parents only cared that I was learning about my faith and the heritage from which I came, and did not try to force any restric-tive lesson or principle derived from current-day methodology and religious practices. I learned from what I read. I understood what I learned. It was, in itself, the purest form of feminism. Absent was all of the rhetoric one way or another—here and now were the stories in their simplest forms. So it was only natural, in devouring stories about strong female companions and civic equality during the time

---

1. SAW is an abbreviation of the Arabic phrase "salla Allah alaihi wa sallam." Like the English translation "PHUB," it stands for "peace be upon him," a statement of respect used after speaking or writing Muhammad's name.

of the Prophet, that I came to the conclusion that feminism in its very essence was a Prophetic virtue.

I didn't need to hear from others about whether or not he was a feminist. His life and decisions told me so. It was in my passion to emulate those I looked up to most that I undertook the values and principles of feminism to be my own.

It was through my faith that I found feminism, and through my feminism that I discovered faith.

I found myself years before I knew I had: a Muslim feminist firm in her understanding of the world's realities and truths. Self-defined and defiant, I saw the world through an unconventional lens, one that seemed to make the most sense to me—yet didn't seem to make sense to those around me.

In my sophomore year of college, almost ten years after 9/11, my community rediscovered me. I finally belonged somewhere. Before then, I was the odd one out at the mosque, not quite fitting in—the girl you said hi to but didn't really know. But one day, everything clicked. It might have been a combination of my role model trying to include me, the volunteering I had been doing for the center, and people feeling particularly benevolent that day—but I finally fit in.

It was when I finally belonged, though, that I lost a true understanding of who I was in relation to my beliefs on religion and feminism. So eager was I to have found a community, I let the loneliness envelope my being, fogging up the clarity I had found for many years. I was abruptly vulnerable to pressures to conform and silence my true self. Suddenly, I was not making decisions and realizations for my own self. Suddenly, my world was about ensuring that those I believed I was lucky enough to call my friends remained happy. Feminism was that guilty afterthought, niggling at my heart at the end of the day, asking why I wasn't being honest with the world about who I truly was. I was so afraid of losing those around me that I lost myself instead. My heart hurt thinking I might be alone again. Wasn't community something that God wanted for us?

I went about it all the wrong way, yet it was the only way I knew how. The floodgates opened for poorly thought out decisions that I felt manipulated into making. Relationships, friendships, family—I found myself stuck in a voiceless and people-pleasing loop. My power was taken from me, my core was shaken, and the choices I pretended I was making were rooted in what everyone else told me to do. For a time, I traded my real self and my feminist beliefs for the approval of others.

Amid my attempts to fit in, I did rock the boat a few times by expressing my truth as a Muslim feminist. Still, it took several tries and a college graduation before I felt able to fully and confidently be myself. I realized then that belonging didn't really mean understanding of who I was, what I stood for, and where I wanted to be. Amidst the pressure to be a part of the community—a conforming, silencing pressure—I reared up and rediscovered who I was all along.

I found God in the silence of the world. And in that silence, I discovered the truths to my faith, and to my feminism. I paid for those discoveries dearly, with years of sadness from always being on the outside looking in. That is a cost I do not regret paying. Through the silence of my community I gained the voice I still draw upon today, an inner flame that burns bright even while criticism faces me from both Muslim and feminist communities.

If I could have it any other way, I would say no. My strength and identity comes from my history, and my friendship with the One that never left me. I am a Muslim because I believe in a God who accepts me. I am a feminist because I believe in a God who accepts all.

# I am CHURCH
## by Corinna Guerrero

CORINNA GUERRERO is a lecturer in Religious Studies at Santa Clara University and Adjunct Professor of Biblical Studies at the American Baptist Seminary of the West. She is completing her Ph.D. at the Graduate Theological Union in Berkeley, California. Corinna is regularly invited to Bay Area churches to speak on the Old Testament, the formation of the Hebrew and Christian canons, and various contextual and advocacy hermeneutics to meet the needs of churches in the twenty-first century. Corinna can be followed on Twitter @cyguerrero and her current work can be found on Academia.edu at https://gtu.academia.edu/CorinnaGuerrero.

In this essay I spell CHURCH in all capital letters when I am referring to the fullest breadth of participating members of the Roman Catholic Church as the body of Christ. I am visually representing the equity and dignity each participant is owed by the whole, regardless of identity, station, or status.

◆◆◆

As a kid my immediate and extended family traveled a lot. The sport of wrestling was the reason for the family weekend travel schedule when I was ages five through thirteen. In fact, it has long been the dominant family sport on my father's side, a legacy now preserved through my brother. Regular weekend and seasonal travel throughout the year bore many benefits. I saw local, regional, and national landscapes. I wrote essays for school at historical sites. I learned how to be self-sufficient in the world. There was, however, one significant religious shortcoming. One disadvantage of regular travel was that at church, on the Sundays when we were available to attend, I sat on what my cousins and I called "no communion row."

Between the ages of five and thirteen most children raised in a Catholic home are participating in catechism so as to be prepared for their First Communion. It is the day that one declares her or his understanding and belief in the identity, redemptive power, and grace of Jesus Christ as well as the role of the Catholic Church in outwardly mediating said grace. Children are less concerned with the theology of the event and more concerned with two practical aspects: 1) *"finally* gettin' some Jesus"—meaning the Eucharist and wine, the transubstantiated body and blood of Jesus; and 2) finally entering the community as an active participant, part of the body of Christ. Regular travel meant that in a very practical sense I was not present enough at catechism to undergo this rite of passage, this sacrament. I was a member of the Catholic Church, but not a participant.

I sat on "no communion row" until I was eighteen. At every mass I attended, my family or friends who had already made their First Communion would get up, walk to the front of the church, and receive communion. I sat there in the pew with those who had not confessed their sins and found reconciliation, those who were not Catholic, non-Christians, observers, visitors, and those who for whatever reason chose not to receive. It wasn't until I was almost eighteen that I started to discover ways in which people could distance themselves from the Catholic Church (e.g. general teenage apathy and angst) or how people could be distanced from the Catholic Church and denied Eucharist (e.g. divorce, co-habitation, practicing homosexuality, practicing contraception). I suppose from the very beginning my experience of CHURCH was among the "sinners." Now I would identify my "no communion row" brethren as those on the margins, on the edge of coming or going, always one reconciliation away from the embrace of mother Church.

I started university as a systems physiology major and soon realized that the decade plus years that I spent on the forced periphery of conversations and questions about the Church, religion, Jesus, and the Bible simply because I had not yet "made my First Communion" had run its course. More than once, my questions about the intricacies of the Bible as sacred scripture or Mary as the virgin mother of the messiah were met with snappy retorts by family and parishioners. *Who are you to ask questions? Who are you to question at all?* I was told that since I had not even made my First Communion, my lack of full participation in the Roman Catholic Church substantiated this treatment. I know now that to be pushed into the periphery is not the same as being peripheral. My questions were not, as I was led to believe by the disregard of those around me, disrespectful, morally bad, or a sign of little faith. My questions were, instead, the beginning of what would become a lifelong relationship with the Church. I changed my major to comparative religious studies and registered in RCIA (Rite of Christian Initiation for Adults) at the local Catholic parish. I sought answers to my questions.

As it turned out, I did not share the same theological and scriptural questions as my RCIA cohort. Being eighteen at the time, I had no interest in conversations about preparation for marriage, nor the baptism of children. My cohort consisted mostly of those who: 1) were satisfying their sacraments before impending nuptials; and 2) those who already had children and were satisfying their sacraments before their children's impending baptisms. I was uninterested in marriage and had no interest in having children. All I had were my questions.

I can now in hindsight say that my questions were never going to be satisfied because with every question answered a new one would form. *Why do we attend mass on Sunday? How is Jesus fully human and fully divine? Why is the Bible so violent? If Jesus is God, then why did he think God had abandoned him at his crucifixion? What is the virtue of excommunicating members of the Church?* My feelings of frustration during RCIA stemmed from the scholastic limits of the program, not the Church.

It was through undergraduate, graduate, and doctoral coursework that I came to reconcile what had been mistakenly taught to me as two disparate halves of myself, my desire to worship God and my intellectual or academic curiosity. The decision to pursue graduate education in the fields of religion, theology, or biblical studies is often met with hesitation, anxiety, or discouragement by some religious communities. Phrases such as "You'll lose your faith!" or "They'll make you an atheist you know!" are common from one's local communities. As a Catholic woman, my personal favorite is, "Why? Do you want to be a nun?" These sentiments polarize religious devotion and intellectual conversations, making it appear as if faith and intellect are opposites. Although some claim that one should forego intellectual pursuits of religion, in fact, intellect and faith intersect to be mutually informative for religion.

As a biblical scholar and literary critic I am fond of expression; whether that be a narrative plot line, a poetic turn-of-phrase, parable, or metaphor. I like them all, every genre, every literary device. The Bible is, for me, humanity's attempt to express adequately the fullness of the divine-human relationship. This statement in no way means that the text is not inspired. It is. Rather, what it does mean is that I take very seriously the breadth of human experience—for example, joy, praise, sorrow, wrath, devastation, bewilderment, wisdom, yearning, poverty, excess, love, torture, and marginalization. I am as committed to experiencing my own humanity as I am in refusing to look away from someone else's.

My identities as US-Latina, Catholic, feminist, lay person, working-class, and Biblical scholar regularly converse. Sometimes they intersect and create a greater synthesis, while other times they illuminate sharp contrasts. For example, as a feminist I am highly aware that my body is a female body experiencing a world that never ceases to remind me that my body is female. On any given day I am faced with cultural, social, economic, political, and religious media and rhetoric that shout at me a fact that I already know—I am female. However, none of what I just said is a universal constant. First, not all feminists are female. My husband is a self-proclaimed feminist, and was so before we met, before we married, before we created a daughter out of our love. Second, not all women are born with a female body. The transsexual experience of womanhood should not be relegated to a lesser status, because trans women have had to fight for the thing that I cannot shut off—for the world to see them as female. Third, not all women want to be mothers. It is a major taboo in many cultures and societies for a woman to say that she does not want children. In many cases it is presumed that being female, a woman, and a mother are a series of progressive realities that one is biologically determined to desire. It is untrue and does not reflect the fullness of women's perspectives on our own choices for existence. For some women who adhere or desire this progression, it is a choice to become a fuller self. For some women who chose any variation of the presumed progression, a new self-determined paradigm for women forms. Each new paradigm is an opportunity for women and femininity to become more broadly defined and authentically presented in the world.

I am brutally aware of how heart-wrenching and complicated it is to sift through the noise of a world more concerned with defining who and what I am than allowing me to form my own conscious self-definition through education, life experience, family, friendship, and love. In the end, it is my identity as the body of Christ, my identity as CHURCH, to which all my identities reconcile. It is as CHURCH that I find the dignity to persevere in my tradition, faith, work, life, and service despite the constant presentation of a better Catholic Church as a smaller, "truer" Catholic Church.

The Apostle Paul introduced the metaphor of the physical body in his first letter to the Corinthian community to explain the deep respect, value, and indispensability of various members to the community as a whole. He emphasized that it is not those portions of our community that are already given the respect, privilege, and honor due them that are to be highlighted or represent the whole, but those who face the greatest hardship, marginalization, and injustice. In brief, Paul and the Church identify this intersect of parts and wholeness, indispensability and dignity, as "the body of Christ."

As a participating member of the Catholic Church, I, in all my identities, am a piece of this complex. At every mass where I freely and openly receive the Eucharist, I transparently acknowledge my participation with Jesus as Redeemer of humanity, the Church as a beacon of hope highlighting redemption, and my existence as part of the body of Christ. Some days one or more parts of my identities already have the dignity acknowledged by the community. I can walk and be seen by the world around me, be acknowledged, and have my needs be heard by those around me. Other days I am called to be part of the dignity-building of those who walk in the world unseen because others refuse to acknowledge their needs as legitimate, perceive them to be outside of the understanding of the community, or are simply unaware.

As the body of Christ, as CHURCH, we are each called to oscillate between acknowledging our dignity and acting in the service of dignity-building. As a former inhabitant of "no communion row," a Latina, a feminist, a lay person within a religious hierarchy, a contributing member of society always a few paychecks away from poverty, and a scholar of the Bible with a commitment to look humanity in the eye, I can say beyond a shadow of doubt that just because one is pushed into the periphery, the border of exclusion does not make one's circumstances or needs less valuable or less deserving of dignity. In fact, it is the opposite. My experience of church with "sinners," those not walking up to receive communion because they won't or can't, opened my eyes to the opportunity and obligation to act as body of Christ.

Given the struggles that I have within the Church, *why do I remain Roman Catholic?* In brief, my answer is this: I cannot leave what I am. I cannot leave the Catholic Church because in the deepest parts of my theological understanding and devotional existence, I am part of the body of Christ. I stay because my existence and participation is a living testament to the constant commitment we all agree to when we chose to be part of this body, this community. I stay because I agree to look humanity in the eye and build the dignity of others. I stay because I am CHURCH.

# My Weakness is My Strength
## by Elizabeth E. Meacham

ELIZABETH E. MEACHAM, Ph.D., is an Assistant Professor of Philosophy and Religious Studies at Ursuline College in Pepper Pike, Ohio. Her research interests include sustainability justice and ethics, contemplative ecology, religious environmental activism, and applied ecospychology. She also facilitates ecotherapy workshops and performs with her jazz trio, PorchSwing.

A dear friend from graduate school said to me at a recent lunch that her husband doesn't understand why I would practice and raise my children in a patriarchal religion. I know that because I seem progressive in so many ways, my attraction to traditional religion is a mystery to some in my life, not least of which to some of my secular Jewish in-laws. Yes, my children read Hebrew and we unplug on the Sabbath.

Some might say that I have a weakness for religion. I love religion. I love liturgy, ritual, communities of faith in many expressions, the search for meaning, meditation-induced shifts in consciousness, and contact with the divine, which I sense around us at every moment. Sometimes it is a weakness; when I feel spiritually disconnected, I feel lost. But, this love for religion is also my strength. The community, passion, faith, and joy of my childhood experiences with religion set the stage for the journey, strength, and meaning of my life.

All the strongest women in my life have been deeply religious. My beloved touchstone grandmother, Adaline, my father's mother, was deeply religious in a very solid, no nonsense way. As I learned from her, her faith gave her power to persevere. She taught me that "prayer is all a woman might have sometimes." My dad's practical, Christian grandmother, Leona, raised eight children in Northern Wisconsin, carving out a farm from the woods, away from stores and doctors. At five o'clock, standing in my kitchen after a long day of work, facing an evening of motherhood, these women give me strength. Sometimes, while nursing a sick child through the night, or when the overpowering feelings and demands of parenthood weigh on me, I think of Adaline and Leona carving food from the earth for their families with their own hands. I pull their strength to me, a strength buttressed by faith.

Varieties of religious experience permeated my upbringing. When I was six my dad had an encounter with the divine in our small apartment bathroom across the hall from where I slept. As he tells it, calling out to God in despair, God answered in the form of Jesus appearing to him. My dad glowed for days, and, in many ways, still glows today, forty years later. After that experience, he could convince almost anyone that God listens and talks back, that God is an all-loving pervasive presence in our lives. He certainly convinced me.

In the years after his life-changing spiritual experience, my dad taught me how to pray; deeply, and for all kinds of reasons. Though my names for God have changed through different phases of my life, I've never lost the glow of an intimate relationship with the divine passed on to me like the nectar of life from my dad. His profound encounter with God led him to preaching, first as an evangelist in inner city Baltimore, and later in our house church in Iowa, where my parents led prayer meetings in the living room and in the back yard under the spreading shade of a five hundred year old oak. Eventually, my parent's commitment to preaching "the word" led them both to an Episcopal seminary in Virginia, where our family entered a different flavor of liturgy, community, and faith. My mom turned in her backup role strumming an autoharp behind my dad's bible thumping preaching, and embraced her own role of power and leadership; a woman ordained to the priesthood when that was still new and controversial.

During my second year of college, a few years after my parents completed seminary, their marriage broke up while they were working as priests in the same church. At the time, I blamed the politics and institutional dysfunction of "the Church." I felt that the veil had been lifted. I had seen what lay behind "the great Oz"—the awe-inspiring beauty and pageantry of the Episcopal liturgy—and it was not pretty. Eventually, my perception of my parent's divorce changed. Twenty-five years of therapy later, I realize that my mom's untreated mental illness was at the root of my parent's failed marriage and our damaged family. At the time, though, the simultaneous loss of my family, faith, and community was the most difficult thing I had dealt with. My parents both remarried within a year of their divorce. Bereft and disillusioned, I couldn't find my way into feeling like I truly belonged in either of their lives for many years.

When I first met my Jewish husband at twenty-four, I was a bird with a broken wing. He had lost his parents young, so we both struggled with deep loneliness and grief. While I felt estranged from and abandoned by my own family and faith, my new Jewish family accepted me wholeheartedly for who I was. The cycle of weekly and yearly Jewish rituals began to create a rhythm of comfort, meaning, and healing. Family, a new kind of faith, and community began to knit back together for me. During the most painful years of my life, the decade after my parent's divorce, I often went to the woods to write music and soothe my soul. As I sat writing poetry or songs, I began to find ways of knowing and being in nature that brought me to the intimate place with God that I had felt as a child, but with God in a different expression than I had imagined before. I began to glow with the nectar of life on my own, without the aid of my earlier Christian belief structures. Driven by a passionate curiosity to understand and contextualize my spiritual experiences in nature, I went to graduate school to get an M.A. in Philosophy, and then a Ph.D. in Philosophy and Religion. This work to explore and express my experiences of the divine in nature—which I call "ecospiritual"—continues today in my spiritual practice, scholarship, and teaching.

At thirty-five, when my first child was a baby, I made a friend at the local library. Since we were both managing Ph.D. work and small children, we became fast friends, spending long winter days together with toddlers and second pregnancies while navigating the hurdles of male-dominated graduate programs. In the way that mothers follow those they trust, I sent my son to the Jewish preschool her son attended, and learned more and more about Judaism. When it was time for kindergarten, my husband and I visited and fell in love with the Jewish Day School her boys attended. We chose this school, full of art and love, for our children. As it became clear that I couldn't go back to being a Christian because it was too painful, it also became clear that my husband, while open to occasional forays into other religions, would only participate whole-heartedly in Judaism. We already had Shabbat dinner at his sister's house or ours every week; we had been having holidays with his family for years. At the time, I couldn't be with my family for holidays because of unresolved tensions, and their busy schedules on Christian holidays. I didn't want my children to be the only Christians in a Jewish family, and I wanted them to have what was the best part of my childhood: the integration of family, community, and religion. So, I chose Judaism for my children and for myself.

On a frigid night in December 2013, on the full moon, Leona, my dad's grandmother, comes to me in a dream. She is wearing a shapeless dress of prairie calico that matches fabric on an inherited unfinished quilt from one hundred years ago. She looks at me and says simply, "I was Jewish. I assimilated. I never told your grandfather. All the clues are there. If you look, it will be easy to see." Then she pulls a kugel out of her antiquated, wood-burning oven. At the end of the dream she feeds me, speaking fluently in Yiddish that I mysteriously understand.

I wake up disbelieving, my axis tilted. Leona's family came from Germany to North Carolina in the early 1700s, homesteaded Illinois is the early 1800s, then moved to Iowa in the 1850s. These were American pioneers, and as I've always been told, good Christian people—hardy midwestern stock all the way back. At 3:30 a.m., my heart races as I register for a two-week trial on ancestry.com. I look up the one name I remember clearly from our family history, Leona's grandfather, our pioneer ancestor. My dad has traced our roots, and I've seen the names of Leona's relatives before, but only once many years ago. Sleepy, with my mind buzzing in the light of the moon, I can't remember them now. As I search, her uncle's names begin to jump off of my computer screen into the darkness of the room: Solomon, Isaac, Jacob, and David Israel. *So what?* I think. Biblical names were common ("but David Israel? Really?" my friend says over the phone from Israel). Whether Leona came to me, or the dream was a memory of names I had seen long before I understood Jewish naming, my mysterious attraction to the ancient rituals and widely expressed culture of Jews seemed answered for me from that night forward.

Like Leona, all the strongest women in my life knew the Bible and referred to it often. As a feminist, I profoundly honor the religiously inspired wisdom of the women in my family. My own strength and vision as an ecofeminist derive from knowledge gained during hours of prayer and meditation in nature. For me, religion, strength, transformation, and justice go together. For my own family, I actively sought out a religious identity and community. These were the strengths of my own childhood, and I wanted to pass something similar to my children. Yes, when I lost my faith, it became my greatest weakness to wander without it, but that base of religious and spiritual identity also gave me the ground to heal and to rebuild my life.

As I sat in a class on Rabbi Mordecai Kaplan led by our rabbi last year, it came to me that although the religions I know well are distinct in many ways, transformative ideas engendered in the last one hundred years permeate them. Those ideas get translated through diverse religious expression, and certainly we maintain different rituals and traditions over time, but conversation across religious boundaries can share a vision of a global spiritual movement centered on social, economic, and environmental justice. I came to believe that this spiritually inspired, global consciousness of justice is an important part of the evolution of our species. It became more important to me to find a place to plug into the web of community, ideas, healing rituals, and work for justice that this emerging global consciousness represents, than to stick to a specific dogma. I believe that we have an ethical commitment to reconstruct our own traditions to meet the challenges of our time. Practicing Reconstructionist Judaism, I feel very strongly a part of that process of transformation. At our synagogue, women lead services, wear *kippot* (skullcaps) and prayer shawls, and read regularly from the Torah. In 1922, Mordecai Kaplan, the co-founder of Reconstructionist Judaism, had his daughter read from the Torah in the first public bat mitzvah. My children are encouraged to see the world and themselves from a feminist, and ecological, perspective in many ways in our religious community.

The night after the Leona dream, I set the table for Friday night dinner, our ritual to bring in the Sabbath. I set out the candle holders and Kiddush cups of various sizes and materials, made in preschool and kindergarten by my children; the challah with the cloth cover hand-painted with flowers by my daughter; and the small white candles that we use only for Shabbat. I feel joy, connection, and some deep longing answered. My story is filled with love, loss, and a lifelong stream of shared meals celebrating myriad faith traditions. For me, choosing religion is not rational, nor does it feel like a choice. It's who I am. While my story is complex, my answer to people who ask why I practice a traditional religion is simple: I grew up that way.

# Finding My Voice in Prague
## by Talia Cooper

TALIA COOPER is a youth educator, organizer and musician originally from Oakland, California. She is the Program Director at Ma'yan, a Jewish feminist organization that works to empower high school girls and the educators who interact with them. Prior to Ma'yan she worked as Executive Director of Jewish Youth for Community Action (JYCA). A singer since birth, Talia can also be found performing and recording original music as "Entirely Talia."

"Welcome to Prague!" my brother Lev exclaimed. He was finishing up his semester abroad, and my mom and I had determined this an excellent excuse for a vacation. "So what do you want to do here?" Lev asked as we bump-rolled our suitcases along the cobblestone streets. I knew exactly what I wanted to do. But I never thought saying so would lead to questioning everything I'd learned about my faith.

I was born in 1985 to hippie-era parents who had never technically gotten married, but had exchanged found stones at a ceremony of their own creation. Both originally from New York, they'd met at a protest at the Israeli embassy in San Francisco, and built their life there together. As a young girl, my parents read to me from a book of feminist fairy tales. They would say, "Women can be anything they want!" And they did their best to model this statement.

My mother became a cantor and a well-known musician who travels the world singing. She told me stories of being a little girl in

Orthodox New York synagogues, watching the men from her spot in the women's balcony, quietly learning all the music and wishing she could be downstairs where her brothers were. And now look at her! On the bimah itself! Leading the music, sometimes even filling in for the rabbi at her synagogue. Smart woman. Strong Jewish leader.

My father also became locally well known as a Jewish leader, first as the owner of a Jewish bookstore and now as a rabbi at a Jewish Renewal synagogue. My parents both made social change central to their teaching. They brought me to marches and we sang "Study War No More!" in groups of leftist Jews, and women had a majority presence at all Jewish events I attended.

My parents always gave me leeway to make Jewish practice my own. During High Holidays I would listen as my mom's voice broke out from the bimah, demanding a place in the congregants' chests. I learned to harmonize along. Some years I even went up and sang with her, adding a round to the prayer Mah Tovu.

At age twelve I celebrated becoming a bat mitzvah on the 150th anniversary of the Seneca Falls Convention, the first ever women's rights conference in the United States. I heard my voice amplified over the congregation as I sang and spoke. My speech was about the biblical daughters of Tzlofchad from Numbers 27:1-11. I told my congregation that what the daughters did was brave—demanding that Moses and G-d adjust the laws so that they could inherit their father's land. I also explained why I loved Judaism. In my mind, Judaism was flexible. Judaism could make adjustments when injustice was revealed. Women were listened to. That was the leftist movement of Jewish Renewal. That was the Judaism I was raised with.

Despite my upbringing, I remember doubting that my form of Judaism was as valid as older, more Orthodox forms. After all, I knew my parents had learned the more traditional kinds of Judaism in their youth. They'd been taught prayers and laws, halakhic texts, and famous quotes from Jewish scholars. They absorbed all of this deep history and information, and then chose to reject it in favor of their own Jewish path. But I'd never learned the original traditions, only my parents' reinvented version. What if the originals were better? Or more real? What was it that we were rejecting anyway? Did traditional mean more authentic? Superior?

Over time, what started as a pinprick of a question grew into full-body wonderment. Did my Judaism count as real even though it was invented later? And not precisely according to scripture?

So, when I travelled to Prague, I was curious to learn about the authenticity I feared my Jewish upbringing was missing, and I told my brother what I most wanted to do: attend Shabbat services at a synagogue. An old one. I wanted to feel real Jewish history shiver through my veins and maybe even feel G-d in my gut.

My brother hesitated. "You know about the *mechitza*, right?" Right, right, I knew. I'd been to modern Orthodox shuls—with the *mechitza* drawing a straight line down the middle of the room to separate men and women—and I'd felt a comfortable kinship with my fellow female *daveners* (daven is Yiddish for pray). I'd heard stories of my mom's childhood in the balcony. "Well, it's not quite like that," Lev said, and my mom nodded in agreement. They tried to persuade me, telling me this wasn't like other Orthodox synagogues, this was more extreme. My determination was a fist in my chest. So come Friday, we put on our nicest travel clothes and headed to the Altneuschul.[1]

As we walked, my mom battered my brother with questions. My attention would land on their conversation and then flit back to the synagogue. We'd toured some of the old synagogues earlier that day. Growing up, our places of worship were mostly rooms rented in churches with carpeted floors, pillows, and references to Jesus covered with draping fabrics. These Prague synagogues echoed with size, the floors and walls dredged up memories of services, whispers, shuffling, and persecution. Details were etched in the windows and walls. The stones cracked and crumbled but stood tall, and I stood tall within them.

There was a hole in my stomach that needed to hear the cantor's voice blast over these big ceilinged rooms, to hear their Czech accented Hebrew glide through the room and land in our ears, to feel

---

1. The Altneuschul literally means "The Old New Synagogue." It is the oldest active synagogue in Europe, though for a time it was converted to a church.

the wooden benches root me firm in this history, plant me in this Jewish timeline. Perhaps I would feel tingles swarm my arms and legs the way they sometimes do when I think I might be in the presence of something big.

At the entrance we showed the guards our passports and answered a few questions proving our Jewishness. My brother moved towards the double doors of the main room, the men's section, and waved goodbye. I followed the throng of women towards the side where they were standing in what appeared to be an additional lobby. I assumed that once the service started, the women would lead us to another part of the main room, or perhaps a balcony where we would witness the service from above.

Nope.

Not at all. This was not a divider down the center of the room. This was not a balcony. Hell, this was not even those cheap concert seats that put you way back in the outfield staring at ant-sized musicians. We were outside the room behind a thick wall. Peepholes to the sanctuary allowed a few women at a time to witness the happenings inside. This was the women's section.

The service began. I took my place crowding around a peephole, waiting my turn to stand on tippy toes to see the rabbi or cantor (or even my brother). Mostly all I could see were men with yarmulkes, standing and sitting, muttering the prayers in a communal buzz, and bowing in all the right places. Next to me other women stood pushing in or sitting off to the side, entertaining the children and chatting.

I was in the synagogue. I could hear that prayers were starting. But witnessing this version of Judaism felt like meeting a distant cousin with features vaguely resembling my own and without any common values.

My first thought: "Okay, this is okay, I can do this." My next thought was to revise my plan. It looked like this in my head:

OLD PLAN

Participate in Jewish Shabbat service in really ancient shul.

Listen to the rabbi and cantor and hear how their voices echo in such a big place.

Feel super holy and have a newfound understanding of my Jewish identity and therefore myself.

NEW PLAN

Squeeze closer to the peephole.

Find my place in this darn Czech prayerbook.

Sing along sing sing sing.

At least catch a glimpse of my brother to feel some kind of connection.

See step three of old plan.

I revised the plan over and over. Maybe I could still see my brother? Maybe I could still focus on the echoing sounds of Jewish prayers? Or on the architecture? Maybe I could still find a connection with G-d? With myself?

My mother pushed her way close to me, found the page, and sang. Loudly. As if she were trying to root me with her breath and her voice. Her voice, which has always represented the depth of Judaism to me. But by then, all I could think was, *why didn't you tell me?*

To be fair, she had warned me of her own experiences with Orthodoxy. She'd tried to tell me this would be different. But this felt much worse than a balcony. This was exile.

Those feminist fairy tales. Miriam's cup on the Passover table. Women leaders. Singing prayers in the feminine. Here, in this cold, ancient synagogue, where there is literally not enough room for me— this must be the truth.

My mom's voice and the chatters of the surrounding women at least gave me enough space to cry unheard.

Afterwards, my brother held my hand, his face a mix of empathy, hesitance, and guilt. It wasn't his fault. Could I place the blame on anyone? My parents for not telling me? Me for not hearing them? The men inside for not caring their loved ones were left out? The rabbis of old who set this in motion? Myself for thinking I needed to come here? For coming here and then letting myself feel so small?

When I returned home after Prague, my friend Rachel Stone asked: "Why did that upset you? Why did that kind of Jewish seem any more real than what you had been taught? Why do they have more of a right to decide what 'authentic Judaism' is than we do?" I drank her questions and held them inside. *Yeah*, I thought, *what is "authentic Judaism" anyway? Who gets to say it is so?*

Slowly, I nursed a Prague-shaped wound.

The next year two big things happened: through Bend the Arc (a Jewish social justice nonprofit focusing on domestic organizing) I joined an interfaith cohort of community organizers; and the Occupy Movement[2] began. With the support of my interfaith peers, I talked about my Jewish journey, and remembered that the tingles I sometimes experience almost always come from singing. I wrote an Occupy anthem and got crowds of hundreds to sing it with me, feeling an energy well up through feet, knees, guts, chest, and burst out of my throat, a wellspring of history. I was once again the girl singing Mah Tovu, chanting Bat Mitzvah Torah, crying "Study War No More," but this time it came from deep within me, and the me I was becoming. In the places I felt silenced by traditional Judaism, music reminded me of my inner voice.

Like the story of the treasure seeker who arrives back home to find gold buried in his very own garden, I wanted the Prague synagogue to plant me in the Jewish timeline, to give authenticity to my Judaism, but it was singing that grounded me in the here and now all along.

Sometimes it's still hard not to see Orthodox and Conservative forms of Judaism as more valid, especially when some people try to argue exactly that. But after rooting myself in music, I'm not likely to have my foundations rocked the same way they were in Prague. I'm not likely to let anyone else's definitions make me feel small, when my voice itself is what makes me big.

2. The Occupy Movement, inspired by the Arab Spring and other international events, started in 2011 in New York with a group of protestors camping by Wall Street in response to a diminishing economy and a decreasing faith in the capitalist system. The movement demanded social and economic justice for the "99%" of the population, no longer just the "elite 1%." The movement quickly became widespread, with Occupy encampments springing up in over nine hundred cities across over eighty countries.

Now a few years have passed since Prague. I live in New York, my parents' homeland. I perform original music as "Entirely Talia," my project of self-reclamation. I work at Ma'yan, a Jewish feminist organization, where I support high school girls as they wrestle with issues of sexism, oppression and liberation. When I teach young people, I say that there is no such thing as a "good Jew" or a "bad Jew;" we are all good and each of us gets to define our own Jewish path. On Friday nights I light candles with my partner to mark the passage of time. I go to shul sometimes, or independent *havurahs* (small, informal prayer groups). I am drawn to the idea of recreating ritual in new meaningful ways. I sing loudly, like my mother. I protest proudly as a Jew, like my father. I crack wicked jokes. I say the *Shehecheyanu* (blessing for new experiences) whenever I do something for the first time, because wow, it really is amazing that I've arrived here.

# Girl, I am So Over Church
## by Nikki Bailey

NIKKI BAILEY holds a Master of Divinity from Union Theological Seminary in New York City. She is a speaker, mentor, performer and author of *Soul Smarts for Day Start: 31 Days of Creative Inspiration and Activities.* For more than thirteen years, she has been helping people leap into lives of spicy spirituality and creativity. Nikki's Spiritual Creative process provides tools for tackling the Big Questions of Life and enhancing the Soul Smarts needed to reconnect to self, community and the God of your understanding. For more information, visit soulnik.com.

My friend Tara dropped a bombshell over the weekend. At dinner with her family, her aunt asked me if I was still singing on the church choir. I told her that I don't go to church anymore. I said it just like that—all simple and blunt, without my usual "I'm between churches at the moment" lie. I said: "I don't go to church anymore."

After a stunned silence, Tara tried to steer the conversation to our Saturday evening theatre plans. I knew she never missed a Sunday service so I offered to get her home early on Saturday night so she'd be prepared for the next morning. She waved her hand in the air as if shooing a fly, sucked her teeth, planted the hand on her hip, cocked her head to the side and announced to her whole family:

"Girl, I am so over church."

Her aunty gave me some serious side-eye making it clear that she blamed me for this blasphemy. I thought I was in trouble but was surprised that she immediately changed the subject. Apparently, the

Real Housewives of Atlanta are way safer to discuss than two forty-something, well-churched, black women coming out of the "I am over church" closet. I wondered for a moment if I should force the issue—make Tara's God-fearing, ultra-Baptist family deal with what had just happened. It was a big deal and the room was humming with shock. And fear. And I . . . I loved it!

See, I'd kinda been waiting for Tara to get over church. It was hurting her. Week after week, she'd show up for Sunday service on time, suitably dressed, ready to praise, trusting the shiny happy belief that if she did righteousness right—dripping with humble, hopeful, and really, really good—she'd be alright. And week after week, she'd call me in tears, wondering how it could be God's will for her to be so sad. How could God expect her to tithe what little money she has, to pay the salary of a preacher who looks down on her single motherhood and condones the bad behavior of men who regularly admire (and admonish) her body, her pantsuits, her make-up, her natural hair?

I know it scares her to walk away from church. I know she wonders how she'll make it into heaven if she "backslides." I know she's afraid of what people will say and what it will mean—for her salvation, for her day-to-day ability to function—if she doesn't go to church. But I am so glad she's leaving. I think she has to do it. It's for her own good. I know how hard it will be for her because it was hard for me too. I left church a long time ago. And it still hurts.

I was raised in church. My dad was a minister, my mom was the church clerk, and my grandfather was the head of the Trustee board. My brother was an usher and I sang in the choir. We went to Sunday school, Bible study, youth group, revivals, and Baptist Training Union. We took long car trips to fellowship with other churches in our denomination. We were in church all the time. And we loved it!

In fact, I loved church so much that, after a successful career in television, I went to seminary and earned a Master of Divinity from Union Theological Seminary in New York City. I wanted to help churches use media to educate their communities about social justice, positively influence youth, and spread the gospel message of love, justice and mercy. So, after seminary, I went to work at a Baptist church in Brooklyn.

Um . . . Let's just say it didn't go well. Less than a year into my pastoral residency, colleagues in my Baptist polity class were calling me a heretic for questioning the patriarchal status quo. I remember being named a rebel and enduring angry lectures from other women clergy because I had the audacity to wear pants in the sanctuary. And I remember the terror I experienced when I realized that I didn't belong there. Standing in that renowned pulpit, preparing to lead the congregation in prayer, I thought: *Oh my God. I can't believe Ms. Smith commented on the length of my dress . . . again. How is that important? Maybe I just don't believe this in the same way they do. How can I pretend that I do? What can I pray right now that isn't a lie? What am I even doing here?* Managing depression, confronted with the ills of church politics and gossip, and just . . . over it, I moved back to my hometown and removed myself from the ordination process.

Back home, I visited a different church each week. I worshipped with Baptists, Presbyterians, Methodists, Catholics, Lutherans, United Church of Christ, Church of God in Christ . . . I tried them all! But each week, I got more and more frustrated. On more than one occasion, I walked out in the middle of sermons so filled with homophobia, misogyny, and bald-faced, scripturally inaccurate lies that I just knew Jesus wept as much as I did. I was loving church less and less. I was exhausted and disappointed and, well, hurt.

As a womanist (committed to survival and wholeness of entire people), I found that there was so much about Christianity that got in the way. Personally, I found it discouraging that, no matter what I did or how hard I tried, I was never able to be quiet or virtuous or respectful enough to merit the righteousness I was taught to seek. It affected my self-esteem to believe that though "God so loved the world," (John 3:16) God still created me horribly and intrinsically flawed. So flawed, in fact, that the only thing saving me from destruction and damnation was a very good man dying on a very bloody cross. It became impossible for me to survive and feel whole as I internalized such demoralizing messages.

So, I stopped going to church. I stopped beating myself up for being pretty and loud and loving my body and enjoying sex and cussing and wearing makeup and showing my arms, legs or cleavage. I stopped believing lies about my value as a woman and a human being. I stopped listening to stories about my sinful nature and the "fallen" state of mankind. I divorced myself from the celebration of violence permeating scripture that many believers view as holy and necessary and praiseworthy. I rejected the notion of the "unworthy sinner" and began to believe that if I am created in the image and likeness of God, I must surely be perfect . . . just the way I am. Unable to suffer even one more comment on women's clothing or conduct, and unwilling to "submit" to "authority" (and a wide range of "authority-based" stupidity), I stopped attending church.

But, honestly, I still struggle with it. I still love church. I still love God. I still love Jesus. I miss the music and the feeling of family and the joy of sitting in a room with people who thirst for connection as much as I do. But I felt I had no choice. I left church for my survival. I left church for my own good. And I miss it, painfully.

It was necessary to leave church but I did not leave my faith or my ministry. And, I've discovered that the purpose of my ministry and the scope of my calling has expanded beyond church. While I still feel called to serve in spiritual community, my ministry is not focused on church. Instead, I help people—particularly those who feel marginalized and unwelcome in traditional religious settings—find faith and spirituality that works for them. Through the exploration of culturally relevant, life-affirming spiritual practices and beliefs, I help people better understand the language of God that speaks most deeply to their hearts and souls. That language may or may not be Christianity. It may or may not be rooted in any specific faith tradition. My ministry is simply to help people listen for how God speaks to them beyond—and in spite of—the dogma, doctrine and problems of traditional religion.

That's what I've done for myself. I've found a way to keep my Christian identity even as I constantly rewrite the meaning and spiritual significance of the faith for myself (and anyone else who's interested). I describe myself as "Christian+" and I love that I've found a way of believing that affirms the best of the faith and supports the survival and wholeness of all people. I've kept my Jesus but left behind the baggage of sexism, violence, and judgment that I found in church. I've kept my Jesus and added acceptance, hope, justice and the radical love of self and community.

# Holding the Keys
## by Rori Picker Neiss

MAHARAT RORI PICKER NEISS serves as
the Director of Programming, Education,
and Community Engagement at Bais
Abraham Congregation in St. Louis,
Missouri. She is a graduate of Yeshivat
Maharat, a pioneering institution
training Orthodox Jewish women to be
spiritual leaders and halakhic (Jewish
legal) authorities.

I had walked up the stairs to the women's section countless times
before, but this time it felt different. Never before had it bothered
me that my section of the synagogue was on the second level of the
building. Never before had I been uncomfortable with the fact that
being on the second floor only allowed me to hear the prayers from a
distance, requiring strategic maneuvering to catch even a glimpse of
the holy ark down below. Never before had I been so acutely aware of
all of the barriers that separated me, as a woman, from the men who
constituted the core of the prayer community.

As I walked up the steps this time, though, I saw all of these elements through new eyes.

It was my sophomore year at Hunter College and some friends
and I, newly bonded after a student government retreat in which we
were the only Sabbath observers, decided we should spend a Shabbat
together over a long vacation weekend. We chose to go to my parents' home in Brooklyn, where I had grown up in a very traditional
Orthodox community. My father and brothers were all away for the
holiday, and the four of us decided to keep my mother company while
enjoying the weekend together.

On Friday night one of my friends suggested that we go to synagogue for Shabbat services. I balked at the idea, knowing that the synagogues in the area where I lived were not as welcoming and friendly as the ones they might be imagining. The Orthodox community in which I was raised was very insular; welcoming of those who chose a similar lifestyle but not interested in making a space for those who had a different practice. My friends had been raised in more modern Orthodox communities and they insisted, pointing out a synagogue directly across the street from the house. It was the start of Shabbat, the holiest day of the week, and they wanted to join in the songs and prayers that welcome the Sabbath.

I tried to tell them that they would not enjoy the services; I knew that the prayers would not be sung joyfully and passionately, as they envisioned based on their own experiences, but rather, murmured mimetically out of a sense of obligation. In truth, though, I did not want them to go because I knew that women were not expected to attend services on Friday night. Women's roles centered on the home; men were needed for prayer, women were needed to care for children and prepare dinner. Those of us who were neither responsible for food nor children still did not attend because that had simply become the expected norm.

Despite my attempts to deter them, I found myself leading them up the staircase. With each step I grew more aware of how far I needed to go. With each step I grew more aware of how far away the women's section was.

Although I knew that the men who attended services that evening might find it odd to see women in the synagogue on a Friday night, I was surprised that we received those men's looks of objection from *within* the women's section. It became clear that men, assuming women would not attend services, had overflowed into the women's section. Some men prayed. Some men studied Jewish texts. Some men lay their black hats on the tables, lay their heads beside the hats, and napped.

We held our heads high and faced the dirty looks, walked to the table closest to the front just behind the wall, opened our prayer books, and began to pray. Some men moved down a few seats to create enough distance from us they felt was necessary.

We forced ourselves to look into our prayer books and not behind us to take stock of the disapproving looks, although we could feel the glares even without lifting our heads. None of us managed to focus on our prayers that evening.

I was incensed. If Jewish law required me to have a separate section for prayer, then, at the very least, I deserved the right to have that section. It would never have occurred to me to step foot in the men's section of the synagogue.

I voiced my complaints to members of the synagogue, who then brought my issue to the board. I requested a formal announcement declaring that that the men's section was for men and the women's section was for women, and men were not welcome to enter the space of women's prayer. Instead, the board offered me a compromise: when I wanted to come to services on Friday night, they would lock all of the doors to the women's section and they would give me the key.

The next time I was home for Shabbat, I decided to attend services again. As promised, all of the doors to the women's section were locked before services began. When I arrived, someone was there to give me the key. I unlocked the door, stepped inside, and locked the door behind me. I then sat down in my solitary space, opened the prayer book, and once again, attempted to pray.

My prayers had no more focus that Friday night at the synagogue than they had the last time. Certain Jewish prayers require a minyan, a minimum quorum of people—ten adult Jewish males in Orthodox Judaism. Judaism recognizes the importance of being in community, and the power of voices united in prayer that can propel words even higher to heaven. Although there was the necessary quorum of men present in the building, the solitariness of the women's section was overwhelming in the silence that surrounded me. At the same time, the silence was shattered by the periodic rattling of the door as people pulled at the handles attempting to enter. My mind wandered to imagine the people on the other side of the door. I envisioned men with prayer books seeking a quieter space to pray, returning back to the cacophony of the space below. I envisioned men with other books seeking a place to study, confused as to why someone forgot to unlock the door for services, shrugging their shoulders and returning downstairs, prepared to continue their learning the following week when the doors would once again be opened. And I envisioned women, choosing to join their birthright and to begin the holy Sabbath in song and prayer, seeking a place to celebrate and to talk with God, unable to enter and returning home dejected. Unable to see through the thick wooden door, I had no way to know who stood at the other side, trying to get in, and so all people, regardless of gender, were barred from access.

That night, it was me who locked other women out of their space.

When services ended, I unlocked the door to exit, locked the door once again behind me, and as I turned that lock, I ended my silent and unnoticed protest demonstration. I returned the key and I vowed that I would never again be the person who locked the door to others who wanted to enter. I would never again be the person who prevented anyone who sought a holy space from finding it.

Four years later, I read the announcement of a new, groundbreaking program being created to prepare Orthodox Jewish women for leadership roles in the Jewish community. It was the first program that aimed to train and ordain women as Orthodox Jewish clergy, and I knew that it would be the key for me to use to unlock doors instead of locking them. I joined Yeshivat Maharat in its first year, determined to create a space in which all people—especially those who felt rejected by Orthodox Judaism— felt that they could access Jewish learning, Jewish texts, and most of all, Jewish community.

I am an Orthodox Jewish woman. I believe in my heart that God gave us the wisdom of the Torah as the path on which we are meant to lead our lives. I believe in my heart that we are bound by a strict legal code, given in the Torah and interpreted over hundreds of generations into the laws we have today. I believe in my heart that we are on this earth because we are partners with God in perfecting the creation of this world, and that the wisdom of the Torah and the laws by which we are bound are the tools which will enable us to do so.

I also believe in my heart that Judaism does not command me to hate others or to subjugate others. I believe in my heart that Judaism does not value human lives at different rates based on race, religion, gender, sex, sexuality, or age. I believe in my heart that Judaism, and even Orthodox Judaism, does not view women as inferior to men.

That is not to say that I understand all of the wisdom of the Torah. It pains me to read the verses that applaud violence, or that ostracize LGBT and other marginalized members of our community. I struggle with those verses. I grapple with those teachings. I do not ignore them, nor do I deny that they are a part of my tradition. Nor do I walk away from that tradition. Because if all of us who struggled with these teachings and sought understanding left, there would be no one remaining to ask the questions.

If every time we felt unwelcome in a space we decided not to stay, then that space would, indeed, no longer be for us. In taking ourselves out of a place, we designate that place as not our own.

Over the course of my journey to become recognized as Orthodox female clergy, a heretofore unheard of designation, there were many places in which I was not welcome. I encountered synagogues, houses of study, libraries, Judaic bookstores, and even friends' living rooms in which people made clear that they did not consider me to be Orthodox, they did not consider me to be learned, and some did not consider me to be religious.

That Friday night with my friends, during services, I was unwelcome in the section that was designated as my own. If I had left the women's section, I would have conceded that the space that had been set aside for me was not mine. I would have allowed the "women's section" to become the "women's section when not occupied by men."

Orthodox Judaism has a place for me. I could take the key, let myself in, lock the door behind me, and hold that space just for myself. Or I could take the key, unlock the locks, open all the doors, and tell all who wish to enter that there is a seat waiting for them.

# Honored to Give an X
## by Hoda Elshishtawy

 HODA ELSHISHTAWY works as a national policy analyst for a faith-based advocacy organization. Hoda has written and spoken on subjects ranging from international religious freedom and national security to free expression and bullying. She has been featured on BBC, Al Hurra TV, Fox News, Voice of America and C-SPAN. She was a speaker at the United States Institute for Peace panel discussion "Religion, Violence and Coexistence." Hoda writes frequently on issues that affect Americans both domestically and internationally, with a particular emphasis on those issues that impact American Muslims. Hoda has a B.A. in Political Science from George Washington University with a concentration on international affairs and the Middle East and a Master's in Ethics, Peace and Global Affairs focusing on Islam, ethics, and conflict resolution from American University's School of International Service.

The "X" chromosome in our family is impressively dominant.

I was born in 1985, but my story really starts in 1969. That was the year my grandparents immigrated to the United States from Egypt. It's no secret in the family that if it weren't for my grandmother's infamous stubborn personality, we all wouldn't be here today. (She still proudly takes all the credit for forcing my grandfather to live outside his comfort zone and move to the States to build a better life for their kids). The '69 pioneers included my maternal grandparents, my grandmother's younger sister, my mom (who was three years old) and her little brother (my uncle).

It wasn't easy uprooting a family and learning a totally different way of life. At the time, my grandparents weren't particularly religious people; they were young and building a new life, and religion could come later when they were old and had time for it.

Their first years in America included decorated Christmas trees in the house, Easter baskets in April, and plenty of Catholic friends from around the neighborhood. My grandparents even enrolled my mom and uncle in Catholic schools because they figured the Catholic schools in Egypt were usually top-notch, so why wouldn't they be here too? My family could have lost our Muslim identity, but my grandparents realized that it was important to impart Islam to their kids as part of maintaining the family identity when my three-year-old mom said her very first English sentence: "Mama, Jesus is in my heart."

Growing up, I loved hearing stories from my grandmother and mom about their lives in Los Angeles as Muslim Egyptian Americans in the 1970s, no less. Financial challenges, struggles of identity, and generational misunderstandings all contributed to a very colorful upbringing in sunny southern California.

Getting through high school is no small feat for *any* teenager. Imagine in addition to puberty, hormones, and teen angst, adding challenges such as identity clashes and cultural misunderstandings between your parents and what seems like everyone else in the world. Those were the kinds of horror stories I heard my mom going through during those four dreaded years. I'm sure those experiences made it easier for my mom to decide to marry at such a young age.

And here's where my story starts. In April of 1985 I was born to my mother, who was newly divorced (and a kid herself by some standards) and found herself with a ten pound baby. We were like the television program *Full House,* but with a different mix of family members: me, my mom, my grandparents, and my two uncles.

My grandmother always taught us that the key to freedom and independence was through education—*especially* for girls. So, while my mom finished her undergraduate and graduate degrees, my grandmother retired early to help take care of me. I spent my summers with my Tiger Mom grandmother, figuring out endless hours of math equations, memorizing multiplication tables, reading books, and learning to write answers to comprehension questions. If that wasn't enough, to prevent another "Jesus is in my heart" moment, I had hours of Qur'an and religious studies with my grandmother. I remember the summer going into the third grade was my first time finishing the Qur'an in Arabic—during a camping trip! (Yes, even on trips I had to bring my summer work.)

I still remember going to my mom's master's graduation at University of California, Los Angeles (where she and I wore matching dresses). She thanked God and the support of our family for helping her get through graduate school. That wasn't uncommon; all of our celebrations and occasions were grounded in the strength of our faith. Without faith, the elders would always say, we have no higher purpose to work toward.

Those are the two themes that have played throughout my life over and over—witnessing the strength of women in my family, and my faith. Those two themes played a tremendous role when my mom remarried and we moved across the country. The power of my grandmother in keeping our family close, regardless of physical distance, always impressed me. My mom and I never let a day go by without talking to my grandmother on the phone. And whenever I was sad, they would remind me that God plans everything for a reason.

During this time, I developed my love-hate relationship with airports. Every summer, winter, and spring break, I would travel back to California to spend time with the family I had left behind. Most of the time, I would travel by myself. It wasn't uncommon to see other kids my age traveling alone; I was seven years old when I took my first solo flight. I remember one flight I missed my mom so much, I ordered an iced tea on the plane because it reminded me of her. Airports made me feel like I had to choose between families; but it was also in airports that I established my independence. I had to be a responsible grown-up in order to ensure I made my connecting flights and sat in the right seats.

On one such flight, I sat next to a man who struck up a conversation with me. He asked where I was from and where I was going. It turned out the gentleman was Muslim. He told me that he didn't pray or really observe the practices or traditions of Islam. He asked me if I knew how to pray, and I responded by reciting the first seven verses of the Qur'an (Surah Al-Fatiha, the opening). I still don't know why I did that; but I remember the man being impressed. When I landed at the Los Angeles airport, I told my grandparents the story of the man on the plane. My grandmother was *ecstatic*! She was proud that I took the initiative to affirm my pride in my faith by taking my response to another level. She was so proud that she called her friends and told them the story (humility is not her strong suit).

That was my childhood for the most part: summer homework, hours of learning about Islam, and loving/hating the airport. Until high school. Just as my mom endured four dreaded years of high school, so did I. I *hated* high school. I was going through my awkward phase (I mean seriously awkward—I thought chopping all my hair off and dying it purple would somehow make me look cuter). And I was the only Arab and the only Muslim in my high school. For four years, in southern Virginia, I was as much the minority as minority can get. And then one day in my United States history class, while I was taking my first exam, a teacher came running into my class crying, saying something about America being attacked. I didn't really get the gravity of the situation, just that something really bad had happened.

And then I went to school the next day. It was an *awful* day. Because I was the only Muslim in school, and everyone knew it (I was never quiet or shy about my faith, as witnessed by my peers and teachers who would ask me endless questions about Ramadan, fasting, and Islam in general), I was somehow connected to the 9/11 attacks. Their reaction was accusatory towards me, and for some reason I wasn't allowed to mourn and grieve like the other students. I heard the typical snarky comments from students: "Do you know Osama?" "We should bomb the Middle East into a parking lot for what they did."

So there I was, an awkward teenage girl, Muslim, and removed from what was considered normal by the other students. What was I supposed to do? Cry? Be a recluse until I graduated? Play victim? Luckily, those weren't even options. My grandmother didn't spend her nights crying when she raised her children in a new country. My mom didn't play victim when she found herself a single mother at a very young age. I was blessed to witness the examples set by the matriarchs of my family and how they dealt with adversity. The above weren't options because it would have meant me going against the grain of my DNA—I was constructed to face challenges head on.

I spent nights reading, writing op-eds, and studying the Qur'an further to counter the incorrect and hateful statements I heard from my peers. It was like my childhood summers all over again—minus the math problems. Reading, comprehension, and Islam.

It was all coming together. I realized that year that my childhood had to happen the way it did for me to become me. I got through high school, and looking back, I still hated it. But I tell people (and this was one of the things I told my husband jokingly when I first met him), "I had four solid years to work on my stellar personality because of my awkwardness."

I grew up witnessing my grandmother and mom using the strength of their feminism and faith to their advantage. They never let anyone tell them "no" because of their gender or faith. Once my grandmother was afraid to disclose to her boss that she was pregnant because she had just gotten a job with the local government; after hours of prayer and consultation with her close Catholic friend, she decided to come clean instead of pursuing other options. Another time my mom co-ordinated a World Religions Day for my younger brother's middle school because of an increase in bullying of students who practiced minority faiths. My mother and grandmother never backed down.

Sometimes I wonder if their lives would have been easier had they been born males. They wouldn't have had to deal with the sexism of my grandmother's generation, or the cultural restrictions and double standard imposed upon Muslim girls when my mother was in high school. Yet the challenges and adversities they faced made them stronger. They turned perceived disadvantages into their primary weapons.

Sometimes it seems harder to be a woman. And yet, I see through their actions and experiences their absolute conviction and pride in being strong Muslim women. I'm proud they've passed on their genetic makeup to me. Our "X" chromosome is a badge of honor in our family. It's not a hindrance. My faith and my feminism complement each other; they serve to act as forces on the same side that keep people from messing with me because I celebrate and am loud about my uniqueness. As I sit and write this, I only hope that the growing miracle in my belly carries on our tradition of finding strength in faith. Regardless of what gender my baby will be, I am honored to pass on my "X."

# Glossary

**Al-Fattah**: One of the ninety-nine names of God in the Muslim tradition, meaning "The Opener," derived from the Qur'an and sayings of Muhammad.

**ammi:** Urdu for mother.

**ameen:** Used by Muslims to end prayers, especially personal supplications, similar to "Amen."

**androgynous:** Displaying a combination of male and female characteristics.

**Ark:** The cabinet where the Torah scrolls are kept.

**ashreis:** Hebrew meaning prayerful recitation of Psalm 145.

**avot:** Hebrew for fathers.

**aylonit:** Hebrew for a female who takes on male characteristics.

**bat mitzvah:** Ceremony recognizing when a girl becomes a bat mitzvah. This means she attains the age of religious duty and become accountable for her actions.

**bar mitzvah:** Same as bat mitzvah, but for boys.

**bedside Buddhist:** One who reads feel-good Buddhist-lite books before falling asleep but does not practice the tradition.

**beit midrash:** Hebrew for house of study.

**betulah:** Hebrew for virgin.

**bida:** Forbidden innovations in Islamic law or teachings.

**bimah:** The pedestal on which the Torah scrolls are placed when they are being read in the synagogue; a raised platform.

**brit bat:** Naming ceremony and celebration of the birth of a baby girl.

**catechism:** A summary of the principles of Christian religion, often in the form of questions and answers or oral instruction.

**chazzan:** Cantor; the person in a synogogue who leads the congregation in prayer.

**chazzanus:** Cantorial style.

**chiddushei:** Hebrew for insights.

**chum-chum:** A popular Bengali sweet dish.

**Communion:** Christian Sacrament where one receives the body of Christ in the form of a host or bread. Also called Eucharist.

**Confirmation:** A Catholic rite of full church membership.

**daven:** Yiddish word for pray.

**davening:** Jewish communal prayer.

**Deacon:** An ordained person within the Christian tradition whose role is to assist priests in pastoral and administrative duties.

**du'a:** Muslim prayer or call to God.

**d'var Torah:** Interpretation of a part of the Torah.

**Eucharist:** Christian Sacrament where one receives the body of Christ in the form of a host or bread. Also called Communion.

**Focus on the Family:** A conservative Christian ministry dedicated to preserving a traditional family structure. Website: www.focusonthefamily.com

**Gemera:** A commentary on the Mishnah forming the second part of the Torah.

**G-d:** Some Jews write G-d to avoid the risk of erasing or defacing the name.

**Hadith:** Muslim prophetic tradition.

**Haftorah:** One of the biblical selections from the Jewish Books of the Prophets.

**Haggadah:** The book of readings for the Seder service.

**halakhah:** Jewish law.

**halakhic:** Hebrew for legal; halakhic arguments are Jewish legal arguments.

**halal:** Permissible according to Islamic law.

**halaqa:** A religious gathering to learn more about some aspect of Islam.

**Hanafi:** Of or relating to an orthodox school of Sunni Muslim jurisprudence.

**haram:** Forbidden according to Islamic law.

**hassid:** A follower of the spiritual-devotional popular movement that took root in eighteenth-century Poland.

**Hassidic:** One branch of Orthodox Judaism.

**havurah:** Small, informal prayer group.

**Havurah movement:** A movement of do-it-yourself Judaism, marked by egalitarianism, communalism, and a renewed interest in ritual and creative liturgy.

**High Holidays:** The Jewish holidays of Rosh Hashanah and Yom Kippur.

**hijab:** A headscarf traditionally worn by some Muslim women.

**Hijabi:** A Muslim women who wears a headscarf.

**hujub:** Plural of hijab.

**imam:** Prayer leader of a mosque.

**Inlakech:** Mayan tradition; I am you.

**Insha'Allah:** Literally, God willing. Said by Muslims when referring to something that will take place in the future.

**jilbab:** A long, loose-fitting coat worn by some Muslim women.

**Kaddish:** Jewish hymn or prayer to God.

**ketubah:** Jewish marriage contract.

**ketubot:** Laws of wedding contracts.

**khutba:** The sermon given during a Muslim prayer.

**Kiddush:** A ceremonial blessing pronounced over wine or bread in a Jewish home or synagogue on a holy day.

**kippah:** Skullcap, more commonly known as a yarmulke in English, traditionally worn by Jewish men.

**kippot:** Plural of kippah.

**kugel:** Yiddish for baked pudding.

**lectionary:** Scripture or texts appointed for worship on a particular day or occasion.

**madrassa:** Arabic word for an educational institution, often used to refer to an Islamic religious school.

**makkaar:** Urdu for scheming, insincere, or untrustworthy.

**masjid:** Arabic word for mosque.

**matzah:** Hebrew for unleavened bread.

**mechitzah:** The wall or curtain separating men from women during Orthodox Jewish religious services.

**mestiza:** A woman of mixed racial or ethnic ancestry.

**midrash:** An interpretation; a haggadic or halakhic exposition of the underlying significance of Torah texts.

**miggo:** Talmudic law relating to a logical principle that someone is considered more trustworthy if they're partially incriminating themselves in their confession.

**mikvah:** Hebrew for a ritual bath used for spiritual purification. It is used primarily in conversion rituals and after the period of sexual separation during a woman's menstrual periods.

**minyan:** The quorum necessary to recite certain prayers, traditionally consisting of ten adult Jewish men.

**Mishnah:** An early written compilation of Jewish oral tradition; the basis of the Talmud.

**mitzvah:** Hebrew for divine commandment.

**mitzvot:** Plural of mitzvah.

**mohels:** Hebrew for professionals who perform ritual circumcisions.

**Muslimah:** Muslim woman.

**nepantlera:** Gloria Anzaldua's concept describing a person who lives with contradiction and can see from more than one point of view at a time.

**Nikkah:** Muslim marriage contract.

**Ometeotl:** From the Nahuatl language. A sacred affirmation; amen.

**paresha:** A passage in Jewish scripture dealing with a single topic; a paresha is read in a bat or bar mitzvah.

**PBUH:** Abbreviation for "peace be upon him." Also abbreviated "SAW." Used after speaking or writing Muhammad's name.

**Qur'an:** Central religious text of Islam.

**RA:** Abbreviation for the Arabic of "May God be pleased with him/her"; used after speaking or writing the name of one of Muhammad's wives or companions.

**rabbi:** A religious teacher authorized to make decisions on issues of Jewish law.

**Ramadan:** The ninth month of the Islamic calendar, observed by Muslims as a month of fasting.

**RCIA:** Rite of Christian Initiation for Adults.

**rida:** A style of Indian hijab specific to the Dawoodi Bohra community.

**Rosh Hashana:** Jewish New Year.

**ruhani:** Spiritual communication from God.

**saris:** Hebrew for a male who takes on feminine characteristics.

**SAW:** Abbreviation for the Arabic of "peace be upon him." Also abbreviated "PBUH."

**Seder:** Home service and ritual meal held on Passover to mark the Exodus of the Jews from Egypt.

**Sefir Nashim:** Jewish Book of Women.

**seudah shlishit:** The meal that closes Shabbat.

**Shabbat:** Hebrew for the seventh day of the week; the day God rested from the creation of the world.

**shahada:** The Muslim profession of faith.

**Shehecheyanu:** Jewish blessing for new experiences.

**Shema:** Prayer affirming a Jewish belief in one God.

**shul:** The Yiddish term for a Jewish house of worship.

**siddur:** Jewish prayer book.

**Sign of the Cross:** A Catholic ritual blessing of oneself; often the sign of the cross is made before or after prayer.

**Simchat Torah:** Jewish holiday that celebrates and marks the ending of the annual cycle of public Torah readings.

**solidaridad:** To stand in solidarity.

**Sunnah:** The teachings and practices of Muhammad which observant Muslims try to follow.

**sutras:** One of the discourses of the Buddha that constitutes the basic text of Buddhist scripture.

**taharot hamishpah:** Hebrew meaning family purity.

**tafsir:** Arabic word for interpretation of a religious text, usually the Qur'an.

**tahajjud:** A voluntary nighttime prayer for Muslims; not one of the five required daily prayers.

**tallit:** A Jewish prayer shawl.

**tallitot:** Plural of tallit.

**Talmud:** The most significant collection of the Jewish oral tradition interpreting the Torah.

**tameh:** Hebrew for ritually impure.

**tefilah:** Hebrew for prayer.

**tefillin:** Black box with leather straps containing a biblical commandment, worn on one's forehead and arm during Jewish weekday morning prayer.

**tikun:** Hebrew word meaning heal or restore.

**tlazocamati:** Nahuatl for thank you.

**Torah:** The five books of Moses given by God to Moses on Mount Sinai.

**tumtum:** Hebrew for an individual whose sex is unknowable because of covered or hidden genitalia.

**two-spirited people:** In Native American traditions the diversity of bodies that simultaneously manifest both feminine and masculine spirits and characteristics are recognized and referred to as two spirited.

**tzitzit:** Hebrew for fringes attached to the corners of garments as a reminder of the commandments.

**Yahrzeits:** Jewish tradition of honoring the deceased.

**yarmulke:** A skullcap traditionally worn by Jewish men.

**yeshiva:** Jewish college or seminary with an emphasis on studying classic rabbinic texts.

# About the Editors

GINA MESSINA-DYSERT, Ph.D., is Dean of the School of Graduate and Professional Studies at Ursuline College, author of *Rape Culture and Spiritual Violence*, and co-founder of FeminismandReligion.com.

JENNIFER ZOBAIR is a graduate of Smith College and Georgetown Law School. She is the author of *Painted Hands* and founder of storyandchai. com, a creative space for readers and writers of Muslim and culturally diverse narratives.

AMY LEVIN earned an M.A. in Religious Studies from New York University and is a Master of Social Work candidate at the University of Pennsylvania. She has worked as a political organizer and writes on the intersection of religion, gender, and social justice.

# *I Speak for Myself* series

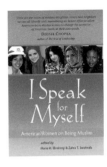

VOLUME 1

## *I Speak for Myself*
*American Women on Being Muslim*

ISBN: 978-1-935952-00-8 / $16.95

VOLUME 2

## *All-American*
*45 American Men*
*on Being Muslim*

ISBN: 978-1-935952-59-6 / $16.95

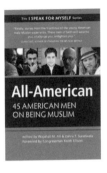

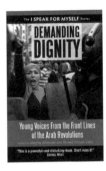

VOLUME 3

## *Demanding Dignity*
*Young Voices from the Front Lines*
*of the Arab Revolutions*

ISBN: 978-1-935952-71-8 / $16.95

VOLUME 4

## *Talking Taboo*
*American Christian Women*
*Get Frank About Faith*

ISBN: 978-1-935952-86-2 / $16.95

VOLUME 5

## *Father Factor*
*American Christian Men*
*on Fatherhood and Faith*

ISBN: 978-1-940468-20-4 / $17.95